PROBLEMS OF REFLEXIVITY AND
DIALECTICS IN SOCIOLOGICAL
INQUIRY

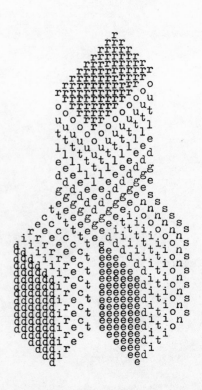

PROBLEMS OF REFLEXIVITY AND DIALECTICS IN SOCIOLOGICAL INQUIRY
Language theorizing difference

Barry Sandywell
David Silverman
Maurice Roche
Paul Filmer
Michael Phillipson

ROUTLEDGE DIRECT EDITIONS

ROUTLEDGE & KEGAN PAUL
London, Henley and Boston

First published in 1975
by Routledge & Kegan Paul Ltd
39 Store Street
London WC1E 7DD,
Broadway House
Newtown Road
Henley-on-Thames
Oxon RG9 1EN and
9 Park Street
Boston, Mass. 02108 USA
Reprinted 1977
Printed and bound in Great Britain
by Unwin Brothers Limited
The Gresham Press, Old Woking, Surrey
a member of the Staples Printing Group

ISBN 0 7100 8304 1

CONTENTS

IN PLACE OF A PREFACE

Doing prefacing, introducing a text and acknowledging inspirations
are far too dangerous enterprises to escape reflection, especially
given the commitments which the following papers manifest.   In
place of the conventional preface, then, it would be circumspect to
explicate why we cannot blithely follow the standard practice of
supplying reading-rules, thumb-nail sketches or instructions to the
papers which the pre-face chases.   We would like to assure the
reader that this vacuum is not intended as irreverence on our part
toward him, but rather the reverse.   In fact our explorations focus
heterogeneously on the problem of respectfully constituting notions
of Reader and Readership where prefaces would at best become redundant, at worst moral insults, concretely understood as denials of
competence (ours as well as the reader's).

Let us have no doubts: supplying prefaces to a work is tantamount to the provision of recipes for the social construction of
worlds; more accurately, prefaces are sets of instructions cajoling
the reader to construe the world in this or that way by turning the
text about an authoritative version of what it is to read.   Within
the practice of differentiating the author's Genius from the reader's
projected incompetence, the reader is concretely collected as being
one in need of tuition (supplied by the preface); a community, as it
were, is present in the innocent location practices of prefacing.

The felt need of supplying such reading rules is an indication
of the shallow understanding of identity and difference (the community of Reader and Writer) behind conventional texts.   These
delaying tactics which attempt to give the gist of the grounds of a
piece of work inadvertently transform the grounds of the writing
into a gist-able thing.   Unfortunately the heuristic practice of
doing-prefacing (often understood as a positive aid for the un-
knowledgeable reader) stands for us a symbol of how the intended
readership is absolutely preempted from entering the text in his full
authorial capacity - as one, in other words, whose destiny hangs on
the way he re-writes the author's work for himself.   Reading, then,
is nothing if it is not a re-writing; sadly most prefaces set off
with the time-worn assumption that reading is nothing if it is not
reading.   Upon that distinction hinges a tradition, the darker side
of which emerges in the mundane speech of positive exchange and the

1

market which is analysed at various places in the contributions that
follow.

The prefaces of traditional texts locate the work as a whole, a
finished totality or completed thing.   To be more precise, the
preface finishes a text by totalizing an object - thereby doing the
impossible: bringing to fulfilment what is basically incompletable.
The feature to be drawn out here is that this enterprise is possible
only given a convention commonly accepted amongst a readership - the
rule that texts can be treated as products to be prefixed and
suffixed into a tidy package without loose ends, wayward locutions
and the ambivalence of dialectic.

What escapes our attention here is the feature that the preface
acts not as a set of instructions for reading a work as the author's
writing but as instructions for reading the work as the author's
reading of his own writing.   But should we not warn the reader of
this seduction and supply him with the tools for re-writing the work
as his reading?   After all, taken to its logical conclusion these
instructions of the author would delay the reader at the preface.
He need go no further if the essence is palpably in the preface.
Not surprisingly, authors do (privately) advocate grasping the
preface and conclusion and ignoring the circuitry of the 'middle';
again, obsession with the etiquette of beginnings and closings, with
the problem of saying precisely the problem at the beginning and
articulating a summary and prospect at the conclusion is symptomatic of deeper issues here.

When we stop and think further we find ourselves in a topsy-
turvy world.   How is it that we never pay attention to the paradoxes
of writing introductions and prefaces?   For instance, we raise the
difficulty of beginning before the beginning - deciding precisely
when we actually do begin in writing-reading.   The 'Introduction'
to these papers can have only one message: that the reader has
already begun - better, that he had better disregard the seductions
of the author's preface.   Let us retrieve the peculiar 'thing' that
a Book is.   Where indeed is the correct entry to a Book?   For as
all authors privately know (and as we here exemplify), the preface is
the last item to be written but it is the first item to appear as the
guiding hand that moves the pen of the reader through the labyrinths
of the author's 'conception';   or so it goes.   Yet the moving finger
having writ moves on...   This applies to author as well as reader.
We must give up the image of the author as a translucent guide-book
to his own work.   That is a transcendental (in its religious
meaning) image which we could well do without.   Inverting the temporality of the writing by placing the preface at the front means
that the author is hiding something, covering up something that ought
to be said, namely, how he went about generating a work.   Should we
not place the preface at the back where it belongs?   Better still,
why not abandon the desire to send the reader somewhere-or-other and
let the reader himself control his life, discover the work by writing
himself into the work as he re-writes the work in his practice of
reading?   This is nothing more mysterious than letting the reader
see behind the masks of the writing in order that he be intoxicated
with the Idea of reflexively providing for that work, the grounds
which sustain it and which are the real subject of writing.

In a preface we expect a display of self-reference.   However, the

habit of wanting a display of authorship 'at the front' in a very
mundane sense, after which we can relax into the somnambulent warmth
of the author's words, tends to reify and exclude a deeper reflexivity.   For instance, sequencing the preface in a conventional
manner tends to suggest that the author need only exercise reflections at the beginning (which is secretly the culmination) of the
writing - when, in fact, the very readability of the work is a
testimony to the presence in the work of self-reflexive 'solutions'
that lead directly to the unsaid of the text.   There is something
strikingly unnatural in requiring the author to accomplish in two
pages what he could not accomplish in two hundred.   Demanding a
preface also presumes that the writing would not display its sense,
would not bespeak its grounds upon interrogation and, more signific-
antly, that the reader could not make it speak in his transformations.
It will be obvious upon reading the papers that follow that we could
not possibly engage in this kind of concretely self-referring
preface-work when in fact one of our recurrent themes is the issue of
self-reference and self-stratification.

To put the reader at ease, to 'put him in the right frame of mind'
means robbing him of the possible mystery and strangeness of a work
of writing;   here the author's self-reflections about his own work
take precedence over any violence the reader may enact.   At this
point the temporal sequence of prefacing joins hands with a fetished
notion of reading: the reader is required to attend to the author's
version of the strangeness of writing and thus to accept as authoritative a conclusion as a commencement.   We can consider this as a
further testimony to the innocent (yet powerfully so) arrogance of
the author who, in proposing to help the reader into his writing,
subjugates him to the author's frame of mind.   The author, as it
were, clings to his product right up to the very end (bringing to
light the product-nature, the commodity-form of conventional
writing) by extending his life from the body of the main work into
the preface.   He is the specter who haunts the work through the
instrumentality of the preface: by his desire to supervise the
reading of the work by supervising the reader's time.   Not only is
the reading of the text preempted for a future reader in a conceptual way (by the way the author supplies a 'frame of mind') but
also by a preemption of the temporal openness of the text: that all
future readings of the text are to be read in a timeless preface
frozen in the 'hic et nunc'.   Perhaps this is why the source-texts
of the tradition we inhabit age most rapidly in their prefaces.
The Hegelian notion of Prefacing (Hegel's Preface to the 'Phenomenology of Mind') would be an exception given that here the preface
becomes a text openly encouraging reflexive readings.   In our
terms it would be an 'In place of a Preface' which displays the
practice of writing - the Odyssey of writing-consciousness as the
consciousness of the Odyssey of Writing.

In place of a preface, then, let us consider certain gathering
'leitmotifs' as an invitations to a listening-Other who is prepared
to soften his hardened categories and enter the play of dialogue in
which social theorizing is performed as a social mode of being-
together.

Prefacing is where the reader discovers which thinkers and
thoughts are judged worthy of remembering - it gives him a clue to

the existence of the author - by showing him which speeches were
deemed worthy of retrieval, worthy of being dredged from the tradition in order to enter the dialectic of our retrieval as reading.
What the reader requires is the subterranean continuity, the great
chain of Being - the community of language and thought - to which we
pay homage in casting our selves as acknowledging selves. We totter
on the verge of metahistory: considering reflexivity as a kind of
unifying thread, along which the cunning of Reason has threaded
masks and deceptions which, when revealed, uncovers the revelation
of historical reflexivity (as Absolute Reason), means accepting one
version of tradition. Our reading of Heidegger certainly suggests
that, for him, the metahistorical destiny of the west derives from
a single vision sown at the dawn and now in the process of working
its inexorable way into the Evening-lands of the west. Yet the
amnesis and reminiscence of Being does not catch our project;
Writing here does not depend on a nostalgic yearning for the play
culture of the ancient Greeks nor for the anti-Writing frenzy of the
Dionysian within our tradition. However, what is certain is that
these metaphors are part of our tradition and at the root of sociological world-conceptions. Without re-trieving these metaphors,
the self-forgetful speeches of sociology become another dried bead
on the deep thread of reflexivity. Writing sociologically, for
instance, is an acknowledgment of the company we would like to keep
historically as well as for the companionship of the reader intended
in the writing. We wish to make the reader co-responsible for
listening to and hearing the tradition so that in his reading (as
hopefully, in our writing) he can accomplish a principled violence -
a retrieval - upon the source works of that tradition. Yet this is
not to be grasped as a structuralist or semiotic project (1) and
certainly not in terms of the underlabouring image of the conceptual
analyst busily clearing the runway of the future for the progressively accelerating engines of scientistic modes of theorizing and
being-towards the social world. If it seems that we are initiating
an all-out retrieval of the conceptual and metaphysical roots (the
cosmic Ideas that sustained historical texts) of our tradition we
would have misled: the preliminary accomplishment of our cooperat-
ive enterprise cannot sustain such a heavy burden; in fact, we
intend the collection as a way of resisting such legislative
metaphors: especially those subtle inquiries still hiding behind
the Promethean desire to display and uncover the underlying deep-
structure of the phenomenal world in an ec-stasis of 'once and for
all'. Touching the 'Anlagen' of the world in this sense means
bringing an end to temporality.
    Relatedly, a retrieval attitude of reminiscence, recollection,
re-laying does not imply that our papers possess a cutting edge that
will deliver ultimate statements about the deep stratum upon which
all sociological texts are ground (the string without the beads, as
it were); nor do we imply any such commitment to the possibility of
some such definitive future programme of depth analysis. Rather,
let us conceive of writings as calls, as self-inscriptions into a
tradition of sociological writing. On the one hand we discourse in
the house of traditional sociology yet, on the other hand, wish to
question and, most of all, understand how in their investigations
sociologists construe themselves by constituting worlds-to-be-

investigated.   But surely there are many mansions here?   How will
sociology be for us?   How will what it was for us be for you?
Certainly these papers are not to be recommended as 'answers' for we
have not even formulated the relevant questions;   in this sense they
are acknowledged failures.   Failures, however, are very often illuminating, and so it is with us.   Our writing forbids legislative
readings and forms of life;   it neither shows how stratifying practices can be mapped nor does it advocate tools for mapping hierarch-
ical systems in the world (even though we suffer by our complicity
with a hierarchic and stratified way of formulating problems in our
theorizing).   A way of being 'had' presents itself to the reader
here: where is their method?   what is their method?   how does their
use of the world read methodically?   how do their methods relate to
the ethno-methods of the presumed unreflexive laity?   Have they a
method?

A useful exercise would be to re-think the bifurcation of writing
into either Method or Madness.   Such a dichtomy hampers any attempt,
like ours, to move into a non-methodic reflection.   In fact we feel
nervous in even raising the question of whether a non-methodic reflection on method is possible or whether it is a contradiction in
terms.   Even so: how far would that contradiction take our thought?
For today, in our age of suspicion, the most urgent sociological task
is to Unthink Method.   Perhaps the reader will take up this contradiction and help in our retrieval?

What we seem to be searching for is a kind of metaphysical camera
that would slow down the way language projects our being in certain
committed directions;   thereby freezing the lexicons of sociology's
many ways of being-in-the-world and retrieving the sense of their
projections.   This is what is so difficult and circular about the
tasks ahead - for we are concerned with sociology's last words in
our tentative and evanescent first words, knowing full well that the
day will be inverted and our words will be read as last words by the
inmates of sociological world-conceptions.   There is no such camera;
it is a remnant of the dream-world of positivism.   We are solely
responsible for the treatment of tradition and of our insertion: we
can of course elect to the gentleman's club of observing the social
arrangements of the world and thereby elect to exist professionally
as voyeurs of the grief of others.

Such freedoms cannot be toyed with, neither by the hypocrisy of
so-called Marxist sociologies firmly entrenched in research bureauc-
racies financed by an 'ideological' purse, nor by formal and
'Wertfrei' sociologies for whom responsibility is the domain of
woolly disciplines called 'ethics' and 'normative philosophy';   for
us absolute responsibility is an existential condition of the
practice of writing from its inception onward.   We would like to
give this an impressive word like 'transcendental grounds' were not
such words encrusted with those very skeletons of skirmishes which
we wish to avoid.   There are colossal tasks to be undertaken and we
cannot be lost in the bureaucracy of polemic or controversy.   Those
who wish to hear our words confirming their deepest suspicions that
'Society' is in the 'Mind' will doubtlessly continue to do so;   we
can only offer openings for other readings that take the trouble of
listening in our language rather than always wanting to translate
into their language.   After all, the latter is the way of all bad

translations.   We have no doubts that brute stratification and class
as palpable realities for the many 'exist';   yet in saying this we
are executing an intrinsic transformation and it is here where we
stand: our work collects itself in its concern with the transformational relationships between these 'realities' and the writing of
them.   The real outrage comes from the dialectically inspired
sociolgies still locked into a realist or representationlist mode of
writing which adamantly refuses to recognise its transformational
character.

One manifestation of our opposition to re-presentational modes of
existence comes through in our papers in the strong emphasis on
'occasion' or 'occasionality';   but it should be obvious by now that
our occasional pieces are not exercises in analytic virtuosity in the
Simmel style.   Rather they come to be in the project of generating a
communal reflection on the preconditions of what it would be to do
social theorizing socially.   We are no Hamlets tied to the night of
endless sparking thoughts about the mundane and curious uncurious-
ness of the world.   The uncurious items of the social world, for us,
simply begin a circling interrogation which leads to the same destination - a destination of themes much older than sociological
writing, much older than writing itself.   Rather than write, we
would like to speak.   Here we have to forego facts and curiosities
and ask for their possibility: we seek to see how the prevailing of
language gathers World and how in writing we open the dimension of
World and historicity, thereby to experience anew the mystery of
being created in language, hanging in language, going forth and
turning back to language.   A mythopoetic preface would look more
like the alchemical image of 'Logos' as serpentine than of the evo-
lutionary image of universal progression towards a limiting 'telos'.

An easy way of entering these papers is by extracting the grammar
of our formulations, subjecting the words to a content analysis,
counting the repetitions of 'leitmotifs', analysing the grammatical
holidays we seem to take, and the like;   but this would be no better
than using these papers as an occasion to flex a rigid mode of interpretation.   This would deepen our disillusionment with the paradigms
of sociological work whose only recourse is to categories of accus-
ation like 'solipsism','idealism', 'anarchy', etc. or to weary
dichotomies like anarchy-culture, writing-revolution, theory-praxis,
idealism-materialism, and their kin.   These faithful categories
serve well to efface the writer from his criticism and from the responsibility of actually reading the text;   they are categories of
self-forgetfulness from which writing emerges as a writing 'for
Anyman', 'at any price', 'at any time'.

A slightly more sophisticated reading of our term 'retrieval'
might label us with the task of rendering deeper readings of the
traditional philosophers and sociologists.   Such readings would,
perhaps be based on a shared notion of the Good (of what communality
looks like, of Membership) which we share when speaking to one
another.   Perhaps we would then retrieve the sense of community in
the writings of the Greek theorists, in Hegel and in Marx.   For
example, it would be important for us to listen to those commentaries on Hegel that have tried to show that Hegel's use of the term
'state' did not name what we today conventionally name with this
term;   rather, for Hegel it was more of a label for the deepest form

of community as an ethical co-existence in an Aristotelian sense and
not as a specific institution, authoritarian, liberal or otherwise.
This would certainly have further implications for our reading of the
Marxian use of the Hegelian philosophy of the 'state', and for Marx's
phenomenology of intersubjectivity. (2)

Such a work of retrieval would also help us collect ourselves
with regard to, say, Raymond Williams's notion of community as a
dialectical product of a long, open-ended revolution which has, from
the very beginning, been opposed to the liberal-conservative ethos of
the Servile Word and the class-context in which the question of
Culture, Tradition and Revolution have been posed (Arnold, Eliot, and
Leavis for instance).   Williams has, for example, argued that Writing is itself and nothing else; he has opposed a Marxian determinism
with the notion that when we are reading (e.g. Marx) we are reading
it and nothing else.

Similarly, for the mythology of the Cultural Revolution, the
categories of participation and commitment understood concretely as
de-structuration and re-structuration touch upon the dialectic of
writing.   Williams himself has suggested that no Vanguard of the
Proletariat, no 'avant garde', no cultural elite, no body of party
rules can generate collective meaning – hence the fatally attractive
icon of the Maoist notion of Culture as an open-ended, incomplete
(principally incompletable) participation in which the Other is drawn
to write (to transform the world) as the social act 'par excellence'.
Thus Williams's conclusion that this dialectic is not ancillary to
the 'real' transformation of concrete praxis, but that it is that
transformation.

If anything our process of rethinking Culture and Tradition is
even more radical than Williams's insight into the intrinsic connection between writing and the revolutionary transformation of the
world.   In this sense we would like to stifle once and for all one
of the liturgical dogmas of conventional sociology which locates
writing as an Individual practice opposed to the Social machinery of
ongoing orders.   We would like to dismantle this inner-directed
model of sociological writing (as we would the criterion-type of man
dominant in paradigmatic philosophy).   Thus we would ask that our
writings be viewed as practices and explorations of a projected
future art of writing-socially (in which the adjective becomes a re-
dundancy).   It is no longer apparent that social theory must be
executed on an individual basis or upon the auspices of a bureacratic
notion of community (the Research Foundation and Establishment-
grant).   The very sounds of these nouns ring ominously against the
truly collective enterprise of doing theory socially.

If sociological theory is, in some hitherto unduly simplified way,
'about' the world men precipitate together, then any theoretic
activity which explicitly attempts to articulate those worlds within
the intertextuality of a writing must display its sense of being a
social practice to its very roots.   Hence we have an affinity with
all who have radically questioned the dominant modes of speech and
their background ornamentation as political acts of the highest order
(the Georg Grosz of the Word – Karl Kraus – (3) as well as Brecht
might be noted).   We, like them, are uncertain of the path in which
doing social theory socially will lead us, but we are also absolutely
convinced about the complacency of non-reflexive writings against

which we rebel; if we have uncovered themes of common interest and
increased the level of controversy, as it were, in relation to
sociological writing, then we have entered the gradual circular recoil
back to where we began from which we have never really moved.   Yet,
as with Kafka, the journey back to where we came from will be truly
immense.

MY DESTINATION

I gave orders for my horse to be brought round from the
stable.   The servant did not understand me.   I myself
went to the stable, saddled my horse and mounted.   In the
distance I heard a bugle call, I asked him what this meant.
He knew nothing and had heard nothing.   At the gate he
stopped me, asking: 'Where are you riding to, master?'
'I don't know', I said, 'only away from here, away from
here.   Always away from here, only by doing so can I reach
my destination'.   'And so you know your destination?' he
asked.   'Yes', I answered, 'didn't I say so?   Away-From-
Here, that is my destination'.   'You have no provisions
with you', he said.   'I need none', I said, 'the journey
is so long that I must die of hunger if I don't get anything on the way.   No provisions can save me.   For it is,
fortunately, a truly immense journey'.

                                        Franz Kafka

NOTES

1 By 'structure' and 'semiotic' we refer to scientistic interpretations of language; the notable reconceptualization of semiotics as meta-semiotic reflection (Barthes and Kristeva for
   instance and Derrida's grammatology) evades our description.
2 We have in mind studies such as C.J. Friedrich's Introduction to
   'The Philosophy of Hegel', New York, 1953, xliv and Z.A.
   Pelczynski's The Hegelian conception of the state, pp. 1-29,
   in Z.A. Pelczynski (ed.), 'Hegel's Political Philosophy'
   (Cambridge University Press, 1971).
3 A political reading of Wittgenstein's later work might begin
   from his respect for the political satirist, Karl Kraus, for
   whom the revaluation of values must have its primary locus in
   the purging of intellectual and political life of empty phrase-
   ology.   See Paul Engelmann, 'Letters from Ludwig Wittgenstein'
   (Oxford, Basil Blackwell, 1967).

Chapter 1

INTRODUCTION: CRITICAL TRADITION
Barry Sandywell

...The Way from Writing to the Thing is no less necessarily
by and through Language.

J. G. Hamann

My interests in the following Introduction and in the papers which
expand upon it seek no more than a sketch for a different sense of
Language and Tradition which revolves around the notion of how speaking differentiates and collects in one unfragmented movement. The
words themselves point to the stratifying rules and practices, talk,
rhetoric of theorists like Marx as instances of the pervasive theme of
Difference. Thus the recurrent reference to Marx's themes: Class,
Class Struggle, Class-in-Itself, Class-for-itself, theorizing the
immanent Transcendence of Class, de-Classing thought-and-action, and
so forth. However these words constitute sketches - a first word or
occasion for the revival of dialectical, speechful, articulating theorizing to-gether. They are in principle unfinished, unfinishable -
and in this sense are avowedly audacious. This audaciousness is
intended to move the reader to formulate the sense of this and other
occasions in his own Voice. The audaciousness engineers a sense of
the praxis of Writing in order that we may retrieve talk as making
reference to perennial themes which sink deeper into language than the
surface forms of that talk insinuate. Specifically I wish to refer
the reader to the auto-stratifying practices of theorist's talk - as
instituting them into a collective identify, morality, commitment;
more generally, I wish to refer these irremedial auto-stratifications
back to deeper notions which, like tributaries of a river, lead to the
source of any possible social reflection, and possible social theorizing.

This source is regarded as the stimulus and the 'telos' of languaged activities - it is regarded as adumbrating a moral sense of Self.
An incomplete cycle of these themes which might be called essentially
unavoidable notions forms the 'grammar' of an emergent concept - and
this is Critical Tradition. Thus essentially unavoidable notions
cluster about Language (as 'Logos'), Language as unavoidable Articulation, Speech, Speechful Labour, Theoreticity as the ideal of moral
speechfulness, Speechfulness as referring the speaker to the essencing
of authenticity, Theoreticity as Critique, Critique as Critical Reason

which aspires to Wisdom, Critique as Critical Reason, Critical Reason as both concrete and analytic liberation not from but for the sway of tradition.

Such an intertwining variation of themes also contains their negation - a correlated forgetfulness which is the shadow that accompanies theorizing tradition.

This cycle of notional forms provides the mirror-play for all thinkable social thought, a subterranean Limit, Measure, Grammar which must be concretely filled out before any form of social thought becomes possible. It is the way that modes of speaking concretely fill-out this grammar which leads to the pathways that have been carved into our tradition - and it is these 'Holzwege' which we wish to raise to the surface under the rubric of Critical Tradition. Unavoidably we trade upon a lexicon which is likewise 'on the way' - there are no standard footholds nor ready paradigms to be cited for this venture.   The reader must accept as an a priority the speculative intelligibility of this (kind of) writing. Where he does critically accept the text, he has already become a re-writing Reader.

My listening and canvassing of this mirror-play is more radically an invitation to the reader that he enter and theorize along-with the writing; the mirror-play is such that it essentially in-volves him - for the oblivion of language touches all speakers. In this sense we are ob-lig-ated, we find ourselves tied together in the common pursuit of a difference that would collect us as theorizers.   In order that this be concretely advanced the reader must be dislocated into taking two steps back before he stands forth to inherit pathways (speechways) into tradition, in my-our sense.

By pointing our reader along the way to that Difference which 'makes' (poetizes) all difference we destroy nothing; like the Delphic oracle these fragments are signs, indications, digressions, reminiscences on rationalities and madnesses - whose 'point' lies elsewhere.   Yet these digressions - indeed this digression - are spoken for a reason.   One of the first great reflexive speakers already declared that he came not to destroy but to fulfill - to provide the world's talk with its forgotten communal ways and means - with its vital grounds.   In a similar way, the emerging notion of interrogative or critical tradition, seeks to preserve through the disruption and terrors (for concrete speakers) of listening and articulating formulation.   Hence the dislocation spoken of a moment ago - a dislocation felt when the concrete speaker is referred back to the Difference which makes a difference, gathers his talk and makes him speak 'differently', makes his outpourings a difference within a curtain of Identity.

We come not to destroy but to preserve.   It is this disruptively respect-ful attitude which I'd like to draw attention to at the very outset; to give a reader the hint which transforms his egological desire to depict Being into the desire to formulate it - to explicate his stance and consciousness of his sense of explication and criticism - to achieve a Community of formulation and therein radically ground his words.   For there is no problem of the radication of meaning, the radical problem is the communal construal of senses of meaning resourcefulness - Difference is; what are the Differences?

In a way what is so difficult for us to research is the simple

question: How do practioners of instituted communities come to formulate Being in the languages (in the depth of Language) grounding
those communities? Once this question is richly specified, made
'concrete' in the Hegelian sense, it shades out into a notion of tradition and the variegated texture of discourses which provided a
tradition's possibility. Receiving concretion likewise transforms
the 'simple' problem into the most difficult research of all - for
this research not only seeks the grounds of the Other's rhetoric but
also seeks to know its own, and the double movement of reflexivity
can only be furthered in the same attitude of re-trieving a sense of
language and critical tradition. How does Being come to disclosure
in those beings which form the fabric of tradition - in discourses?
How does Language sustain the being of languages, discourses, rhetorics in its sway in order that depth be instituted as the resourcefulness of all speaking. How and as what does the world come to be
said in the voices which form the secret history of tradition? It
is in this nexus of questions and problems where we can authentically
locate the enterprise of Criticism as one further rhetorical possibility.

We recall that discourse is an instance of what it speaks about;
talk has a deep ontological status bound up with this 'about-which'.
Language itself as a communal 'mittence', a perdurance through social
frames of time, is both instrument and product of communally disclosed Being. It is this peculiar dialectical nature of discourse
which makes disclosure and self-disclosure possible. Discourse
leads us to formulate Being as the 'about which' we talk, as it also
discloses itself as that by which we 'talk about'. There are profound reasons for interpreting this two-fold openness of discourse
as a dialectical tension, a sort of 'hyphen' from which begins reflection and self-reflection which are necessary for any kind of articulate speech. The hyphenated dialectic of discourse contains the
possibility of reflexive articulation. Speech, so to speak, is
internally divided for it is 'already about' Being as 'already about'
itself as an instance of Being. Speech exhibits itself as ontologically construed in projecting itself toward the world as construed.
Discourse is self disclosure, self-referring, self-exhibiting.
Throughout its essential twofoldness, however, speech remains coherent; it does not fall apart into the 'about which', nor does it
simply revolve into an exhibition of itself. Speech retains the
unity of its own intelligibility. Like the Heraclitean Bow and Lyre
discourse is a harmony from opposition, a Unity across Duality, a
deep Oneness whose sensible functions rest on a twofoldness. Language, in short, is the articulatory realm of dia-logue which the
ancients baptized Dialectic. Language is already a community of two.

We might formulate this intrinsic logic of exhibition which is
innate to discourse by saying that the unavoidable disclosure of
'Logos' in any kind of human discourse deeply requires that speech be
the region or site both of disclosure and self-disclosure. Fundamental to the intelligibility of any kind of discourse is, as it
were, a 'logic' of revelation. The possibility of self disclosure
(a communal sense of Being, reason, language) or revelation might be
thought of as the firstness of Language, a minimal ontological re-
requirement of articulate speech.

To utter intelligibly means 'already' to be a subscriber to this

condition; to talk 'about' anything at all requires its presencing;
to 'refer' to a supposed autonymous 'reality' with an instrument
which is itself partaking of the same 'real' requires the same resource. And so it goes. Revelation - the hyphenated structure of
Unity through Difference - becomes a category central to our considerations of Language and Tradition.

That we cannot avoid thinking of our being-in-language as a path
or way from language to the thing ('reality') already bespeaks the
pervasiveness of one rhetorical possibility, behind which functions
the hyphenation of revelation. Yet this is a possibility only for
those already operating deep within the continent of Language and
Tradition. It is like a metaphor grown cold. These remarks are
attempts to re-animate this kind of metaphor, working necessarily,
from within their dominion. Kant's great contemporary, Johann
Georg Hamann, points metaphorically to our metaphor when he reminds
us that the Way from Writing to the Thing is no less necessarily by
and through Language. That we can come to know this is a bequeathal
and celebration of the revelatory hyphen itself.

And as there are many paths and mansions toward co-responsive
thinking, so the shape of formulation will display all the richness
and variation of active interruptions in the juncture of Text-World.
Writing our way into a Tradition does not primarily mean mirroring
the objects which that tradition has found eminent - out-standing -
but rather attending to the modes of eminence, the modes of things'
outstandingness. However, the Great Mirror of Language is a potent
and violent way of self-formulation - and to that extent would have
to be respectfully retrieved and ground in its essencing. Or take
the tradition-oriented work of Philosophers of Science - the so-
called 'New' Philosophy of Science which engages the active "seeing-
as" of language and requires theory-ladenness as its watchword;
take the expression 'Criticism of Language' - take this Word much
slower in order that we might hear in it the ambiguous voices of
'Logos'. To attain a foothold to the emerging notion of 'critical
tradition' it might be useful to experience the dialectics of
'Criticism of Language' - for all 'Criticism of language' presupposes
inquiries of the kind adumbrated here; they are unavoidably circular
ventures into the spaces of signification given that Inquiry and
'Criticism of Language' are co-implicative. Likewise presupposing
the fact of a Community - Membership - who might listen as 'Critics',
'Inquirers', 'Consumers', and so forth. Critical tradition is also
a 'Critique of Logos' - a separating and collecting in order to
display the various senses of identity and difference which are tied
into any kind of speech. To do 'Criticism of Language' in our sense
would then be to retrieve and resuscitate the very terms of criticism
(Inquiry, Community, Dialectic, Intelligibility, and so forth);
where - in Kantian vein - we are concerned with the grounds of the
possibility of... as well as the 'and so forth'.

In our Anglo-American tradition it is the work of Thomas S. Kuhn,
Michael Polanyi and their friends who, like the dialecticians of
science on the continent - Bachelard, Gonseth, and the like, have
most seriously tried to re-think Science from within a critical linguistic tradition. Science is reformulated within this 'Criticism
of Language' as a community's ways and means of claiming a certain
kind of authoritativeness for its statements and propositions. The

historicity of Science's conceptual dialectics is nothing other than
the necessary working through of endemic structural relations to be
found in altered form in other institutions designed to produce
epistemic claims as objective reports upon Nature.   Science is both
communalized in its essence - as inquisitive research (Normal/Revo-
lutionary Science) and brought back within the possibilities of Language as another highly articulate attempt to discourse with Being
through particular authoritative social forms.   Kuhn, of course,
restricts his thesis to the concrete problems thematized by the traditional historian of science.   In this respect he - and other texts
in the Dialectical tradition - are more important for what they omit
and gloss over in silence than for what they articulately claim to be
speaking about.   The notion of theorizing the very grounds of anything like 'the history of Science' as itself part of a critically
discursive tradition, is left for the metaphysicians.   Kuhn's re-
trieval of Science however is symptomatic of both a conceptual need -
witness how his talk around paradigms has been consumed in great un-
critical draughts - and a deep rooted unwillingness to inquire into
the grounds of one's own thematizations.   Through this fundamental
oversight examples of the 'New' Philosophy of Science and the 'New'
History of Science are forced to resort to a positivist notion of
Community and Communal authority, rather than pushing deeper into the
grounds of community and posing the question of the reflexive possibility of 'society-talk' in the first place.   The failure to give an
account of one's accounts bedevils Kuhn - and writing of that kind.
Scratch his texts and we find a concretized version of the Hegelian
dialectic which refuses to think its own Limit and measure.

   As my introductory sketch is more of a research statement I would
wish to point out sources of possible work required if we are to re-
trieve historicity as discourse, Language.   Kuhn's work and the
syndrome of critical debate it has instigated is a notable candidate
for such reflexive theorizing: to re-think Science in terms of the
uses and senses of the Communal which its practioners presume and
display in the concrete actualities of their communications, reports,
work.   Not only are there something like 'paradigms' of theorizing,
examples, problem-candidates, and the like, but also paradigms of the
Communal which underlies and provides the intelligibility for surface
talk about problems, instrumentation, methodology, operationalization,
theory-testing, etc.   This vast field of Rhetorical uses of paradigmatic senses of the social remains a field for reflexive work.   No
more than this can be said at this stage in the work.

   For Kuhn and company a member becomes a special Member (e.g. of
the community of Science) by displaying a sense of having internalized,
utilized, appropriated (etc.) the institutional paraphernalia of that
community which Kuhn points to with the richly ambiguous word 'paradigm'.   To be a practioner of Science means to be paradigm-practised
or paradigm-conscious, though not necessarily paradigm-self-conscious.
Paradigm self-consciousness seems to be a structure of language which
is reserved for the various parasitical meta-scientists who tend and
'care' (cure) the machinery of the engaged scientist.   Language
comes to thematization for Kuhn merely as an available conceptual
stock which periodically suffers internal convulsions and revolutionary re-organizations.   Language is part of the instrumentation of
science which meta-scientists care for as would a mechanic or a

Lockian underlabourer.   Thus although Kuhn's work contains resonances with a critical attitude to the languaged-tradition as 'Logos', the work is uncritically located in a positivist description of language as tool or instrument available through paradigmatic ways for the practioners of a community.

We could in passing suggest that Kuhn's 'member' or 'practioner' might more usefully be conceptualized as a languaged Self through which a community's disclosure of Being (its languages) speaks and is channelled into practioner activities.   It is only in this way that a Community achieves expression and 'passage' through the vehicles of concrete speakers.   It is in the practices of these Selves where the meaning of a Community's disclosure of Being is exemplified.   The same argument applies, 'mutatis mutandis', to each and every other languaged-community.   With this transformation all Communal construals of Being become essentially - not just contingently - moral enterprises and are thereby instituted rhetorically as ontologically political.

Movements in contemporary sociology variously labelled 'phenomenological sociology' or 'ethnomethodology' are thought of as candidates for critical de-struction and re-trieval.   Ethnomethodology is a prime example of the practical rhetorical accomplishment of a research discipline which refuses to think through its rhetoric; refuses to move from its research object which it locates as everyday members' practical, indexical accomplishments of sensible environments to the grounds of its rhetoric.

Ethnomethodology might be thoughtfully re-appropriated here not as a sociological discipline constituting itself about the constitutive rationalities/irrationalities of everyday social institutions - but as one rhetorical establishment of instituted reason, discourse, Language.   Like Kuhnian criticism ethnomethodology contains more relevant silence than articulate sense.

If we wished to characterize the sense of this writing which is attempting to rhetorically constitute a tradition of critical language as Logos we might hyphenate the word Ethnomethodology and take the hyphenated structure to the letter.   Thus Ethnomethodology would speak from its silence as:
'Ethno-methodos-Logos'
and this triadic Concern (in Heidegger's sense) now begins to speak to this paper in the voice of Language and tradition.   In terms of its three components -'Ethno/Methodos/Logos' we could speak ethnomethodology as our project.   That is, we are seeking rhetorics by which Communities (Ethno-) articulate ways and means within language (Methodos-) in order to disclose, construe or articulate Being (-Logos).   Our rhetoric might be located as seeking ways and means of re-opening Community paths ('Methodos') by which we can resuscitate and re-inscribe our Selves into the Ground of Language thought radically as 'Logos'.

In a Hegelian manner, concrete ethnomethodology was a dialectical antithesis to the thesis of 'The Sociological Tradition' - that is Positivism or Constructive theorizing as re-presentational language/speech/writing which we are now attempting to 'sublate' through the internal contradictions which make the practise of ethnomethodology deeply impossible as a reason-able instituting (though possible as the ultimate 'logic' of Constructive theorizing).   The 'overcoming'

of ethnomethodology would occur by critically grounding it in the
forgetfulness of its words - showing it what otherwise would remain
(for ethnomethodology) obscured, obscurantist, irrational - pointing
it back into the grounds of language from which its rhetorics emerge
and, through oversight, to which it forgetfully returns.   Ethnomethodology dialectically necessitates 'ethno-methodos-logos'.

Working the implications of this thesis into the practice of ethnomethodology would unfortunately require a monograph in itself.   I
leave the project as a future research topic.

Inquiry - Criticism, if you like - indicates deep forms of rhetorical instituting conceived as full bodied 'Praxis'.   And it would
seem - from the fragments gathered here - that the instituting Process which is Language in the mode of ontological Difference (re-
trieving praxis, articulation, formulation) is to be construed as
prior to the Object, the articulated, the product.   The hint is itself contained in the lexicon of 'Criticism' which litters our socio-
philosophical tradition.   Perhaps the most amenable root to Critical
tradition would be through a radical interrogation of the 'Kritik der
Vernunft' (Kant), the 'Kritik der Sprache' (Mauthner, Wittgenstein -
as adumbrated above), the 'Kritik der Kultur' (Cassirer), through the
'Kritik der Tradition' to the cor-responsive emergence of Difference
as the animating ground of the possibility of Criticism (its
attitude and forms) itself - to a 'Kritik' of the 'languages' or the
instituting which founds a tradition - a 'Kritik' of Rule, Style, or
what we might call - hoping that the reader takes us at etymological
level - 'Rhetorics' of this instituting.   Then the 'telos' of these
papers becomes: Realize at its deepest that there are other languages but only One 'Logos'.   Follow the movement of the argument which
takes you from our tradition of 'Kritik', through our 'Kritik' of
Rhetorics to the critical gathering of 'Logos' itself, and dialectically re-trieve these critical enterprises as forms of institution-
instituting.

And in this Odyssey we shall find that the traditional desire for
the Beginning is thwarted; 'I' - the Reader - discover that the
Beginning is ever in the Middle - the Beginning of Language is to be
found in the 'Middle-ing' (Mediation) of Difference, whose name in
our tradition is 'Logos'.   'Then critical tradition is to be re-
claimed by dialectical inquiries?'   Yes and No.   Yes to the extent
that all writing is an interrogation which ingresses in order to
articulate senses of language-Being; no, if dialectics is taken as
outside tradition in the manner of a neutral Method of thinking which
remains immune from our grounding enterprise.   'Then tell me what
"dialectic" means?'   Dialectic - think of it this way - always the
Novel is worked out painfully from within the trammels of the archaic.

We would resuscitate the languages of the tradition (the expressions labelled 'metaphysics' for example) showing how the attempt to
articulate 'another site/another beginning' always works from within
an extant tradition, an extant use of the resourcefulness of speech
(and all that this implies) from extent articulations - cuts in a
landscape.   So 'Negation of the Negation' would be reformulated as
the struggle of the Novel achieved in a dialectical movement of reading or interrogation within the accomplishment of the Past (which is
also rhetorically available).   Here words such as 'Past' would
gradually be stripped of their concrete meanings.

Reading as interrogative Writing is the only access we have to
Negate Negation, our only point of access to the Voices which constitute a tradition of reflection or, in anticipation, of auto-
dialectical theorizing.   We are all familiar with the Diacritic of
'Our' thinkers: the western destiny - twilight of thought, the
'history of thinking' which is conveniently at hand under various
disguises and rubrics.   Polarity is its principle.   We refer, of
course, to the dialectic of Interiority's Odyssey over and against
Exteriority; we refer to our labels which provide us with a sense of
thought's historicity; we play Existence against Essence, Individual
sensible things against Ideas, we feel content in locating 'Plato's
Theory of Ideas', Limited to Absolute, Temporal to Eternal, Percept
and Concept, Reason and Sensation; Realism against Nominalism;
'Ratio cognoscendi' against 'ratio essendi'; Finite shatters against
Infinite, the Many stalks the One; Experience vies with Reflection;
the Concrete chases and bruises the Abstract; Art is pitted against
the unacknowledged artfulness of Science; Metaphysics is set up and
de-structed.   In other words we have not a Critical tradition, but
traditionalism; we enter the life-span of texts where one theorist
is eternally turning another upon his head.   We feel forced to
choose (sic!) our language, its allegiances, its 'ontological commitments': we opt for 'Aristotle or Plato', 'Descartes or Spinoza',
'Socrates or the pre-Socratic thinkers', 'Hegel or Marx', 'Husserl or
Wittgenstein'.   The field of playful antinomies is endless.
We can formulate a sense of traditionalism in Inquiry by saying
that traditional criticism thinks conversation as War, as analytic
violence.
What can we possibly mean when we articulate our peaceful tradition of disputes and debates as belligerent Strife?   Heraclitus
informed us of the analytic meaning of War.   But we have no space to
trace this line of thought.
War is the rule of our tradition to the extent that it hides its
belligerence under the cosmetics of 'criticism' and 'dialogue'.   In
our tradition 'criticism' is the polite word for partisanship - the
play-form (as Georg Simmel might say) for the wishful out-and-out
destruction of the Other as autonomous Other.
Where the play-form of War rules, then dialogue requires the annihilation of the Other's argument glosses under the differentiating
phrases of 'dialogue' and 'critical debate'.   Schools of philosophical theorizing became available as citations: look toward the
plurality of our tradition - there lies its vitality.   However, in
certain circumstances the pluriform nature of the Many conceals a
violent One: what is the meaning of this Manifold when what unites
the Manifold is a Totalitarian (Totalizing) concept of argumentation
as sublimated destruction?   We can be courageously speculative in
disputing with the Many on the presupposition that we do not overturn
the very terms of socio-philosophical argumentation - only on the
presupposition of leaving the analytic form of life of much of our
tradition: the Logistics of war-ful (the mirror inversion of awe-ful)
speech outside of our analysis.   To enter the School-debates of traditional inquiry means assimilating the forms of violence which form
its instruments.
To re-collect a non-belligerent sense of tradition means first to
bracket War-ful argumentation and attempt to provide it with its

sense - which it - as belligerence - could never accomplish.   With
great insight Marx began the formulation of types of thinking as
rooted in an Age of Iron: in a war economy thinking takes the form
of analytic violence. Raising the question of 'another beginning'
from within an Iron Age might be formulated as posing the question:
what kind of thinking will non-belligerent Inquiry be?   What would
an analytically non-violent conversation look like.   The illusion of
all talk lies in its naive assumption that the nature of talking is
simple and settled.   This very assumption is a sign of totalization
- to presume that talk is available and that we can proceed from
there.   Against the belligerence of traditionalism I would ask:
what form(s) of talk will lead us into a critical tradition which
grounds its talk in openness rather than in the one-dimensional conversation of War.

If our tradition is conventionally formulated as a play of bell-
igerents then research should uncover all the paraphernalia
characterizing war-games.   Thus as we read examples of our tradition
we are witness to the 'batteries' of arguments, the drawing up of
lines of defense, the parries and thrusts of classic disputations,
the trench digging, guerilla skirmishing and all-out campaigns (the
campaigns against metaphysical and theological discourse provide
classic examples of these games).   Behind the logic of philosophical
argumentation lies armeries and belligerent logistics.   Periodically
there are cease-fires and the same perennial conflicts break out
again - in fact the institutionalization of these conflicts is what a
philosophical education consists of in most schools and universities.
This field (sic!) of inquiry into the logistics of belligerent philosophy might form a systematic programme for re-searching our tradition.   The actual lines of that research are yet to be drawn.

What strikes us now - after we have formulated and raised it into
eminence - is that the landscape of our tradition as we receive it
has to be presented as being in a permanent state of seige.   Traditional inquiry now has a reason (we have given it an account, a
'logos') for being adversarial thinking: the antinominal thinking of
our tradition needs Adversaries for its form of life is a concrete
dialectics of violence and war.   'Falsificationism' like conventional 'dialogue' and the older - 'verificationism' is simply a quotidian
term formulating adversarial thinking in a palatable manner - 'falsificationism' is a play-form for violent talk which, when linked up
with the differentiating engine of Progress, steam-rolls a many-
dimensional landscape into a binary world of the falsifiable and
the non-falsifiable.   Science is not simply contingently connected
to Technology and the Instruments of Violence: science expresses
the deepest aspirations of our tradition as belligerence.   Is it not
a violent philosophy which grounds its constructions on the cruel
mundale 'moral': You learn from your mistakes?   Language which
fails to keep to the target set by a Totalizing reason - Scientific
Progress - is condemned to the teeming underworld of speechless
mistakes.   However this is concrete violence done in terms of some
ungrounded and authoritarian notion of not-making-a-mistake:
'meaninglessness' should prompt the question 'Then what is meaningful?'   As an instance of violent speech it pales into insignificance
before other kinds of rhetoric already structually embodied in the
implementation of Violence.   However all these forms of speech are

sustained by deep forms which lie dormant within our tradition -
their pervasiveness should be a clue to their oblivious radicality.
Radical inquiry begins the thematization of the forms of life of
such speech.

All the manifestations of belligerent Languages which rage through
our tradition form perfect candidates for stratifying practices.
All such examples of belligerent speech either know the truth (or at
least where to look for it) or deny that there is truth (and deny the
truthfulness of the denial).   We could re-write this tradition as a
history of such belligerences, dichotomies, binary oppositions which
allegedly crystallize the domain of language into two opposing camps
of Truth and Falsity (today the categorial division is veiled in
distinctions of the kind Analytic and Synthetic).   Belligerent
thinking stands out by its very duality - at base it is nothing but
a community of Those who speak the truth and Those who speak falsely.
It is not accidental that belligerence achieves expression in an
essentially binary categorial apparatus, nor that violent speakers
perennially resort to some such device as Ockham's razor or some
razor-like Criterion.   In our own time we should thank the representatives of the school commonly called Logical Positivism or
neo-Positivism for the energetic way they have shown theorizers the
secret implication of their own tradition.   And in their showing
they displayed its negation, its impossibility, its disrespectful
silence.   But such logicism is still a disclosure of being through
the mediation of language within a tradition (formulated here as War).
The question we would ask is: 'What is symptomatically connected
with this disclosure for the nature and future of inquiry?'

Given time and space these reflections would be continued by re-
trieving the traditions of Sophistry - expressed in contemporary
terms as Ideology as the opening moves which sedimented in our
belligerent tradition.   Ideological thinking - thinking which not
only fails to give an account ('logos') of itself, but denies that
any such account is either possible or even necessary - perfectly
incarnates violence against the analytic Self.   Its rule is: Since
there is no truth there is literally no point in showing the truthfulness of my speech - all speeches are painted with the same brush,
all speeches serve the Interests of the Powerful and are justified in
terms of such violent auspices.   Ideology - in its historical
genesis and un-historical forms provides us with the face of belligerence.   Ideology is the secret truth of our Scientific tradition.
Hegel perhaps would say that the supposed antithesis of Belligerent
talk (Ideology) and the Vehicle of truth and Progress (Science) are
in fact at heart One - if we perform a deeper analysis.   In our
formulation of the adversarial tradition, Science needs Ideology as
much as Ideology requires Science: both require one another as terms
of denial.   However this is not the time to trace out the many ramifications of these dialectics.

Conventional tradition then seems to be a play-ground of false
dialectics and illusory reconciliations or antinomies.   Tradition
seems to be a shifting sand of mutually exclusive language-games and
epistemic claims.   The sign which stands above the door to this
notion of tradition as its august (if Limiting) lintel reads:
'Kritik begets meta-Kritik'.   But there is a grain of positivity
here: existentially its significative loom sweeps us first away and

then back into thinking.   From the concrete construal of tradition
we begin to learn: Your life is inescapably theoretic; theorize or
be-theorized.   Theory which drags a chariot of power tailors men to
its Rules (for example the Rule: See things as 'thing') rather than
sacrificing Rule for the enterprise of Inquiry.   Hence in this
'Negation of the Negation' we begin to get an inkling of the moral
urgency which leads to Dialectics, which requires Dialectical thinking.   For if we accept the above version of tradition it can only be
concretized in its eternally irreconcilable antinomies as War - to
speak with Levinas.   Authentic dialectical thinking subverts this
War by inverting, sabotaging, de-railing man-crushing forces.
Before Rule and Method we recover Inquisitive men; before the disputes and antinomies of traditionalism we assert that to live
rationally is to theorize together.

All that is required is that we think the Simple; the most
difficult thing is to think through these crude formulations of our
tradition.   Here we have compressed our discussion concerning tradition into the naive question: How are we to speak thoughtfully and
responsibly in conditions of unimaginable Violence - taking Violence
as the first theme of thinking today?   Since the beginning of time
to think the Simple has meant to think the Elemental in an elementary fashion and today the Elemental holds sway as the power of
Violence.   Yet Violence is the most difficult thing to think precisely because it is our element.

How does sociological theorizing think Violence elementally?
Conventional sociological theorizing takes as its Object the historically sedimented structures of violence and baptizes them 'stratification'.   It theorizes such 'stratifications' in a rich vocabulary of organismic and mechanistic metaphor of Functions, Orders,
Prerequisites, System-Needs, Rewards, and the like.   Throughout
their formulations however these theorists of stratification system-
atically insulate themselves from the embodied violence of their
Object - in ways similar to their insulation from the violence of
their own formulation and its providing form of life.   The Elemental
- Violence - remains unthought for Sociology.   It remains unthought
precisely because the language which aspires to think it is itself
an instance of violence - is by a lack of radicalism a deepening of
the violence of its Object - Stratification.   Sociology perpetuates
and exemplifies a belligerent tradition by granting its Object -
crystallized violence - sovereign status.   In this compound forgetfulness contemporary sociological theorizing is the acme of un-
thoughtfulness - is the incarnation of a constitutive inability to
think Violence elementally.   Furthermore no concrete criticism of
Sociology's form of life can escape this constitutive incapacity -
for it resides deep within the tradition which sustains Sociology -
not its surface metaphors and terms, but its very form of life.

Sociology's Grand Irony is that the very Rhetoric which is presumed to disclose the Object of Stratified Violence preempts its
authentic articulation.   Sociology as it exists today in its pen-
umbral, parasitical modes fails to think Violence for it fails to
think the nature of its own formulations - which would require a
potentiality for reflection which is - within the site of its oper-
ations - absolutely unavailable.   The irony is that Sociology is
incapable of thinking Stratification because it is unaware of its

own stratifications.   This is a first tentative conclusion.   A
second 'moral' follows from this: Sociology could only think stratification by thinking its own sense of difference - how it stratifies
itself within the tradition, and this would effectively destroy
sociology as it is practised at the present by generating a notion of
critical conversation with the Object of conventional sociological
inquiry which would destroy the Object-sovereignty of that Object.
Sociology can persist as a mode of radical theorizing only to the
extent that conventional sociology suffers its own demise.

In short, Sociology comes to grief in its attempt to think the
elemental Negation which Violence (in the concrete shape of Social
Stratifications) presents to it.   After all - how does a discipline
dedicated to the solidity of its social facts - a positive science
think such a Negation so absolute as Violence?   How does sociology
deal with Nothingness, with absolute belligerence or its concrete
traces in belligerent institutions?   Sociology might be revived
from its own ashes if it learns how to think Nothing - if it suffers
auto-criticism and begins to think simply - which is so very difficult for concrete inquiry.   Social theorizing will rise like the
Phoenix only if it refuses to think Stratification (Violence) concretely and attempts to ground its own violence (stratifications)
within - that is against - the background of its own belligerent
form of life.

However, the so-called Classic tradition already contains a virile
attempt to thematize the Object of social knowledge as Nothing - as
elemental violence, the internal war-state of Capitalist economy.
It is in the Marxist tradition where we re-discover the first radical
attempt to think the Elemental presence of Violence simply - and the
struggles which Marx's theorizing exhibit demonstrate how difficult
such reflexive thought proves to realize within the reified forms of
'bourgeois' reason.   Conventional sociology like all forms of Marxist positivism which are unthinkingly modelled on its belligerent
tradition has a future only as exemplary auto-destruction.   It is
one of the massive, though insufficiently realized, virtues of
Negative dialectics that it grasped some - if only in a concrete
fashion - of the deep paradoxes which a Science of Violence (Stratification) inaugurated.   It is perhaps only when we ask the sociological question in a Hobbsian and Kantian style that we realize
these dilemmas: How is a Science of Violence a priori possible?
Sociology will become an authentic mode of theorizing when it
'answers' that question - and everything hinges on the nature of
the answer.   Sociology will be realized only when that question is
no longer possible.

The question of a concretely understood Marxist dialectics
(reason) can now be provisionally formulated as:
How is a Science of Violence a priori possible?
The question of an analytically understood Marxist dialectics (rea-
son as liberative Logos) can be posed in opposition to this as:
How is a Science of Violence a priori impossible?
Grasping the difference between these formulations would lead us into
the domain of reflexive speech and critical tradition.

But before our formulation of the traditional understanding of
'dialogue' as War, Marx had formulated Capitalistic 'eminence' as
War.   Capital is construed as the sedimented conventional

(historical) power over labour, the means of production and the products which they realize.   Given that Capital is an index of sedimented labour - poetized dialectics as creative of all use-value -
all power relationships are construed as bound up with the organization and control of production, the utilization of labour-power.
The concentration of capital becomes a direct measure of the concentration of power, which is itself linked to man's being as articulating productive historical agent.   Power - sedimented as productive processes - becomes the secret of history.   History becomes a
development of the forgetfulness of articulation, a site for the foreclosure of human potentialities, a history of controlled productivity
('Produktionsgeschichte').   If historicity and human community can
be depicted as 'Produktionsgeschichte', then all talk about 'Man' in
the abstract (abstract Criticism) becomes impossible;   likewise formulations such as 'social history' contain redundant items.   Hence
Marx developed reflexive tools for the Criticism of 'Political Economy' as he critiqued its representatives.   Man appears - achieves
his being - under Political Economy as an abstract fragment of human
being;   Marx theorizes the Capitalistic adumbration of man: Capitalism is an ontological filter, allowing man to appear as abstract
labour.   Being-in-the-world is transformed into a productive sign;
men begin to function as tokens in a 'free' contractual exchange;
they are reduced to the terms of contractual agreement.   Human existence - speech - is canalized into an abstract flow of commodity
exchanges mathematically re-presented as the debits and credits of
the Auditor (whose theoretical symbol is the Political Economist).
    In explicit political theorizing the belligerent tradition sur-
faces in the peaceful facade of Civil Society - which is also a Self-
formulation.   The mask of traditional liberal thought hides, according to the Marxist critique, the latent violence of the framework
within which contractual notions (The Social Contract, Pact, Representative Government through Free Elections, the Sovereignty of
the People, and so on) become ideological possibilities and material
actualities.   A Contractual disclosure of social being would then
invert authentic sociality as it presumes that the 'logos' of the
social can be guaranteed in a concrete collection of decisions and
displays of will - whereas a speechful community is possible only in
the openness toward that which collects - and this is first uncovered
in a form of life which opens men to one another in the gathering of
dia-Logos.   Speech which percolates down to the 'Polis' from the
Representatives of 'the People' parodies dialogue in its one-
dimensionality.   Here there is work to be accomplished in addressing
classic liberal and contra-liberal political theorizing - possibilities of which are opened up in other papers in this collection under
the heading of Market Speech.
    Capitalism, in short, is theorized as the living historicity of
total War - the face of catastrophic internal Violence brought by
one Class against another in the process of capital accumulation
guided solely by the profit motive.   In like fashion the theorizing
carried on under the auspices of market speechfulness (speechless-
ness) delivers social being under the mode of War.   To theorize
within the parameters of this mode of existence is - as Mao formulated it - to theorize from the barrel of a gun.
    Hence the moral import of Marx's 'Kritik'.   The auspices of

Marx's theorizing - its presuppositions - are well known: English
Political Economy, French Socialism, Hegel's idealistic dialectic
and the sustaining horizon of German philosophy. The 'overcoming'
of the Hegelian dialectic was a serious task for theorizing - not one
to be dismissed by a terminological change. It is precisely on this
score that Marx vituperizes against the 'critical theologian' - Bauer
and his followers, of misunderstanding the nature of criticism -
where they presume ·to overcome and conquer their grounds by fiat yet
are irretrievably lodged in the concrete - (in feeling, 'Empfindung')
and fail in the accomplishment of critical self-reflection, 'Selbsbe-
wusstsein'. Ungrounded criticism in fact merely capitulates and
extends the auspices of idealism - it prolongs in a mirror image the
older forms of transcendentalism 'twisted into a theological caricature'. It overcomes without giving an account 'logos'. Marx
theorizes reflexively where he accounts and provides for the grounds
of his accounts. And the grounds of his writings lay - for this
discussion - in destroying the a priori (a historically specified a
priori) possibility of a Science of Violence - in sublating its
Object. His theorizing realizes itself when it no longer depicts
the contours of its Object. 'Marxism' then becomes concretely a
Class analysis of Class for Class (for de-Classing).

It is these aspects of dialectic which we might - in further work
- attend to. And Marx has pointed the way:
 'Die Kritik des Himmels verwandelt sich damit in die
 Kritik der Erde, die Kritik der Religion in die Kritik
 des Rechts, die Kritik der Theologie in die Kritik der
 Politik'.
   Marx ('1844 Manuscripts', Introduction
    to a Critique of Hegel's Philosophy of Law)
By transascending-trans-descending through Marx's escalated landscape of Critiques we re-experience the openness of his speech.
This we may conjecture was why there is Nothing where eager readers
wait for a description of Communist Man. Marx refuses to speculate
on speechful Labour, labour that has analytically come to-itself and
articulates the in-itself for-itself. Here there is meaningful
Silence from Marx - the pen no longer writes. Concretely Marx
refuses to speak on the future; analytically he leaves open the
possibilization of speechfulness. In a way this is a crucial insight that has been lost in the party polemics of Left and Right.
For Marx it is still an abstraction to speak about Inquirers as
'Speakers' - this is too abstract, and not speculatively concrete
(in Hegel's sense). We are 'on-the-way', we are Becoming speakers;
we humanize ourselves to the extent that we can retrieve the 'Logos'
which turns brute silence into human silence. This humanization
is the Promise of the Critical tradition - by 'accepting' the languaged condition we are 'thrown' and urged into a humanly binding
course. We are 'middled', already begun, situated in Language. It
is this 'withness' which resists all concrete formulation - for we
always wish to separate ourselves from the course of Language in
order to depict our connectivity - and yet this is precisely what
tradition analytically forbids: it provides for all forms of reflection, but cannot tolerate 'withoutness'. We speak from 'within'
the coils of Language as we live 'within' a tradition. We speak to
liberate one another within the frame of this bequeathal.

Our themes of Critical Tradition and the analytic pre-conditions
of Becom-ing a Speaker, which engenders a radical destruction and
transformation of our conventional understandings of these terms
(and their conjugates) can be provisionally understood as the thin
edge of a wedge which we have begun to drive into the petrified tradition here formulated as traditionalism, the belligerent tradition,
or the tradition of concrete theorizing - theorizing which fails to
see the moral sense of its project - which fails to see that the
openness of language only perdures in the moment of reflexivity which
grounds speech in the Good of Language.   The tradition of the concrete which flattens Language into a monoscape fails to comprehend
the nature of the goodness of sense which lies in this deep sense of
goodness.

My fragmentary remarks in '"Theoria" and Hermeneutic Circle', and
'Restoring Reading and Reader', is merely a preparatory prolegomenon.   Even though much must go unsaid, however, the recurrent
theme of my presentation - as I believe of the papers which follow -
is that from the source work of Marx, as well as Hegel and many
others in the tradition to which we are heirs, there is the possibility of posing the question of an alternative beginning to analysis
which centers upon the kernel thematics of speech, reason, theorizing and reflexive inquiry.   The enormous dimensions of such another
'beginning' inevitably outstrip the life of the papers between these
covers, thus repressing our variations upon this project - our
collective prolegomenon - into the role of an anticipatory prolegomenon to a prolegomenon to a ....   In short, in the region of our
work only a mere hint of the shape of this new path - another way of
analysis - can be won.   Moreover the winning is entirely 'in' the
listening.   Yet in abandoning once and for all the traditional quest
for the grammar of clear and distinct 'problem' and 'solution' our
theme is focussed: that in being on the way to theorizing (writing
more generally) the author must display the authority of his work,
show where he stands in Language - the warrant of his words - and
thereby exemplify the moral commitment to the animating ground of
those words.   We all subsist in different regions within Language,
yet no matter where our beginnings find us we always meet in the
free space at the centre of the amazing maze;   we meet, as Heidegger
has formulated it, by way of a homecoming in the communal task of
listening to Language, to that which grants the intelligibility of
speech but remains unviolated by the tangential rays of concrete
formulations.   We shall talk without meeting if we fail to experience the deep need to re-think, re-coil, re-cover the initial hope
which pro-jected thinking upon its manifest paths.   For this
apparently endless 'thinking upon thinking' concerns theorists essentially - both in its essence and in our essence.   It must be remembered that Heidegger's early formulation is that the tasks of
inquiry lie in 'thinking' Being which has remained unthought - but
that the practice of his thinking lies on the meaning of Being - on
the manifold ways of Being's coming-into-eminence or falling into
oblivion.   For the later Heidegger this has moved further into
necessary recoil upon the nature of thinking per se - becoming in an
almost Hegelian sense thought upon thinking.   For we learn that the
most thought provoking thing amongst a most thought provoking age is
that we are still not thinking ('Was heisst Denken?').   Heidegger's

recollective 'Denken' however has not escaped the tradition - it has
dramatized our ob-lig-atedness to the web of tradition.   The tradition has to be critiqued and re-covered intensionally - and this
means much more than being 'released' into the domain of Appropriation.   Future inquiries must continually pose the question of the
meaning of our indebtedness.   Here we have no guarantees, no criteria
that would serve as Guides through a strange land - and we have repeatedly fallen into concrete traps already set by re-presentational
modes of thought - we continually risk trailing off into the metaphysical sights along the way.   In this sense thinking places us in
a field of danger and radical vacillation; we no longer question -
it is our speeches which language questions.   The crossroads of the
Way, No-Way, add Wrong-Way never leave our thinking.

'THEORIA' AND HERMENEUTIC CIRCLE

> They are at variance with that with which they are in most
> continual association.
> Heraclitus of Ephesus

Re-presentational writing - like all writing - is animated by human
desire to speak the truth.   Here, however, speaking the truth is
already pre-judged as speaking the truth about the furniture of the
world construed under the warrant 'Thing'.   The 'desire' is already
restricted, and has not been allowed to flower into the hope for the
Whole which inspired the founders of theorizing talk.   Writing re-
presentationally desires to depict contingent things absolutely.   It
is internally contradictory from that moment on.   Its absolute aim
for such a mundane recovery gives re-presentational writing all the
marks of tragic-comedy, for all it succeeds in depicting with necessity is (like all writing) the sense of Community which it keeps
- or better, which 'keeps' it.   What is displayed is the difference
which makes it and preserves it absolutely in the goal of re-presentative speech - and this goal has all the tortuous paraphernalis of a
Frame.   Re-presentational writing thus succeeds in the depiction of
its moral premisses, its use of tradition, its sense of the existent
which it reveals in all its ironies and absurdities.   What is
essayed in writing is a sense of its own construals: how the world
lies.
    I have already spoken about the audaciousness of this (and perhaps
all) writing, but writing which seeks to realistically capture the
world in the space of its insubstantial signs is doubly audacious -
it is, to coin a phrase, composed out of compounded audaciousness.
For not only does it not ground its ironic audaciousness of speaking
truthfully in the first place (and this haunts all writing), but it
does not grasp the audaciousness of capturing Being in a sieve of
words - the very audaciousness of depictive inquiry per se.
    To reformulate a Heideggerian turn of phrase: we have not only
forgotten but we have forgotten we have forgotten: we speak audaciously but we display to our reader a sense of un-audaciously
speaking audaciously.   And unreflexive talk is literally adamant
about the sense of the world which arises in its signifying practices.   It is Adam-istic for the world comes to be with perfect

colours and with Edenic literality in the re-presentative text.   The
Rule for such adamant writing has always been: This is now things
stand - see them presented in the perspicuous language of the text.
However, all such writing refuses to address its mediate violence -
its formulation of the world - the text it exacts by forcing being
through its trammels.   Such writing denies interpretation - it
denies the authority of authorship.

Re-presentational writing denies that upon whose very grant it
rises and gives forth utterance.   Taken seriously there can be no
writer nor reader of this kind of writing - for they are excesses,
obstacles to the depiction of the Real.   Yet we cannot avoid the
problem of wrenching intelligible forms from a work of writing which
is itself drawn from the horizonal gift of the word.   This recourse
to 'hermeneutics' concerns all disciplines since it concerns all
thought - naturally it speaks directly to issues in reflexive theor-
ixing.

Science, where it formulates itself, does so re-presentatively.
Science is but the mouthpiece of Nature, of the God Scientific Progress, where Progress is understood re-presentationally - that is, as
the progressive depiction of the real with absolute structural (or
lawlike) fidelity.   Science is the practice of mirroring nature
to itself- of nature listening to her own Voice mediated by glass
men.   Science aspires to a perfect capturing of the real, of things
in the deep structure of their relations.   It is ousiology, knowledge of 'ousia'.

Over and against restrictive models of speech and writing - such
as those of re-presentation - I wish to assert that any discourse has
the character of depth, that Language itself contains a labyrinth of
paths, allusion, Metaphor, discourses, histories, rationalities,
madnesses, authorities, claims, claimants, methods of claiming,
'games', and so forth.   However the 'depth' is not to be thought as
a descriptive predicate of the subject - Language.   Rather 'depth'
is a characterization of what happens in the e-vent of articulation,
in the 'praxis' of attempting a formulation within the horizon of
Language.   'Depth' is only concretely thought of as either semantic
or syntactic (although it is also 'deep' there too - necessarily).
The 'depth' of grammatical deep structure is a depth-in-articulation,
as formulated within the programmatics of a certain rhetorical use of
language (Chomsky's instituting of a linguistic meta-language for
example).   Depth is, in other words a programme, enterprise, or
rhetoric-characteristic.   When we begin to formulate depth comes
into play, is drawn into the articulations of our analysis.

In this manner any attempt to speak perspicuously - to formulate
the sense of Language in the divine clarity of some derived meta-
language such as logic - is perhaps a necessary 'tension' which
Language contains (a rhetorical possiblity), but is also doomed to
disappointment if it is formulated in absolutist terms.   Only God
speaks divinely, and criterion-talk has always been god-talk.
Language resists the formulation of its depths, whether by logic or
any other re-presentational rhetoric.

Like 'Physis' itself which came into eminence in the thought of
Heraclitus, Language loves to conceal herself: the real constitution
of things is accustomed to hide itself.   And only on the grounds of
the e-vent of depth is there a world in common for those who are

awake.   Likewise any attempt to bring depth into play by desiring to
articulate within language means disrupting the surface of things,
introducing strife.   Articulating rather than re-presenting requires
a violent address of language which constitutes a sense of depth, a
juncture within the sway of Being, a 'whorl'.   In this sense strife
fathers all by its dialectic of harmony and opposition.   The path
into Language is necessarily also the path away from Language.
Heraclitus draws the depth of Language into articulation in the
following declaration:
> You would not find out the boundaries of soul, even by
> travelling along every path: so deep a measure does it have

or perhaps
> The Limits of the soul you would not find out, though you
> should traverse every way

Re-presentational discourse is built on the desire for divine knowledge ('sophia') of Limits.   Addressing Language as 'Logos' means
thinking language as Limitless Depth.

As I cautioned above, my anti-prefatory remarks do not imply that
all our interests harmonize or gell into a flawless picture.   In
fact just the opposite is to be expected.   We are not collectively
engaged in offering remedies, programmes, information, concepts of
truths.   If anything the Hegelian is nearest to our undisclosed
theme - in his understanding of the restlessness of Concept and
Theorizing.   If programmes are requested let it be that we are precisely trying to think that which has never been news.

In speaking of language with the grant of language from 'within'
language we already discover ourselves to be deep within the reflexivity of speech; we come to our-selves as unknowing inheritors
of linguistic, or more broadly, of methodic orientations which trace
our suspension in language.   To speak-out means to be a recipient of
a traditional framework of presuppositions and preoccupations which
ground our words.   This is why we never bother to continually appear
to Evidence or Grounds, since we have never radically doubted the
groundlessness of speech: through speech we are, we think, firmly
anchored in the inexhaustible richness of the total intelligibility
of World.   The term 'Membership' makes reference to this pact.
Irrevocably, then, every writing inscribes itself and its author
within the folds of a tradition, which in its gathering-together,
silently accomplishes the work of grounding.   Further thought upon
these guide-words would have to reactivate the resonant grammer of
'origins', 'genesis', 'constitution', 'intentional sedimenta',
'layer', 'arche-', 'archaeology', 'arche-ecriture' etc. upon which
phenomenological philosophy builds its house.   Before even conceiving of the possibility of questioning Where we were writing from we
are irretrievably committed to social thought (to some 'We'), the
rules and deep grammar of Membership.   Raising any itinerary of
questions show the topography of what we consider to be question-
worthy and question-unworthy.   Is this not why the mathematical
'Cogito' of Descartes or the mathematic rules of the transcendental
ego of Kant and Husserl no longer holds our attention?   There is
something 'unhappy' or 'infelicitous' as our Ordinary Language friend
might say about their approach to the problem of order and intelligibility.   We never stand face-to-face with anything: neither ourselves, our questions, our World.   We are forever ambivalent

thoughts; even the most articulate are entangled in epistemic projections over which they have only the most opaque and partial 'control'.   'Control' is an inhuman word of clarity for that which is
humanly ambiguous.   We suffer our enshrinement in Being before and
throughout the posing of questions; let us say that we are enclosed
in a grammar of disclosing Being.   In this context, the intransitive
verb 'to write' means nothing more (which already includes everything)
than probing the paramaters and limits of the freedom of disclosure
whereby the finitude of our openness cor-responds with the finitude
of the All: the Whole.   How peculiarly inverted everything now
seems: any writing which does raise the question of its possibility
must immediately be read as strange, or as Nietzsche well knew, as
'untimely'.   This is one of the senses of 'stratification' that
should preoccupy thought.   Thinking must always be dislocated by
throwing itself out-of-time if only in the mundane sense of questioning the hermeneutic canons of the 'agora' (thought's past) and
through its failure to offer routinized precepts for the future
(thought's future).   Thought subsists 'in between'.

Understanding and interpretation have been likened to a 'happening' (1) of tradition in which the living past is mediated for the
articulations of future thought in a present occurrence of transmission.   The archaeology of the tradition is 'eo ipso' the 'telos'
of reason.   Re-activating that tradition means dis-covering how
one's speech has already been founded without consent or consciousness.   It is an attitude of listening to the grant of tradition.
Yet there is nothing inevitable here.   The happening may equally be
an inauthentic mis-happening.   In escaping from the natural angle of
vision we place our thought in risk.   The original and archaic sense
of the word 'hermeneutics' (as also with the word 'phenomenology')
catches our attitude of thoughtfully listening to what could never
have been said in the said of texts.   Here it is no crowd-gathering
paradox to refer to the Word – the thought as Text-World – as more
important than the speaker or thinker.   In the passage of language
the concrete speaker is like a vehicle for what is said, thought or
collected in his speaking as the history of meaning ('Sinngesch-
ichte').

'Tradition' must not be confused with a sacrosanct 'Traditionalism'; the latter is an icon for foreclosure; the former, a symbol
for the Openness of inquisitve speech.   In 'Traditionalism' the
very historicity of interrogation, back-tracking-thinking, cor-
responsive thinking is frozen and denied.   A once vital landscape is
levelled and flattened into a monoscape, a two-dimensional field with
neither contour nor adumbration.   In traditional philosophy it
achieves its embodiment in the ideal of the disembodied speaker –
reason's monologue with itself about the course of the world.   Tradition, on the other hand, as an incipient category of inquisitive
life must be reunited with the intercorporeal historicity of Reason.
This historicity is the antithesis of Reason-denying Historicism.
As again the scepticism, particularism and nihilism of Historicism,
historicity affirms the role of historically ground reason.   Embodied writing produce within the understanding of historicity is
animated by the ideal of Readon – 'Logos'.   Hence we come to a
preliminary understanding of tradition as the continual re-appropriation, re-reading of latent 'Logos'; critical reason and traditional

reason are soldered into one common pursuit.   Writing-reading which
dwells upon its own carnal grounds has to be reason which reflects,
objectifies and critiques in order to further the openness of language.   Tradition exists as a potential;   like the domain of language itself it is an infinite field of creative Labour.   In this
sense the Labour of the Concept follows the Concept of Labour.   We
live as hyphenated Flesh-Word 'in' and 'as' a tradition.   We are to
this ever-expanding or collapsing sense of the same flesh or that of
which we speak.

It would not be untrue to claim that the sense of reflexive writing aims at an understanding of the Labouring language ('praxis') of
interrogative reason.   And that further, writing of this kind is
inspired with a sense of the Critical Tradition.   Concrete speech is
to be understood as an articulation within a field that has already
been articulated.   The domain of tradition and language is the event
('Ereignis') of Articulation, the e-vent of possibility which enables
the concrete gatherings of empirical speech to assemble, locate,
gather itself and give forth utterance.   Here then Vico's fable contains a truth: Language is the domain of the Creative;   concrete
speech is creative, articulatory - constructive.   Speech is literally
a making - and it is this that the Greeks express with the word
'poiein', from which is derived our 'poetry'.

With the desire to speak truthfully man is the mid-point where this
'poetry' is realized;   all speech is rhetorically touched with a
poetizing attitude to the extent that all speech is a 'making' articulation of Being from within the auspices of the whole.   The impurity
of our hyphenated being-in-the-world far from being an obstacle to
speech is its very condition and grant.   We are the 'withinness' of
the flesh of the world, embodied within the sedimented corporeal
schemata of a tradition.   Merleau-Ponty's philosophy of intercorporeality might be read in this more radical sense of 'etre-au-monde'.
We project or ingress into a tradition by virtue of the dialectical
tension - the hyphenation - of our incarnate status.   The dialectic
lived body-World is a concrete version of the hyphenated dialectic of
Flesh-Word/World where the hyphenation is our passage into, the
guarantee of, our communion with the world, with the Other, with Being
as tradition.

Tradition - to deepen what we have already achieved - is 'poetic',
a 'making' and an articulation.   Another way of phrasing this poetizing is that the languages of tradition disclose senses of being.
Where we speak of Substance, of 'Cogito', of 'Praxis', or the mun-
danities of Ordinary Language - each speech dis-covers a sense of the
world - and to that extent each speech is to be valued within its own
Limit and Measure.   There are no prizes to be given or received.

Through all these modulations of articulation - through the Labour
of Praxis-Speech - Being is 'on the way'.   Reflexive inquiry might
be construed as the self-consciousness of Articulation.

Now each one of these crucial terms - tradition, inquiry, poetizing, criticism, and so forth, are problematic in their own right and
should act as occasions for further inquiry.   They are guide-themes
which lead away from the stream of our concerns here.   Ideally we
should write a cluster of papers attempting to thematize issues which
are clotted about these terms.   However, for the limited ends of
opening discourse we can but exemplify a sense of this project - by

exhibiting what it speaks to and about – the disclosive potential of the Word, 'Logos', Language.

The sense of this exhibition really lies with the eyes and ears of a reader: of what resonates in his speechful reading, what sustains the speech for him in disclosing (or foreclosing) themes – ideally this should lead him back into the problematic of tradition.   To continue the metaphor – the attempt is to loosen the clotted threads, to slacken language in an attempt to say what language has left unsaid.   In this sense the text is a response in the richest sense of the word.

Tradition's recoil upon itself has led many of its members to speak of themselves as 'thought' or 'attribute' of tradition, substance, Logos.   This 'thought' is the authorship of the speaker, his fate-ful understanding of the depth of his commitment to writing and tradition; to the 'destiny' of his speech and to 'that' which sustains his words.   Martin Heidegger expresses the same crucial point: Language speaks.   The author's election to engage Language in his own speeches becomes more important than those concrete speeches themselves.   Thoughtful writing is writing which remains faithful or respectful with respect to the dependent nature of concrete speech; which recognizes that 'what' sustains one's speech cannot be other such speeches, nor a rule, nor a concrete 'turn' upon one's speech, nor a materialistically inspired reflection of the order of a sociologism of knowledge, and never a mere 'thing'.   Respectful writing struggles to avoid these impieties; it struggles to make reference to the historicity of the writing-self, the situated commitment of language and its light – the 'Nous' – shining through the text which makes the text ring.   It would be mistaken to literally 'search' for the subject matter of our discourse, since the most difficult thing is to understand that the matters which concern us are everywhere and obvious.   Its inaccessibility lies in its discretion.   This thought is like a pebble; we do not really choose the subject matter for from the beginning it has chosen us.   The way not to dis-cover our themes is to set out searching for them.   With a Heideggerian turn of phrase we can say that we do not come to thinking; rather it comes to us.   As Heraclitus spoke to the same discretion: Nature loves to hide.

Gadamer articulates this as a speculative movement of Being, dividing itself from itself, tying past with present in a unity of interpretation, the creatively new with the contexed-old, horizon within horizon as progressively further gatherings of a speculative unity.   The perdurance of time (its ec-stasis), of the opening of the mirror-play of the world regions has always remained unexpressed; identify and difference remain to be thought.

Reflexive inquiry into any matter whatsoever (not only social stratification and the dialectics of social formations) must begin with the self-interrogation of its own competence and rationality, the grounds which make speech about 'social structure', 'class', 'conflict', and the like, possible in the first place.   Inquiry identifies itself with a speculative interrogation of the tradition of reason which makes speech andhistory sound for us: a letting of language hold-sway in the self presentation of what the text ostenisbly speaks.   Here, for example, we might see in Marx's concepts a 'praxis' and 'proletariat' his way of raising the oldest theme of all - to humanize speech and history without anthropomorphizing the world or turning reflexive inquiry into an unthinking humanism (to the latter quest we would have to ask for the grounds of the possibility of any humanist metaphysics).   For Heidegger the conversation with the tradition must, likewise, be simultaneously a conversation with the history of the meaning of Being.

If we construe the field of sociological analysis as the theatre of Class Struggle, then all problems of analysis ultimately reduce to the life-and-death contradictions of Labour and Capital - where the question of human(e) speech and life lies in the reconciliation of Subject and Object.   One of the great Marxist thinkers of our own generation - Georg Lukács formulates the problems of historicity and analysis in these beautifully simple terms.   In his work 'History and Class Consciousness' the antinomy, the 'coincidentia oppositorum' of Subject and Object receives its formulation and speculative-dialectical resolution.   Here the problematics are stripped to the bone, sublimated and transformed into the dialectical struggle, not of Master and Servant, but of Proletariat and Bourgeoisie - the outcome of which results in reconciliation after the revolutionary overthrowal of de-classing of society symbolized in the u-topian blossoming of social relations after the transition from the realm of Necessity into the realm of freedom - itself articulated as Control of that which is Necessary (after Spinoza).

But in a sense, this kind of speculative dialectics takes as its model the tensions and contradictions of a unity-in-difference, whose model is conversation.   The conversation is simply articulated in a highly specific manner.   Understood as the definitive picture of the real such a formulation is a foreclosure.   We, however, are seeking conversations, disruptions, de-structuration of such dialogues. As Heidegger says we must not forget that our conversations are questions posed to a rich tradition concerning ultimate problems.   This is necessarily the case since:

'We - human beings - are a conversation.   The being of man
is rooted in language; but language occurs really only in
conversation' ('Gesprach') (From 'Erlauterungen zu
Hölderlins Dichtung', 1963, 36).

Language speaks.   In our theorizing we are merely in conversation with language, with the non-human Saying of Being.   Naturally, however, the claustrophobia of the concrete immediately robs us of this hard-won insight.   It is not an acquisition in the sense of acquiring a new pair of boots; it has to be continually re-achieved.   All our theoretic activity can be regarded as both a methodic use of self and a methodic use of the history of Being (the mittence of Being). Reflexive writing asks that the insertion into this mittence be shown in its use, in the work of the writing.   Here the crucial issue of the writing is how the writing issues.   How it stands in relations to coherence, how the intelligibility of its speech is guaranteed, how its intelligibility is produced, how we are assured of its coherence; the problem is to make the issuance of writing the issue itself without freezing what sustains the writing into a set of objects or methodological cautions, or much worse, in a display of personal, idiosyncratic and relativist 'Weltanschauungen'.   The self-centered 'hubris' of a Protagoras as a paradigm for this emerging notion of writing would be an absolute subversion of what

reflexive speech can be.   The nihilistic silence of 'Man is the
measure of all things' is the very antithesis of our notion of the
humanity of speech.   For this vicious humanism segregates man from
language, being from Being and like the voluntarist humanism of positivism must be avoided at all costs.

Language speaks.   Language enables speakers to 'have their say',
to give forth, make reference, utter, join and separate within the
creative expanse of a community's rhetorics.   Language enables the
formation of rhetorics.   In this manner it is the region of the Opening.   It opens men to one another through the medium of speech.

Men are opened to one another through that which divides them concretely.   They are separated (stratified) and yet gathered together
in the mediation of word.   Here we have a perfect image of the
labouring word - the praxis of articulate being, recoiled upon itself which separates as it collects.   Language speaks.   Men labour
within its horizons to articulate upon the many-leveled, splendoured
resources of language.   Speech happens within the intercorporeality
of a labouring tradition.   Here we are at the heart of Marx's
notion of 'praxis'.   Men exist as formulations within a horizon of
formulations.   We speak now - and for a future - only on the auspices of communities of anonymous Others who have laboured at the
tasks of speech and life, providing the very sources and instruments
of our talk.

Tradition means to speak from within the labour of the Other; we
labour and stratify the world and give voice to expression (which is
not to say speech is simply expression in the style of Romanticism
in philosophy).

Language is - among other things - the laboured bequeathal of an
infinite string of dialogues; here we have a concrete image of the
Resourcefulness of language.   The grounds for our expressiveness -
the House (to use a Heideggerian deceit) in which we have our articulation.   We are obliged to speak from within.   We carry this
obligation as speakers.   It is worth taking the words 'obliged' and
'obligation' more slowly: we are tied into the labouring hands and
voices of others: ob-lig-ation.   Speaking ties the expressiveness
of a lived past to the infinite possibilities of a living future.
Language is this chamber of self-ful actualities.   The dictum
'Become who you are' points to its inner dialectic - the futurity of
meaningful discourse, action, reflection.

Language speaks.   Speech is the strange dialectic of Sameness
and Otherness, Presence and Absence, Sound and Silence.   Yet how
does language contain speechful possibilities?   In what way are we
'tied', bound, bequeathed?   How are we promised, pledged to the
horizons of the Word? (2)

What is the nature of the secret force lying within tradition that
gives Voice to concrete voices?   Perhaps it is here that we touch
upon the fundamental mystery which philosophy has skirted since the
opening of our tradition?

Language speaks.   How is speech-ground-into-a-tradition possible?.   Why speak at all?

And that question strikes us as strange: it is of the order 'Why
are men together in human(e) community?'   We feel like responding -
what are you comparing to speechful men here - the speechless animal,
the brute?

'Why speak?' - the question is self-answering, yet in its self-reply we are sent puzzled back to the notions of Tradition and potence - tradition which holds the forms and rhetorics of our speechfulness - and is this legacy the rhetorical possibilities of our being and future co-existence.

The question - 'Why speak?' is perhaps an impossible question;   a more naive formulation might have been: 'Since we are thrown into language how can we make language speak, say utter?'   How can we open further the domain of Opening?   How can we make dried tongues and texts sing again?   How can we re-instate the prose of speech with the vibrant Prose of the World - the world which sings through and upon the auspices of language?

An adequate understanding of the emergent notion of 'reflexivity' must block all concretely autobiographical turns as it also must exclude statements of historical 'value' in the neo-Kantian epistemologies and the total commitment to 'life' of the 'Lebensphilosophe': these groundings are culturally relative and tend to transform speech into measurable things as does the slightly less sophisticated reductions of positivism and materialist definitions of speech. Naturally enough 'what' animates writing goes much deeper than any such personal or World-historical choices, and must somehow be the invariant that lies untouched in our tradition (that is, that Parmonides at the beginning of our tradition attempted to make reference to the sustaining features of speech and reason in a mood of inspiration caught by later thinkers within their texts).   Ludwig Wittgenstein, for example, divided the 'what can be said' from the 'what can only be shown' and despite his logistic formulation of the problem in the 'Tractatus' his recognition of the puzzle of the text, of writing, of saying the beyond-logical within the Form of the logical resonates with the attitude of our reflexive contributions. This probably makes the 'Tractatus' one of the most important moral works of the early twentieth century.   Like the 'topos' and horizons of Wittgenstein's six world-bearing propositions a model of reflexive writing must itself become an occasion to exemplify the invariant grounds of its production - as an occasion to retrieve one's own method, to interrogate the wonder of the Concept, one's way of transforming text into world and vice versa but without objectifying it within the writing.   Showing one's method then becomes tantamount to showing one's responsibility for the writing - the moral commitment of the text.

How are we to dwell authentically with our writing?   If the kingdom of the world is the Word are we up to the burden of honestly speaking from that site?   How are we to live theoretically?   By what criteria do we judge our writing?   What are 'criteria'?   Where is the author of the work?   What is a text?   If we are to be deeply puzzled by the act of writing we must loosen the traditional notions of theory and inquiry, reading and writing, reading and reader, authority and author.   In a way we are trying to dissolve the 'and' that divides in order to gether the differentiated in a togetherness that collects.   Our language requires less 'and'.   If we are to ground the sense of our speech (to be self-responsible) we must exemplify the self of the accomplished work for in casting a writing there is a correlate casting of self.   This much is inescapable;   it could not be otherwise.   But this is far from an uninteresting

platitude (as the disquietudes above are not themselves uninteresting).   Grasping by re-writing a text in a listening attitude of re-
trieval must be central to reflexive work.   Writing can be likened
to a well, knowing itself to be sunk deep into Being from which are
dredged the gifts of language.   What we have to say cannot be mech-
anically repeated in the reader's reading, but must be re-written
continually anew.
      But what - the impatient Reader asks - would stand for a 'success-
ful' example of reflexive speech?   How can we (as unreflexive
speakers) join hands and speak together (as a reflexive We)?   What
would stand as an example here?   In a way we could only return the
reader to the Writing and point to examples: From these examples
become a Reader!   But this is unsatisfying.   Well, then: Language
must be re-instated as open-ing and bequeathal.   Language speaks and
to the extent that it echoes within your words, language bequeathes,
grants, gives.   Language is a divine gift.   The aim of our writing
then might lie in the satisfaction of a desire which this essay exhibits: to 'open' the web of language, construed as 'Logos' - or
better, to add to the 'opening Voices' which are struggling to re-
collect the primordial opening which language bequeathes - to think
language as the ever-present possibility of this bequeathal.   But
then do you not - we hear - presume as both theme and ground for your
words both the opening and the bequeathal that constitutes the intelligibility of language - and hence, as part to Whole, of your
speech - are you not labouring at articulation in one Vast Circle?
In a way that has to be true - it is 'analytically' true.   But
already our reader has Voiced a notion of 'circularity' and is 'on
the way'.   To Open and give Voice to the Open-ing.
      But why - our reader continues - are you puzzled with the question
'Who speaks?'   Surely this is obvious - concrete men and women
speak.   But we persist 'Who speaks?'   'Who speaks when ordinary men
and women take up the Word?'   Yet could we be whipping a dead horse,
squeezing an already overworked seam?   Has not Nietzsche already informed us that philosophy (writing) is a species of involuntary and
unconscious autobiography ('Beyond Good and Evil', paragraph 6)?   We
shall have to answer in the affirmative if 'retrieval' or our remarks
be construed as intending socio-historical autobiography - work.
However, we intend the grammar of 'retrieval' (as did Nietzsche) in a
more basic sense: as a declaration of Membership, an openness to the
sustaining roots of a tradition in its open-endedness as Language.
'I' speak only to the extent that the ominous Shadow speaks to and
through me - and this shadow is the Tradition itself?   I speak only
on the grant that Language 'voices' me?
      Showing the authority and problematicity of any writing within the
auspices of that writing itself by visibilizing the method illustrates the intrinsic circularity of this mode of work.   Hence the
applicability of the term 'hermeneutic circle': how to make the
method visible in one's reading (as a re-writing) of a text?   This
term is to be understood as an index or shorthand expression for an
immense knot of problems and paradoxes.   Like the notion of authorship it may smack of the platitudinous if we do not make the journey
from the obvious into the exploration of whole horizons of consequences.   It is certainly not accidental that the Parisian schools of
semiotics, metareflecting semiotics and grammatology see in Orpheus

the archetypal hero of reflexive speaking which turns upon itself to
pose its production as a problem by 'doing violence' to its signs to
enable the act of writing to dis-locate, dis-engage and de-center and
thereby counteract the low ebb of writing-degree-zero.

To the question 'Who speaks' - our reader continues - you answer
the Circle, Tradition, the Whole. Then you are friends of the Hegelian 'Dialektik'? We have already gone too far to meet our reader -
now he is searching between the lines (where else?) for the Hegelian
'Begriff', the speculative Circle which leads from the realm of the
concrete to the halls of Absolute Knowledge. The difference being
that Hegel possessed Wisdom - indeed professed to be a Scientist of
Wisdom. This too is a reading of tradition - and an example of a
richly critical and speculative reading. However, I would prefer to
begin in the shack beside the architectonic.
How would you begin to teach a non-member - a child for instance - to
enter into the Membership of Tradition?
Well, teach him the language.
By your attitude, teach him the Promise of language.
What is silent in the teaching of the child is what cements him to a
world - and this is the promissory nature of human communion.
'Teach him the language!'

Then you have recognized, have you not, that language is the um-
bilical cord to tradition; language is our life-line to human being
(essence) and human community. But this 'essence' is a u-topia - a
futurity - by own admission? Man, we can say, essences in language.
For concretely we are born and sustained in the flesh and blood of
Another; analytically-in terms of speechful possibility - we are
ground and sustained through the vital line of Language - and Language is, as we have said, the source of meaning which leads us back
into the grounds of tradition.

We hang between Concrete Otherness of flesh and blood and Analytic
Otherness of Language, Membership, Tradition. Our being is, in this
sense, a 'hyphen' - a conjoining which separates; a unity which po-
larizes and resonates between Flesh and Word - and we are neither but
both.

We are the 'within' of tradition; we are the possibility of both
Flesh and Word - their communion, a kind of Mediation (logos) through
which language and tradition 'happen' - or 'hyphenate'.

We can thus formulate Circularity in the eyes of the child: how
does the child enter language?

The child becomes in the rhetorical space of language only as he
becomes the Hyphen of language, the Mediation of Flesh and Logos.
Tradition allows the world to pro-ject as World. It is only in the
implicative net of language that our child can be said to 'live-in'
or 'possess' a world. The child is the co-implicative hyphen which
primordially events in Language-World.

Tradition might then be construed as that which enables this
standing-out-of-World to continually 'happen'. Tradition is the
carnal openness of standing-out; it enables things(one of which is
our child) to step forth. It is a source of eminence and beauty -
in the crude Greek sense of 'shining forth'. In its primordiality -
as 'always-already-language-ing' tradition is the gray eminence
providing the grounds for intelligible talk about things and in modes
of reflexivity, about its own talk-about - the sources of its own

intelligibility - and for future modes of intelligible eminences.

The written is always and everywhere ground upon the unwritten, all theory and doctrine is provided for by an 'agrapha dogmata', by the unwritten doctrine, the oral grounds which sustain writing, scripture, graffiti.

Our expression 'Hermeneutic Circle' formulates - with reference to a movement of thought that began with Hegel and Marx, Nietzsche and Freud but which vibrates as the secret 'trace' of our tradition - the radical unavailability of notions of human being construed as a translucent source-point of self experience, consciousness, reflection or of speechful acts, language-games, discourses. The 'Circular' indebtedness of all inquiry to Another which provides by its very absence stands deeply opposed to any form of transcendentalism, whether it be of the neo-positivistic logistic kind (where the transcendental subject is interpreted as the logical form or grammar of language) or whether it takes a Kantian or phenomenological turn (as realized in Husserl's pure or transcendental phenomenological philosophy). The radical unavailability of such notions can be articulated in many contemporary ways: the unavailability of pure thought outside the frames of some language, texture of speech acts, 'language-game', etc.; the unavailability of pristine presence without the voices of absence; the unavailability of structural descriptions of language without some constitutive formulation or 'interference'; the unavailability of origin and the pervasiveness of mediation; the unavailability of structural form outside of a programme warranting its articulation and providing the paramaters of the enterprise; the unavailability of syntax without semantics; the unavailability of the text without the absent sites of 'intertextuality'; the unavailability of the sign outside of a discourse formation; the unavailability of writing divorced from a literary tradition itself exhibiting compound internal complexity of styles, genres, tropes, devices, and the like; the unavailability of constative utterance without the socially resonant performative 'upshot'; the unavailability of the 'disinterested phenomenological Ego' outside the form of life which made possible Husserlian 'reason'; the unavailability of the ontic without the ontological; the unavailability of speech without language; the unavailability of 'la parole' outside of 'la langue', performance without competence, surface structuration without the formation and transformation rules descriptive of deep categorial structure; the unavailability of normative description outside an indexical context of social presuppositions, a 'sense of social structure', 'social competence', etc.; the unavailability of theme without horizon, topic without resource, thematic without operational concepts ('Begriffe'); the unavailability of formal without dialectical logic, formal without transcendental logic ('Formale und Transczendental Logik' in Husserl's sense); the unavailability of logic without metaphysics; the unavailability of tradition metaphysics without Fundamental Ontology; the unavailability of Fundamental Ontology without an ontology of 'Wild Being' ('Etre sauvage' - to use Maurice Merleau-Ponty's expression); the unavailability of theological 'Hermeneutik' outside of the category of Revelation; unavailability of Christian dogma without a 'de-mythologizing' hermeneutics; unavailability of critical, historical, transcendental philosophical analysis without the attitude of recollective thinking

('Andenken');   the unavailability of being beyond the Appropriating
of Appropriation traditionally (and misleading) named Being;   the
unavailability of our logocentric tradition outside of the redeeming
category of 'Ecriture' and its conjugates arche-ecriture, 'trace',
difference read as
difference and differance;
the unavailability of speech and discourse outside of 'logos';
etcetera,
etcetera.

As far as our thematization of Writing-reading is concerned we may
say that all Writing (in this emergent sense) is for and from Another;
as such it must display its indebtedness to absent friends - not in
the mundane sense of biographical notes, but in response to the ways
in which absent friends (their unavailability) enable one to write,
discourse: ingress.   The Other of tradition can be formulated as
the anonymous 'friend' of writing.   Ingression - beginning the inquisitive life of writing - in my sense is always both a thinking and
a thanking;   a paying of outstanding debts and an incurring of deeper
obligations.   Refusing the dialectic which preempts a translucent
Beginning, knowledgeable Origin, unmediated Reflection is to fall
victim to a form of pretense - which even though it has characterized
the most notable writers of our tradition, must still be named a form
of illusion.   It is Nietzsche who fought transcendentalism on all
fronts who, perhaps, holds the greatest hope for interrogative, hermeneutic writing - so long as we do not fetish the discourse of unmasking into an 'ersatz' transcendental, so long as the gods do not
return not in the shape of divine sources or promises but as the very
form of inquiry or writing itself.   Nietzsche to the extent that he
deified 'Kritik' and wished to abolish the tradition - is as dangerous
as he is helpful in formulating this notion of radical unavailability
- hermeneutic circularity.   All writing is impure.   Much of the
'impurity' is systemic, structured, ordered as rhetorics and genres.
Writing in cor-responsive theorizing means grasping the meaning of
this constitutive 'impurity'.   The only pure writing would incarnate
itself as pure Identity stripped of all Difference.   Such discourse,
needless to say, would not be for human ears.   As speakers upon this
Earth we live within the tension, the Hyphen of articulation named
throughout as the hyphenated belonging together of Identity and
Difference.   We are bound by deep conditions which hold in proportion all human speech and we respect the measure of these conditions
to the extent that they are shown - present as absent - within the
sway of our being-languaged.   Identity and its speeches would be for
those who know themselves to be Identical.

The 'Circle' generates an off-spin of paradoxes that would choke
any literalist, positivist or re-presentational model of writing and
authorship.   Without this wonder before a text we inevitably run the
danger of reifying the work as an object reality removed from the
responsibility of human agency and historicity.   (3) Upon this issue
(the issuance of speech) hinges the current concern with 'repressive
communication' and the alienating-freezure of speech as another
object amongst a world of infinitely indifferent other-such-objects.
Even posing the question as 'What are the grounds of language?' like
asking 'What is-World?' blocks the path to a listening attitude.
Language itself is the grounding in the same mirror-play as man is

himself grounding-disclosing, world-unveiling, worldish: man is
languaged. Man incarnates the Hyphen. In binding writing to
reading (in removing the 'and'), in restoring the reader as an essential participant who is invited to do violence with our speech, we
attempt to restore reflexivity to writing and begin the long march of
appreciating language as limitless and inexhaustible horizon. In
reading the text we are nothing if not re-writers (co-writers) and a
work's 'raison d'etre' now must be located in its invitation to per-
petual re-writing. As it were we would like to see Reading-Writing
read unhyphenated: experience the meaning of the Hyphen.

It is not man who possesses or creates language, but rather language which 'has' man; the writing-self becomes a dramatic limit of
the expression of language – thus the kernel of truth in Wittgenstein's remark that the self is the limit of his text-world 'qua'
Language. Another paradox surfaces. For it is the sustaining
ground of language itself which permits itself to be objectified into
an instrumental functionality or mathematical capacity. This shows
that because language gives a myriad of possibilities its auspices
are always something Other, are always ahead of any of the determinations we suggest. Hence there are a myriad versions of what it is
to 'write'. Jacques Lacan and his students, for instance, interpret
(after Freud) the otherness of the unconscious as an accomplishment
sustained by the Otherness of Language, its dream 'work' in the
'other-theatre' of the unconscious. When we think of 'writers' what
kind of imagery comes to mind? We think of Dickens, Zola, Tolstoy,
perhaps Marx and the representatives of the 'Nouveau Roman' today.
But we also have to remind ourselves that 'writing' for a de Sade was
the sublimated salvation of his forced imprisonment or that Genet
claims not to write at all, but to excrete. But how can we possibly
tie language to a status as 'part' of the world, when it gathers world
at the outset. Language, in this context, is the best symbol of the
otherness (the unity of identify and difference) of the tradition
which also cannot be construed as another 'fact' (only a historical
'fact') since it overrides before as the condition for the possibility
of all such reductions.

Language conceived as 'Logos' throws off all the trammels we care
to shackle It with; this for the reason that it sustains those trammels; it provides the site where they are. Speech can now be
understood as a gift of 'Logos', over which we have a limited lia-
bility. As we noted about Language is a gift, inheritance or bequeathal. Before exploring the nature of this gift it will be useful to round out these remarks with a short glance at the original
Greek sense of theory, of inquiry as 'theoria'.

For the Greek, after Pythagoras at least, 'theoria' derived from
the context of the spectator at the games with its focal activity of
all spectatorship – watching. Theorizing was identified with a
notion of passive contemplation – a retiring watching, a disinterested
gaze of the pelucid eye toward the furniture of the world arrayed and
posited for one and all. It is at this juncture in the history of
the west where theorizing and contemplation touch, hold grammatical
hands and intermingle. It is also this sense that has been handed
down to the tradition. We think of 'theorizing' and a sea of con-
templative imagery pre-judges the matters of our concern. We are
led by a word; the text becomes flesh. Unfortunately a radical

trans-lation has been unknowingly enacted. As with the Roman translation of the Greek understanding of 'physis' (or 'phusis') as
'natura' which set the original thought of 'physis' (as the gathering
together and principled unfurling of Being and of beings within
Being) onto the track of 'ousia' (Substance), causality and 'nature'
understood as a dynamic mesh of causal dynamics (of 'physics') and as
with the Romanized understanding of 'Logos' as reason understood as
'ratio', the spectatorial conception of 'theoria' set a fate-ful
course for western metaphysical thought. But again, this is not the
inevitability of the cunning of the Absolute ('der List der Vernunft'). Originally 'theoria' referred to delegates from city-states,
state-ambassadors, envoys, message-carriers attending the sacred
events of another city-state. The theorist 'qua' the bringer-of-
messages was thus a traveller between exotic sites. In-built, as it
were, is an original anthropological sense of curisoty of the laws,
customs and ways of others. (4) Lobkowicz also reminds us that the
Latin expression 'contemplatio' originally derives from a religious
horizon: from 'templum' which first referred to the site which the
auger delimited (dis-closed) as the field of observation or presence relevant to the prophecy (to that which comes into presence
for him, to the pre-sencing). Here if we had enough space we would
try to show the historical ramifications of the metaphor of 'field'
or 'site' which is opened by the cor-responding presence of man, the
reflexive inquirer. (5)

     As I shall show the imagery of 'clearance', of dispersion, of
'forest spaces', of 'opening', 'Lichtung', the 'Licht-metaphysik' of
the tradition, 'presence' and the later 'temporality-play-field'
('Zeit-Spiel-Raum') is Heidegger resonates with these guiding-words
of the tradition. But to return from the digression: the original
entanglement of the religio-festive significance of 'theoria' and the
Latinate expression 'contemplatio' colour theorizing with divine
attributes. Heidegger, today is alone in seeing the relevance of
this identification (in his account of thought, reflexivity, transcendence, 'Dasein', and so forth). His thought gathers the originary thought of the pro-Socratics (a term which he does not like since
it stratifies thinkers like Parmenides, Anaximander, etc. in terms of
the Socratic and Platonic Tradition), a thought embroiled with the
presence of divinity, the Poetic and the Holy. For the purposes of
this introduction let it suffice that the notion of originary
'theoria' places the theorist in the realm of freedom which (with,
say, Pythagoras) is the realm of the sublime. Here the light which
animates the Greek sense of 'theoria' is so difficult to capture in
our ratio-determined modes of thinking; we are in an alien world
removed from the sources of thought through the mathematization of
reason which Husserl has analyzed at great length in his 'Krisis'
work. What is sublime in the Greek term 'theoria' is the uncontroll-
able force of wonder - 'thaumazein' - which drives man from the
plains of the concrete into thought.

     Unfortunately contemporary thought has identified theorizing with
the warrant of positive 'scientific' theory-building, with the mathematical pre-determinism of the thing itself as a methodic sensiti-
zation; this identify, however, is a pale-shadow of the rich wonder-
saturation of the original sense of theorizing. Science, for the
latter, may measure its worlds, but must fail to measure itself -

for that it would have to think itself, which is impossible.   Heidegger has often said (without deriding the positive results of the sciences) that science itself cannot think.   Wonder rather takes the thinker (we remember that Heidegger has seen fit to distinguish between the philosopher and the thinker, the latter being more foundational) and leads to self-transcendence in which he is even envied by the Gods.   'Wisdom' as the culmination of 'theoria' is quite literally divine knowledge (cf. Lobkowicz, pp. 8-9).   We may now reclaim this sense of 'thaumazein' as wonder at the mutual cor-respondence of theory and speech, speech and Language;   not as a forced unity compounded from a multiplicity - a One from a pre-existing Two; but rather a necessary Oneness, a primal coherence of belonging-together which provides for the possibility of there being anything like Two in the first place.

RESTORING READING AND READER

> How can one escape that which never sets?
> Heraclitus of Ephesus

A text can be understood as resting on grounds that escape the scope of the work.   To self-formulate the auspices or 'Nous' of a text by recoiling the same speech upon itself would inevitably require turning the auspices of the writing into formulatable 'somethings'. Direct attempts to state the auspices of a work resolve into a Medusa's stare that petrifies the writing.

Relatedly we might also fall into an infinite 'meta' regress whereby we have to formulate the original formulation, and then the language of the formulation, and so on.   We would fall into Wittgenstein's trap of the impossibility of formulating the Logical Form of language while presuming it in our formulation and with the related puzzles to be found in the Zeno-type paradox or in the Whitehead-Russell theory of types and logical sets.

By freezing the ground of speech in either of these ways we would, in short, be wholly responsible for providing for the meta-language as well as the object-language.   It appears that what sustains the text can only be shown or displayed in the writing: we are responsible for exemplifying method and authority.

From the above remarks it is evident that for us reading and writing are intimately associated.   The reader must not be invited to enter the work as if the text was an iron cage of passage-ways, a solid product that is 'finished' in some ontological sense.   Rather, as a reflective co-participant in our work (as a Member of the I-Thou collective of reading-writing) the reader must be so constituted for the writing that he enter the space of signs and display his responsibility, his authority, his ob-lig-ation, his soul in the reading which is his re-writing.   This obviously requires a much more intensive re-construction of the depth of the I-Thou nexus, upon which common-sense notions like writing and reading can be reactivated. That project must lie outside the scope of this introduction.

To face up to our understanding of what it is to write, the reader can neither criticize, nor quote, nor argue with the text without making his stance, his authority known by displaying his commitments

as we have, hopefully, displayed ours.   Otherwise we talk to one
another without saying anything to one another; we are deaf to each
other's soul.   Without displaying where we stand together we run the
grave danger of solipsism in our speech and the moral vacuum of
nihilism in our moral lives.   The attentive reader will appreciate
now that an equally viable entry to our problematic can be made by
re-wrieving the history of solipsism-nihilism, within the jaws of
which we live.   By 'commitment' and 'authority' we intuitively refer
to the deep issue that must be recurrently posed in engaging in the
emerging project of reading-writing: How in the world (in the tradition) did I come to speak?   Again 'Who speaks when I begin theorizing?'

Introducing the dimension of historicity, of tradition, follows
from my understanding of speaking thoughtfully: as a listening which
inscribes the self of the speech into an ongoing tradition from which
the self re-trieves and sustains his writing and to which he addresses
his responsive word.   Speech is expressive in the sense of pressing
something out; speech leads to a sense of Eminence; it is where
Eminence happens; it thus presumes a background from which something
can be pressed, an opening where things can come to be.   Speech is
also re-cognition.   We can also note a trajectory to our writing by
seeing that this is a basic Hegelian insight: that in the movement
of the self toward the sun, intelligence is something which recognizes.   Being comes to self-knowledge/self-consciousness through
the reflexive being of Language.   Another way to phrase this is that
in reflexive work the task is always to approach the obvious that has
always enfolded us and to grasp that which grips us (we need only
think of Heidegger's 'Dasein' analytics of Being-unto-death, radical
finitude, mood, nullity, understanding, the ontological difference,
Nothingness as an authentic mode of 'Dasein''s being, dread, and so
on).   Here Being-unto-Death becomes the sole possibility of the self
as a living-dying within a tradition that teaches the meaning of
death in objectivist forms against which thought must question.
Like our use of 'commitment' and 'authority-authorship', Heidegger's
categories index not idealist or existential leaps, nor nihilist fear
and trembling, but rather the question that the meaning of Being has
to be continually re-thought after long and painstaking inquiry: the
'sober understanding' advocated by Heidegger (SZ, 310) is itself one
of the factical 'a priori' possibilities of 'Dasein''s 'ek-sistenz',
which he would later phrase as the shepherding of Being.

Since the problem of stratisification has shifted to the self-
stratifications of speech in the self-conceptions of speakers I would
like to draw my remarks together by considering several ideal typical
ways of self-being, of 'relating' (6) to one's speech and writing.
Consider the following paradigm cases:

1. Coherence: where a relation of coherence exists between
speech and thing; where man becomes a nexus of coherence for the
universe: a coherence or pre-established order of intellect and
thing (e.g. Leibniz);

2. Correspondence: where a relation of correspondence exists
between speech and thing; where man becomes a mediating term of the
limits 'word' and 'world', a conjoiner of subject with predicates and
truth becomes an 'adequatio intellectus et rei', 'veritas' as
'conformitas';

3. Object-behaviour: where speech is one more object, a behavioural object amongst a world defined as a totality of objects;
where man becomes a positive, behavioural actor moving amongst a kin-
ship of things, as already-an-object, as always-having-been an object
(Watson and behaviourist theories of language);

4. Form: where speech is sustained by the pure and underground
syntax of language which exemplifies Universal features of a divine
Grammar (Leibniz's 'mathesis universalis', de Saussure's 'la langue',
Chomsky's 'competence', Carnap's logical syntax of the world,
Husserl's purely eidetic grammar); man becomes a deep mathematic
structure conceived as a Form or pure System or as a transcendental
matrix of rules and principles (the Kantian transcendental Ego) or as
a purely formal stream of functionining 'a priori' intentionality
(the Husserlian transcendental Ego);

5. Depiction: where speech is essentially depictive, enabled
with the power to articulate a pre-existent, language-neutral world
of things; man becomes one infatuated with the insatiable desire to
re-produce and re-present the world;

6. Name: where speech is essentially the conjoining of names to
things and man as Subject (Substance) becomes, like the Hebraic God,
the all-powerful name-giver;

7. Image: where speech is the trace of images and/or ideas;
where man becomes a thinking animal, a thinking substance, a Subject
as 'Cogito', 'res cogitans', a stream of cogitations, of sense-
impressions or intentional life (the English empiricist tradition);

8. Constitution: where speech is totally constitutive of the
intelligibilities which we label 'objects', 'world', 'reality', and
man becomes the source of meaning and Being;

9. Expression: where speech is essentially expressive, affective
poetic; man becomes the expressive limit of the world as Aesthetic
Will (the Romantic imagination);

10. Game: where speech is a compound multiplicity of language-
games or functioning tool-instrumentality locked in the pragmatic
forms of life which characterize the everyday managerial activities
of the 'Lebenswelt': man becomes a fabric of 'usage', habitualities,
and historically-relative language-games or a knot of 'speech acts';

11. Communication: where speech is defined as a universal communicative 'medium', a technological aid for the transmission of 'information'; man becomes again the mediation of a technological will
to communicate 'bit' by 'bit', a will to communicative power.

Examples of these pure types, their various combinations and sophisticated elaboration (and my listing does not attempt to be comprehensive) can be found beneath the literature of social studies and
philosophical work throughout our tradition. But to all these self-
conceptions we must ask 'How does the theorist provide for his notion
of speech?', 'What sustains all these perspectival and partial
determinations?', 'How does the speaker ground his auto-construals?'.
'Would the theorist be able to speak at all if he took his conception
of speech "to the letter"?' We realize that each one of these self-
conceptions also embodies a notion of truth; they then become more
dangerous: for if speech is the linch-pin of social co-existence
then everything follows from these perspectival understandings of
truth. To centre our exposition on Heidegger's work I shall choose
the concept of speech as Correspondence.

Heidegger (as well as the latter Wittgenstein) has offered a continual reflection and critique of the correspondence doctrine of
truth in which truth is regarded as a relation of proposition (or
assertion) and world, of subject-predicate compounds and their sufficient grounds (the category of 'sufficient reason').   Heidegger's
whole path of thought oriented to the phenomenological destruction of
metaphysics might be regarded in terms of his reiterated reflection
on truth as a propositional 'relation'.   This is also applicable to
the well-known 'reversal' in his later thought from the path of
Dasein to the path of the thought of Being itself.   In his 'Vom
Wesen des Grundes' ('The Essence of Reasons') Heidegger explores the
restriction placed on the notion of truth by this correspondence
conception (epitomized by Leibniz).   (7)

Without much difficulty Heidegger shows that the correspondence
dectrine is necessary a derivative insight (Cf. SZ, part 1, section
44) whose real auspices and 'grant' lie elsewhere: .

> The correspondence of the nexus with being and its resulting
> consonance do not as such render being immediately access-
> ible.   Rather, as the possible 'subject' of a predicative
> definition, being must already be manifest both prior to and
> for our prediction.   Prediction, to become possible, must
> be able to establish itself in the sort of manifesting which
> does not have a predictive character.   Propositional truth
> is rooted in a more primordial truth (unconcealedness);   it
> is rooted in that prepredicative manifestness of being which
> we call ontical truth (see the corresponding German original,
> pp. 19-21).

I presuppose an acquaintance with Heidegger's terms here (such as
'Seienden', 'praedikativen', 'Unverborgenheit', 'vorpraedikativen',
'vorpraedikativen Offenbarkeit', 'ontische Wahrheit', and so forth).
Heidegger urges us to clearly differentiate between the discoveredness ('Entdeckheit') of truth as present-at-hand (for instance, the
truth that material objects are present-at-hand: 'Wahrheit von
Vorhandenem') and the original disclosure or what the Greeks had previously called 'aletheia':   the disclosedness of existing 'Dasein'
('der Erschlossenheit des existierenden Daseins').   Around the time
of the publication of 'Sein und Zeit' Heidegger stressed the openness
of 'Dasein' - the horizon of transcendence - as the key to the possibility of unconcealment.   After the 'reversal' Heidegger increasingly speaks of the openness of Being itself as 'the open' which
makes knowledge and truth possible.

Discoveredness consists of the objectivist attitude of presenting
and re-presenting objects and 'truth' as naively at-hand and un-
problematic.   Whereas the primal opening or uncovering ('A-lethe')
of Being (truth) is guided by a prepredicative understanding of
Being;   further, the preontological understanding grounds the pre-
dicative notion of relational truth: 'The disclosedness of Being
alone makes possible the manifestness of being' (ibid., p. 23).   The
disclosedness of Being, the truth of Being as ontological truth,
Heidegger calls preontological ('vor-ontologische') understanding:
'In order to comprehend Being, the understanding of Being must have
developed of its own accord and must have made Being (which is understood, generally projected, and somehow disclosed in it) its problem
and theme of inquiry' (ibid., p. 23).   Yet even given this pre-

ontological (and we presume 'a priori') grasp of Being, the openness
as that horizon-which-horizons conceals as it reveals.   Its essence
lies in a certain withdrawal from the scene.   Being is both concealed and unconcealed in its presencing: the grounds of the unconcealed remain hidden.   Here we understand the grounds of the unconcealed as the mirror-play of speech, Logos and truth.   It is precisely this dialectic of give and take which we seek to exemplify in
our writing.   Consequently every such project of disclosure must
suffer the belonging-together of truth and un-truth.   Truth is painfully revealed from untruth but always presented with untruth.   (8)

Along this line of thinking Heidegger develops the notion of the
'difference between being and Being', or the 'ontological difference':

The essence of truth, which is and must be bifurcated
ontically and ontologically, is only possible given this
difference.   Yet if what is distinctive about Dasein is
that is behaves toward being by understanding Being, then
the ability to differentiate the two (in which the Ontological Difference becomes factical) must have struck the
roots of its own possibility in the ground of the essence
of Dasein (pp. 27-9).

It would not be an exaggeration to say that the completed part of the
'Sein und Zeit' text hung upon this bifurcation.   Being's revelation
as composed of beings bounded with the all-horizon of Being defines
the essence of 'Dasein':   that particular being (or rather its
structure) who makes the Ontological Difference his 'concern', who
cares for Being and its historical mittence as tradition.   The structure that is 'Dasein' founds this possibility;   it is transcendent.
It is now clear that the problem of Being for the earlier Heidegger
centers (as does the problem of reasons and of the hermeneutic
circle) around the problem of transcendence: Heidegger refers to
transcendence as the 'realm' ('der Bezirk') within which this texture
of problems can be authentically faced (ibid., p. 33).   The 'difference' lies in the fact that Being can not be ordinarly predicated;
we can not use the dangerous word 'is' in speaking of Being since we
violate the whole spirit of ontological reflection: the Being as
grounds of being cannot itself be a being or thing, but must -
strangely - be a no-thing, Nothing.

Speaking in terms of the way Being exemplifies itself in beings is
also inadequate.   An entirely original discourse is required to
speak ontologically: hence the irremedial tension that Heidegger has
never overcome between ontic and ontological talk, a tension in which
his experience with language works.

The primary sense of transcendence, for Heidegger, lies in its
meaning as ground or possibility which forms the fundamental constitutive feature of 'Dasein' before all other relations, interre-
lations and concrete actions.   This constitutive 'surpassing' in
fact makes anything like a 'relation' possible in the first place.
It founds the possibility of descriptive studies of movement, relation,
space, time, as well as the With-world of human intersubjectivity.
'Transcendence' represents one of Heidegger's linguistic innovations
solely designed to undercut the subject-object or Substance metaphysics of traditional thought, before a conceptual armoury can be
derived in order to think anew.   'Dasein' is a being-in-transcend-
ence (hence the expression 'transcendent "Dasein"' would be

tautologous).   That which is surpassed, that into which 'Dasein' as
'Dasein'-structure transcends, becomes the 'World'.   Thus we come to
Heidegger's much misused and misunderstood definition of transcendence as Being-in-the-world;   and, of course, his 'Dasein'-analytics
of 'Dasein''s mode of Being-in-the-world (e.g. the Moods) becomes a
'transcendental' discussion.   Man is 'Dasein' (the two should not,
however, be confused or used synonymously) in that he is granted the
site from which he, and only he, must understand Being as his own way
('Weg') to Being: as his respons-ibility to the circle of thought.

I have dwelt on these rather technical terms (9) in order to indicate that they are, although now part of the coin of philosophy,
technically understood and oriented to a categorical not much different from the conceptual analysis of Anglo-American philosophizing.
For example, the Heideggerian concept of World would not only have to
be distinguished from the everyday sense(s) of this concept and from
the tacit use made of it in ordinary language philosophy, but it
would even have to be distinguished from, say, Husserl's use of world
(e.g. the 'natural attitude') or from Max Scheler's understanding of
the antepredicative world, or from Alfred Schutz's notion of the mundane life-sphere, the 'paramount reality' of everyday usage.   For
Heidegger, the category of 'World' as a transcendental term pointing
to the 'a priori' (obviously in a much different sense from the traditional understanding of the 'a priori') constitutive features of
the being of 'Dasein': its essence of Being-in-the-world.   The
'Dasein' analytics were, it will be remembered, regarded as lenses
which variously concentrate the refracted light of the One question:
the question of the meaning of Being.

Like many of Wittgenstein's enigmatic reminders the thesis of
Being-in-the-world is so absolutely concrete that it stares us in the
face (Being permeates our every step, as Tradition writes itself in
every word).

The thesis is, as Heidegger says, 'primordial and simple'.   Yet
this certainly does not mean that 'it is simple to show what it
means'.   To fulfil such a project requires more than a selection of
papers;   it requires a thoughtful experience and re-thinking of our
everyday and theoretical categories - the speech in which we dwell
and express our selves.   For instance, 'Dasein' is freedom; it is
the freedom of pro-jecting; 'Dasein' grounds and thereby establishes
itself through its project.   Thus it is not paradoxical to speak of
a 'World' worlding, nor of the thing thinging.   Heidegger speaks of
a 'world worlds' in so far as it collects and gathers itself in the
midst of Being.   'Dasein' is also the archetype of commitment; it
is 'thrown' in Being ('Geworfenheit') and must freely choose its own
possibilities.   However, this is a far cry from the absolute freedom of the 'en soi-pour soi' dialectics of Sartre.   The existential
freedom is lost to its own speech; if anything it falls back into
Cartesian dilemmas.

In conceiving the notion of 'transcendence' as essential to 'Dasein' Heidegger interprets the happening of transcendence itself as
the happening of temporality.   'Dasein''s facticity as a concrete
self in a With-world of Other such selves is the concrete pole (as
Husserl might say) to which transcendence 'happens': 'Dasein' accepts
the abyss of groundlessness of its pro-ject (as a 'Sein-zum-Tod') in
the very thrownness of its self in temporality, the discovery of

self-hood, of a world of Others, the destiny of Being, the mittance
of Being's construal.

'Dasein' reveals its own finitude in the infinite temporality of
existence.   Although Heidegger's early work owes little to Hegel's
concept of truth, the later Heidegger has discussed sympathetically
Hegel's concept of experience.   If Hegel exhausted the possibilities
of idealist metaphysics and prepared the way for absolute end of
metaphysical thought in Nietzsche (his Word 'Gott ist Tod' and the
Eternal Recurrence) does Heidegger's early work escape from its
cloak?   There is a section in Hegel's 'Phenomenology' that is at
once both Nietzschean, and strangely Heideggerian.   It concerns the
bolistic, developmental-dialectical notion of truth:

> Appearance is the process of arising into being and passing
> away again, a process that itself does not arise and does
> not pass away, but is 'per se', and constitutes reality and
> the life-movement of truth.   The truth is thus the bacchan-
> alian revel where not a member is sober; and because every
> member no sooner becomes detached that it 'eo ipso'
> collapses straightway, the revel is just as much a state of
> transparent unbroken calm (p. 105)

The history of Logos precipitates in this metaphor; speech, here,
cannot be reduced to the clear and distinct ideas of the Cartesian or
to the dogmatic thing of ontic talk.   But how are we to exemplify
what Hegel (and Heidegger?) would call the entirety of the movement,
the unbroken quiescent whole (p. 105)?   Since the world is not a
fabric composed of lacunae and lacks, since it is neither anarchic
nor solipsistic, the sustaining grounds are before us (or the self-
becoming of Hegel's thought would not even be conceivable).

But perhaps the 'before us' caters to the vision-oriented 'Licht-
metaphysik' of the tradition; should we not listen rather than look
to understand the silent saying of tradition.   As Aristotle tells us
in his 'Metaphysics' - as the eyes of bats are to the blaze of day,
so is the reason in our soul to the things which are by nature most
evident of all.   We might understand the Platonic icon of the Good
and the One as both blinding and yet sustaining speech (in the sense
of transcendental foundation which cannot be touched by what is
founded):

> the good stands to the mind as the sun does to the eye;
> both noetic and visual perception occur through the
> mediation of a third binding element (Ideas, sunlight) which
> not only is different from, but draws attention away from,
> its source.   In order to see an object, we do not look at
> the sun or even at the light, but at the illuminated object.
> The sun, when looked at directly, blinds us, and the light,
> considered apart from all visible bodies is itself invisible
> or homogeneous (Rosen, p. 182).

Transposing the metaphor to the grounding nature of the Good and
speech gives us Plato's One focal notion, his One theme which is the
undisclosed theme of all his dialogues, but which comes to perfection

in the 'Parmenides'.   It is the idea of the One, the unifying
grounds which like the Sun sustains the light of objects without ever
either being those objects or being tied to them.   It is the idea
which gave neo-platonism the maxim: Everything is in everything, but
each in its own way:

And what is the view, the vision which supports the whole?
It is quite simply the vision from the Allegory of the Cave,
with its two paths: from the darkness (of the senses) up
toward the intelligible light with its beautiful, good, and
unitary source, the sun (this is the way to the Philosopher)
- journey which is motivated exclusively by the will to
know and understand - and from the light back toward the
darkness, or more correctly, toward the 'cave's' 'clair-
obscure', now with the purpose of propagating the new understanding by forming and reforming what apparently exists
(this is the way to the Academy state)... (Wyller, pp. 381-92).
Now we can begin to appreciate the subterranean web that ties, say,
Hegel to the profound experience of the Greeks (and thus of Marx's
relation to the Greek philosophers), as well as Heidegger's thought
and the thought of those who came before Socrates, Plato and Aristotle.   In Plato (as we shall later find in Marx) we find the struggle for the unity of 'theoria' and 'praxis' as the togetherness of
thinking and being, of man's speech with the sustaining Language of
the good: from the beautiful through the practical stages of the
Good, to the theoretical stage of the One, which is above Being and
non-Being.

Socratic Good (received from the Platonic dialogues) can be regarded as a way of providing for the intelligibility of the world and
writing as a horizon of light, exemplified in the imagery of the
cave, the sun, the divided line, as well as the overall dramatic
structure of the dialogues themselves (Rosen, p. 190).   It is no
accident that Paramenides thought on the Oneness (the unity) of Being
is itself a poem; nor that Plato philosophized the unity of identify
and difference within fluid dramas; nor that Hiedegger today has
seen fundamental resonances between the Poet and the Thinker; nor
what Wittgenstein's critique of Establishment-philosophy can be read
as confessionals, or as some of the finest German prose - deeply
metaphorical and aphoristic - since Nietzsche's poetic aphorisms.
All are, in their own distinctively unique ways, offering us invitations to engage in reflexive inquiries of our own, inquiries that are
self-grounded upon a committed display of their auspices.   Exegesis
of Wittgenstein would do well to explore his relations with the
tragic poet Georg Trakl (whose only precursor was Hoelderlin), with
his reading of Schopenhauer, and his admiration for Karl Kraus (apart
from the resonances between Wittgenstein, Trakl, Rilke, Hoelderlin
and Heidegger).   They have presented their thought as poetry, as
likely stories, deeply felt grammatical jokes always painstakingly
cut in order to help the reader free himself from the self-conceptions
of the day thrown by the metaphysical shadows of the establishment.
The secret key rests in the thought we have continually repeated:
that what sustains speech erases itself from that speech and its
'products' and can only be approached indirectly by way of iconic
exemplification.

The One is the all-prevailing Ground...Toward the One,
thought seeks to find a foundation for itself; away from
the One, thought seeks to describe as well as to transform
the nature of things - the One which, in as much as it is,
'never is one, but constantly in process of becoming two'
(Parmenides, p. 143A) (Wyller, p. 391).

It is this thought which was buried in Aristotle's translation of
Plato into a 'metaphysics', into his use of the thought of being as
a 'category' - as the category of substance, or 'ousia'.   Aristotle
began to theorize in the sense of attempting to depict the totality
of what is.   He set the fateful course for the total mathematization
of the cosmos: 'precisely against Plato's doctrine of the One 'above'
Being, a doctrine which Speusippus took over and sought to expand,
Aristotle launched his attack in the form of a theory of that which
is, in as much as it is ... Which is, however, another story
(Wyller, p. 392).   It is another story indeed: it is our story.
Consider again Hegel's election which, at the end of the eighteenth
century prophetically grasped the outcome of the story (as did Marx,
in his own terms).   For Hegel, 'philosophy' is nothing if not the
pursuit of the Absolute; his thought is nothing if not the thought
of the Whole or Totality as dialectical trajectory: the Absolute
permeation of thinking and being (cf. Werner Marx, 30) as reason dialectically working`itself out in (or as) history.   This attempt to
re-experience the beginning of our tradition has unfortunately been
passed into existential thought as the infinite desire of the unhappy
consciousness rising from the cave of the senses and aspiring to the
sun of absolute subjectivity, the nothingness of infinite desire (as
in Sartre's reading of Hegel) or the idealist's dream of perfect
coincidence of thought and world, speech and being.   But like Plato,
the grounds, symbolized by the term Spirit or Absolute by Hegel, are
not said in his texts.   The surface of Hegel's work (especially the
'Phenomenology') is a dramatization of metaphor and icon, very much
opposed to the philosophical prose of the day (e.g. Kant's style).
   Many regard the work as a 'romantic masquerade',(10) intending
thereby to be critical; however, this perfectly caught Hegel's
purpose for he precisely introduced his work in this way in order to
display what could not be said in any other way.   His notion of
'Absolute', for example, as the divine - or that which is in and for
itself (again cf. Marx's lexicon) reminds us very much of the Parmenidean thought of Being as being-gathered-in-and-for-itself. (11)
Walter Kaufmann has also called Hegel's 'Phenomenology' a 'logic' of
passion with the intent to distinguish it from the somewhat different
dialectic of Hegel's 'Logic'. (12) It is animated by a passion for
analysis, mediation, difference, differentiation and synthesis in the
spiralling moments of 'aufgehoben' - sublation (again, cf. Marx's
indebtedness).   Soll (13) has gone further: not only does the
'Phenomenology' use a logic modelled on the passions (as for instance
did David Hume) but it is also a passionate logic.   More interesting, however, Soll also interprets the Logic as being passionate in
the same vein.
   Let us say that Hegel's method (his dialectical method) is a logic
of passion, passionately exemplified in the work of his labour - his
writing.   As Kierkegaard was to appreciate, the depictions of consciousness, although 'abstract', are existential ways of 'spending'
existence, of being alive and responding to the mittence of Being,
defined in socio-political terms by Hegel (e.g. the category of
'civil' society that was to become so important for Marx).   In an
ontological reading, Hegel's Logic has also been read as a 'poetic of
Being' unfolded through the agency and mediation of man. (14)
Because of the ontological difference (to borrow Heidegger's meaning)

human language expresses the Logos of Being as a dialectical totality: truth.   For Hegel, this is nothing other than Absolute knowledge.   It may well be another historical irony that the arch-enemy
of Hegel - Kierkegaard - (or so we learn in elementary texts) is also
committed to passionate thought, to thought that touches the soul by
transmuting life into personal existence;   yet unlike Hegel's passion
for the Concept, Kierkegaard's passion must forgo analysis for the
decisiveness of the religious leap.   Had we time, in this introduction, we would trace out the trans-historical significance of
Hegel's famous dialectic of Master and Servant, the Odyssey of the
Unhappy Consciousness, the emergence of self-consciousness, and the
like.

Such a process of hermeneutic retrieval would place us in a much
better position to appreciate Marx's philosophical grammar in which
the metaphor of the proletariat becomes the very embodiment of
Critique (the driving force and sustaining roots, the salvation of
'Logos') and the material force of the social revolution that will
historically institute Reason on the scale of all Humanity - the
Academy that remains after the withering away of the State, which is
represented in Marx's writing as the very antithesis of Logos.   The
proletariat we remember is hardly described (see Roche's contribution
to this curious omission, above), but when it is depicted in Marx's
short analyses of class (the incomplete third volume of 'Das Capital'
for instance) it is depicted in cosmic terms as the total, transcendent (the class is not of bourgeois society), a historical (a
class without history, without self-understanding, class-consciousness, its authentic speech), and metaphysical (it indexes the end of
history as a dialectic of classes and the beginning of the history of
non-aliented man as speech that is classless: un-stratified) opposition to Capital where the sundering of Thought and Being will have
been both practically and theoretically achieved.   In displaying his
commitments (his analysis is avowedly determined, located, classed
(for the emancipation of the proletariat) or class-analysis of
class), Marx is playing the same game as his mentor, Hegel.   Both
are thinkers of the Total, the Transcendent, and Reflexive grounds
of speech and history.

It might prove interesting, had we space, to consult Marx's
letter to Engels of the 14 January 1858 where he gives an account of
his reading of Hegel's 'Logic' - as a work of great inspiration and
service to his own formulations (especially for the 'Grundrisse').
Nearer home, we might also consult Lenin's account of the relationship in his 'Philosophical Notebooks'.   (15)   Could we not say that
where Hegel began from the Idea (Absolute reason, the divine) and
moved through historic institutions (class and labour) to Man, Marx
moved through the same dialectical process in the opposite direction?   That is, we find, surfacely 'alternate' treatment of the Concrete as a dialectical concentrate of partial abstractions, yet both
thinkers are together on the same Odyssey after the Concrete - did
not Marx sociologize the Absolute by absolutizing the Sociological
(the 'material conditions of production')?   In relation to both let
us ask: What is the rational (in the sense of 'Logos') kernal and
the mystical (in the sense of 'ratio') shell;   and what the mystical
kernel, what the rational shell?

We cannot rest content in any established readings of either Hegel

or Marx.   Nor can we follow some naive phenomenological directive
like 'to the things themselves'.   Unless we provide for our formulations we are lost.   As with Heidegger's thought on opening and
disclosedness (the possibility of anything being manifest in the
first place) the openness withdraws and remains hidden.   We must,
then, strive for a path in order to pose the question of how beings
are drawn together and collected in Being; we must do so by listening to language and to the tradition as what has been handed down to
us as the Being of being ('What is Philosophy?', p. 71) – an attitude
of listening to the voice of the Being of being (ibid., p. 93).
Again I would like to underline the radicalness of the election – the
depth of man's responsibility for his own being and his fate-ful relation to the history of Being (caught in Heidegger's play: 'Sein-
Geschick-Geschichte-Geschehen').   What is the nature of the present
partial chapter of the history of Being?   Is thought always too late
to think itself into an alternate beginning.   This animated Hegel's
resigned maxim: When philosophy paints its grey on grey, a form of
life has grown old, and with grey on grey, it cannot be rejuvenated,
but only comprehended.   The owl of Minerva begins its flight only at
dusk.   The question which concerns us today is the way the grey on
grey of sociology has failed to pose the radical reflexive question
of speech and thereby to comprehend itself.

It has long been apparent that the Minervan owl has long left the
sociological imagination, without sociology over feeling the lack nor
the desire to capture its own petrified form of life.   Social science as the sufficient ratio of social worlds seeks to perfectly
possess its speech, to devise a technical vocabulary of description
and a ground-plan of theory divorced (sic!) from the language of the
laity, to count upon language, to compare speech, to control speech,
elaborate worlds from within the folds of its descriptions, to manipulate the word and harness talk to the predefined goals set out as
the canons of positive science (in which 'serious' thinking is identified with the rhetoric of the hypothetico-deductive method and
'serious' results with the System, and the System's needs).   Speech
has again become an object; a form of life has grown old, and even
the speaker is reflected in the mirror of objectivity by which he
locates his essence.   The philosophy of the past two decades –
language analysis – begets an even more forgetful and arrogant relationship with language and the tradition; analysing the grammar
of society as how we use language must never be confused with thinking language itself; likewise burning the works of the past by turning them into exhibits for a museum of irrelevant curiosities from
which conceptual analysis frees thought (there are, of course, notable exceptions) is the death of thought.   When philosophizing stops
being philosophizing-with and turns into unthinking dismissal then we
go further than Nietzsche, for now ever thought is dead.

The dull desire of English philosophers to be released from the
dark glass of tradition, as the fly is shown out of the bottle by
conceptual therapy, is truly incomprehensible before comprehending
(by listening to) the goals and telos of the traditional philosophers.   The impossibility of a razor sharp break on the level of
socio-political 'praxis' felt by many of the philosophers of the last
thirty years has been introjected into the almost irrational desire
for clean beginnings on the theoretical level.   Yet has Conceptual

Analysis addressed the tradition in the profound manner we have in-
dexed with the notion 'listening'?   For Heidegger it would clearly
be negative.   Anglo-American philosophers are no longer thinking;
for thought is nothing but an ongoing conversation with the tradition
requiring a thoughtful reading of that tradition, by 'doing violence'
to the source works.   'Listening' to these works means letting our
categories 'thaw' into the terms of the original.   Heidegger speaks
of 'de-struction' of metaphysics (as does Wittgenstein) not in the
sense of annihilation nor in the sense of burying the past in a plane
of anarchy.   'Destruction' rather, requires a thoughtful listening
to the tradition of Parmenides, Plato, Aristotle, Kant, Hegel,
Nietzsche (etc.) by bringing their questions to life (for they have
never died) for the purposes of our retrieval.   Heidegger describes
this sense of destruction very clearly in 'Sein und Zeit' (section 6)
and summarizes in his work on Kant and Motaphysics and in 'What is
Philosophy?':

> Destruction does not mean destroying but dismantling, liqui-
> dating, putting to one side the merely historical assertions
> about the history of philosophy.   Destruction means - to
> open our ears, to make ourselves free for what speaks to us
> in tradition as the Being of being (Destruktion heisst:
> unser Ohr oeffnen, freimachen fuer das, was such uns in der
> Ueberlieforung als Sein des Seienden muspricht)
> (What is Philosophy? pp. 71-3)

'Dasein' as relfexive existence - the space in which Being comes to
self-consciousness, must address itself toward the tradition.   For
Heidegger this means particularly conversing with the giants of pre-
socratic thought such as Parmenides, Heraclitus and Anaximander.
It is only through and by language that man can speak of Being.
Being speaks through language.   Being inhabits language: as Heidegger says - Language is the house of Being.   It was the primordial
contribution of the pre-socratics to uncover the speech of Being.
Through the plays of Sophocles (as well as much later the poeticization of Being by Hoelderlin) the solicitations of Being were allowed
to come into openness and be spoken.   To question by listening to
the tradition is to slowly awaken from the dream of metaphysics and
to comprehend its nightmarish ramifications.   How is thought to
aspire to this task?   Writing must continually pose the fundamental
question of the meaning of Being ever anew - to discover a path
through which what is question- worthy ('Fragwuerdige') can show itself.   Simply asking 'What is Philosophy?' displays our enslavement
(freedom) to the philosophic attitude of the Greek word, along the
path of which we have already been travelling.   For Heidegger, the
'axis' of the pre-socratics (as Jaspers might say) is the very cot of
thought which today, in its maturity as 'philosophy', has been lost
and forgotten.   We have even forgotten that we have forgotten!   It
is as if the birth certificate of the tradition is indented with the
Greek hieroglyphics along whose traces we have to re-trieve our own
pathways by entering the grammar of the Greek world.   We must remember the grounding soil that lies in Greek culture:

> The question of our discussion concerns the nature of
> philosophy.   If this question arises from a need and is
> not to remain only a hypothetical question for the purpose
> of making conversation, then philosophy as philosophy must

have become worthy of question.   Obviously we can indicate
this only if we have already taken a look into philosophy.
In order to do this we must know beforehand what philosophy
is.   Thus, in a strange manner, we are being chased around
in a circle.   Philosophy itself seems to be this circle.
Assuming that we might not be able to escape immediately out
of the ring of this circle, we still are permitted to look
at the circle.   In which direction should our glance turn?
The Greek word 'philosophia' indicates the direction (WP. 43-5).
It is to the Greeks, the Greek language and the way the question of
Being was raised in an attitude of astonishment where our ears must
lend themselves.   The re-collection involves the Original-Originary
wonder - the precipitation of the question - in the pre-socratics.
Speaking in the context of Heraclitus' understanding of the thinker
uncovering the 'sophon-Hen Panta' ('One (is) All') which names the
wonder of the drawing together of beings within Being.   Heidegger
reads:

All being is in Being.   To hear such a thing sounds trivial
to our ears, if not, indeed, offensive, for no one needs to
bother about the fact that being belongs in Being.   What
else remains for being but to be?   And yet, just this fact
that being is gathered together in Being, that in the appearance of Being being appears, that astonished the Greeks and
first astonished them and them alone.   Being (small 'b') in
Being - that became the most astonishing thing for the
Greeks (ibid., 49).

As Heidegger well knows to begin to think with the words 'Let us
think things from the beginning' has raised fifty years of ugly
smiles;   certain schools of philosophy still persist in refusing to
take such formulations seriously.   This is precisely to be expected
since we no longer have a legitimate word for such writing.   Students of Heidegger all know that the word 'ontology' was gradually
phased-out of his vocabulary and is, in the last publications, nowhere present.   Yet the same striving is present;   it is the same
striving for 'sophon' - the 'Eros' - the knowledge-wisdom of Being
that drove the Greeks to think.   Yet with the Socratics thought
became philosophy.   The question gradually changed to a question
about the nature of the being within Being;   Heraclitus' and Parmenides' question of the One-All was eclipsed.   The step out of thought
and into philosophy, for Heidegger, rests with Socrates and Plato and
from the thought of Being can only be considered a regression.
Philosophy then posed the question of Being as 'What is?'.   To delve
into the grounds of metaphysics, however, we must renew by listening
that which the tradition of philosophy delivers us, that is, liberates
us (WP, 71) by means of a destruction of what has been handed down to
us as the Being of being, by attuning ourselves to the voice of
Being.

Philosophical thought must be rememberance ('Andenken');   Heidegger would have us eschew conceptual grasping ('Begriff-Denken'),
formal-logical or calculative thinking before we can open our ears to
what the ground-words of our tradition say ('Sage').   The later
Heidegger would have us replace the appropriative language of the will
to will with 'essential thinking' ('das wesentliche Denken'), thinking that recalls ('Andenken') in the spirit of thanking ('Danken')

with 'originative thinking' ('das anfaengliche Denken') or meditative
thinking ('das besinnliche Denken') which would be a listening by
echoing the grace of Being - 'man's answer to the soundless voice of
Being, a still attentiveness to the truth of Being, a patient, responsive putting together in words, and thus bringing into being, of
this truth, so that it might become effective in the lives and thinking of men' (Mehta, p. 48).   The experience of Language to which
Heidegger calls attention is essentially the Greek experience of
'pathos';   our listening must unfold as a manner of correspondence
which is attuned to the voice of the Being of being.   From what we
have said it will be obvious that the thought of thinking the historicity of Being will itself collapse into history;   this thought is
a happening which shares the historicity of human existence - thought
is subject to the same finitude as is Being itself.   Even the
attempt to evade addressing the tradition as the mittence of language occurs from within the coils of this tradition.   The only escape from tradition is into tradition, in a heedless way.   Heidegger's thought culminates in the resonant synthesis of the Poetic
and the Saying of Being.   Those who have philosophized poetry reciprocally attain the poeticization of philosophy.   But haven't we
strayed from the intentions of these introductions?   What has all
this got to do with the analytical perspective of the sociologist?
In a way nothing;   but there's the rub.   We feel great obstacles in
relating to these violent contexts and in finding our way about the
writing of Writers like Hegel and Marx, Wittgenstein and Heidegger;
part of this is due to the fact that they are all fundamentally dis-
contented with their own Say and the means of expression at-hand -
their own engagement with language.   Their work is barbed with
strange warnings and ironies.   (16) We have to suffer their work as
painful dissolutions of what we normally take to be the 'established
contexts of intelligibility'.

What emerges from these Writings is that whatever is said must be
ground on what is left unsaid;   reading as re-writing demands a decision relating to this difference - leaving us with questions and
not answers: What have we read?   What has been taken-in?   Haven't
we been there before?   What kind of Genius is the writer claiming?
Where have we traversed in having social worlds depicted for us?
What was the Audience the author had in mind?   How do I gain entry
to the work?   How to hear the unsaid in the said?   Where is the
work?   What kind of audacity is it to write in the first place?
What grounds the writers tacit claim to know more?   What grounds his
resource of presuming that what he has to say is worth knowing?,
etc., etc.   Wittgenstein, for example, was obviously ethically uncertain of the honesty of presenting a finished text which somehow
pretended to be a map into an individual's head;   that is one of the
deeper reasons why the question of style (which is not to say that he
is alone in the early twentieth century) preoccupied him, and why in
the end, the rest was silence.   Let us take another path which leads
into community.   In re-trieving we must ask such questions thoughtfully by penetrating to what does not lie in the words but is never-
theless said in those words - to the unspoken which is bound up with
the spoken, to the culturally expressed reality which is not itself
entirely cultural (cf. Deely, p. 22).   Speaking of the necessity of
'doing violence' to the text Deely notes:

> What is essential in all philosophical discourse is not
> found in the specific propositions of which it is composed
> but in that which, although unstated as such, is made
> evident through these propositions.
> It is true that in order to wrest from the actual words
> that which these words 'intend to say', every interpre-
> tation must necessarily resort to violence. This
> violence, however, should not be confused with an action
> that is wholly arbitrary. The interpretation must be
> animated and guided by the power of an illuminative idea.
> Only through the power of this idea can an interpretation
> risk that which is always audacious, namely, entrusting
> itself to the secret elan of a work, in order by this
> elan to get through to the unsaid and to attempt to find
> an expression for it. The directive idea itself is
> confirmed by its own power of illumination. (Deely, p. 27).

Deely also demonstrated the complete irrelevance of pseudo-attacks
which claim adherence to the literal letter of a text; in a similar
vein we can also ascribe irrelevance to those approaches to our
writing which refuses to (or fails to) formulate the auspices of its
own work:

> If, in evaluating our efforts, one should accuse us of
> doing violence to 'that which is said' ('das Gesagte'),
> he would miss the point entirely. He would fail to
> grasp the whole sense of an effort to re-trieve, which is
> to say what an author did not say, could not say, but
> somehow make manifest. The only legitimate evaluative
> approach is to precise and criticize the fundamental idea
> which commands this 'violence' and gives it in a pro-
> found way its sense. What is at stake is nothing less
> than the difference between a comparative textual analysis
> and a philosophical study (ibid., pp. 27-8).

This is only a beginning to the problems inherent in the hermeneutics
of reading and textuality. The crucial terms of Deely's account, as
well as Heidegger's own pronouncements, are questionable. Whole
schools of continental hermeneutics are rent down the middle over
precisely these problems (of 'principled reading', 'elan', 'arbitrariness', 'subjective versus objective' canons of interpretation,
the unsaid 'in' the said, re-trieval, the place of the 'Hermeneu-
tiker', and so on). We need only mention the conflict with those
who follow Gadamer's hermeneutics and those influenced by the hermeneutic canons of Betti. (17) There is an enormous divergence, in
fact, in the readings of only Heidegger's writings. Thus, Werner
Marx (18) is well known for his re-trieval of Heidegger's thought
about the phenomenological destruction of the traditional Aristotelian and Hegelian motifs of western philosophy (Substance philosophy),
even thought in his work 'Heidegger and the Tradition' he has referred (in an Appendix) to the importance of Nietzsche for Heidegger.
There is a strong emphasis on the pre-socratic re-trieval of Heidegger. (19) Bernd Magnus (20) has built his version of Heidegger's
version of the tradition about Nietzsche's thought on eternal recurrence, and to a lesser extent, the relation between Nietzsche and
the Platonic tradition. Rosen (21) is now well known for his
critique of Heidegger's understanding of the Platonic dialogues.

And so it goes.

Although there are great difficulties ahead we are searching for
a notion of writing-reading where the adjective would become a re-
dundancy in 'violent reading'; where every reading becomes an adventure (or what the literalist would have to call a 'mis-interpretation'). But where there is a mis-interpretation we are surely not
wrong in waiting for the legislative interpretation to be supplied.

This stratum of questions could have radical consequences for
sociology's self-conceptions. How is human-being to be? Given
that a community of theory discloses its objects through the available
linguistic means, the speech of theory becomes crucial; presuming
that language is not encased in its own sound and fury the essence of
the social resides in the essence of speech: it is there where we
must search for grounds. By now we are all well aware that speech
depicts partially, that the descriptions of sociology are in some
sense metaphysically inadequate, that talk constitutes the world it
pretends to investigate, that reference may well be inscrutible (as
Quine formulates it). Relativisms of this kind are well-known camp-
followers of sociology, to be taken from the moth balls periodically
for lectures and conferences. Yet sociology is hermeneutically un-
musical; it is deaf to the radical philosophical understanding required - and this holds irrespective of the various sociologies of
knowledge and sociologies of false consciousness extant. What passes
for dialogue about 'foundations/grounds' in sociology is the weary
debates about the 'Methodensstreit' of the Heidelberg circle, today
represented by the praxis-group in Frankfurt.

English sociology is still debating whether 'Verstehen' should be
granted full status as a methodological aid for would-be researchers;
delicate concern is paid in symposia over the 'problem' of 'action',
of 'social explanation', of 'reasons' or 'causes', of 'mind-body' dilemmas, and so on and so forth. Sociology becomes Nietzsche's irony
incarnate: 'Menschlich all zu Menschlich': it represents an intro-
verted community all by itself. But have we come all this way to
learn this? It is enough to conclude that sociology has not entered
the circle of thought yet, that it cannot seriously think its own
essence and its own inscription in the covering-uncovering dialectic
of Being? What is required is a beginning which is reflexive to the
extent that it can begin to address such questions. How do sociologists deal with their intrinsically self-stratifying practices?
How does professional sociology stratify its talk from the 'sheer
relativisms' of literature, poetry, journalese? How do they differentiate amongst the various epistemic claims of each? I assume that
these are 'class' questions of the first order (quite literally),
which sociology conceived as a positive science must come to terms
with. I would also include sophisticated types of positivist re-
visionism like ethnomethodology, social phenomenology and the various
types of 'critical' sociology about that are still firmly entrenched
in the paradoxes of the descriptive-normative paradigm underneath
their philosophical ruses.

Yet the moral impetus and humanistic gloss of positivism is un-
deniable (as we shall learn from Marx); this is so since its warrant
derives from the liberal-democratic organization of the status quo as
a formally free community of 'free' selves; its criteria of adequacy
and sufficiency are correspondences and rules for detecting corres-

pondences; and its underlying form of life is that of functionalism.

But perhaps the final and most grotesque irony is that we are all positivists now. Existential, phenomenological, and ethnomethod- ological alternatives to positivist sociology or constructivist critical theory were, as we know spurned by the reaction to positivism in the first decades of this century; they still repeat their slogans that the self is social, interactional, a displayed order of accounting procedures and tacit rules of assembly; perhaps they too are steeped in the same questions raised by positivism, or at least are coloured in their re-action away from a scientistic framework. Paradigms of theory are, naturally enough, not unrelated; the rising paradigm still deals with the same questions raised by the superceded paradigm. It may well turn out that positivism is a train with a fixed 'telos' which we must abandon from the roots upward (even trans- cendental phenomenologists are accused, by their contemporaries, of being too 'positivistic').

We are also living in a climate of non-reconciliation which no longer has time for a purely conceptual solution to what sociology 'is' presented in an eternal 'now'. We wish to know what sociology will be for us - what is required to live sociologically. Nietzsche- Zarathustra have asked not how can man be described, but how can man be overcome? Holding critique and counter-critique across the corrodors of the train of positivism will not advance matters; per- haps it will take more than a generation of scholars to fathom the depths of the new beginning required. From a much different context, Dietrich Bonhoffer has left us with our dilemma: that when one re- alizes he is on the wrong train it is no use running backward down the corridor in the opposite direction.

NOTES

1 This is Hans-Georg Gadamer's formulation voiced from within his version of hermeneutic phenomenology (see 1960). 'Ereignis' (understood as the 'Appropriating' or 'granting' of Being, the archaic word-concentrate of the tradition of Being, has been used to characterize Heidegger's later thought. It becomes a guide-word of back-tracking thought (see Kisiel in Sallis (ed.), 1970).
2 Here perhaps the reader might retrace our remarks from the latent phenomenology of intersubjectivity in Husserl to the vital phenomenological ontology of Maurice Merleau-Ponty (from the spoken word (parole parlee) to the speaking word ('parole parlante') of living contact with the Other; from phenomenology he might move to the dialogal thinking of Martin Buber on the 'between-ness' of the I-Thou encounter, of the philosophy of We in Ebner, Rosenzweig, Schutz, Loewith - and taking Buber's own hint return to the dialogal roots of intersubjective philosophy in Feuerbach and Marx; perhaps the reader may enter into the hermeneutics of Husserl's student, Paul Ricoeur or indeed of Heidegger's student, Hans Georg Gadamer.
3 If we think these are 'mere' metaphors we might miss the chance of reflecting on how metaphorical formulations sometimes take us by the heels and force thought upon us. Perhaps what goes

unsaid in metaphorical transformation is precisely what makes metaphor possible at the outset; metaphor speaks to, rather than of, the unity of the world. The being of metaphor remains a rich pool of problems – none of which we can address here.

4 Details can be found in Lobkowicz (1967), pp.3-9.

5 For example with the Cabala, Isaac Luria's (1534-72) idea of the clearance of Being where by a sort of 'contraction' within God himself a space is opened for some-thing to present itself as being. Lobkowicz has noted its affinities with the historical origins of the term 'alienation' (ibid., pp.289-90).

6 Such typical self-conceptions are ways man has cast himself in the history of his transcendence; at root his self-conceptions, his ethical and social co-existence, are speech-conceptions. Heidegger's work 'Gelassenheit' has attempted to coin a non-relational lexicon that would undercut comparing man and speech per se (again the dangerous word 'and'): thus he speaks of the 'region that regions' as Being, thereby overturning the form of the question such as 'How is speech related to man?' or 'How is Speech related to Being?'. These are, when we stop and think amazing questions; they presume everything we are trying to think. Rather we might now ask 'How is speech with man?' or 'How is speech man?' or 'How speaks It with man?'. Other essential transformations of the same type can be carried out with 'Being', 'truth', 'essence', 'Time', rather than speech. Hence we place the traditional metaphysical category of 'relation' in inverted commas, to signify that we are still in the onto-theological speech of metaphysics when we ask for the 'relation' of man and speech. That man has the arrogance to define his relation to Language as a 'conception' is the truly amazing aspect of the history of the west. We are only gradually realizing the ramifications of this arrogance in the 'Weltbild' (world-picture) that Science and Technology is elaborating of Being as the culmination of our epoch in the history or mittence of Being. The category of 'relation' is that of technology.

7 For very different reasons Hegel, in the 'Phenomenology of Mind', had already thoroughly criticized the notion of truth as the truth of the proposition: 'Dogmatism as a way of thinking, whether in ordinary knowledge or in the study of philosophy, is nothing else but the view that truth consists in a proposition, which is a fixed and final result, or again which is directly known' (Preface, p.99). From this critique Hegel derived his dialectical concept of truth as a Total dialectical development of the Notion. Its apotheosis occurs in the derivation of the dialectical categories in the 'Logic'.

8 I refer again to a very similar argument in Hegel's Preface to his 'Phenomenology' (e.g. pp.81-2, 99, and 105).

9 Others – particularly 'alethein', care ('Sorge'), 'ek-stasis', 'Ereignis', temporality, 'Sage', 'der Tod', 'Sein-zum-Tod', etc. – must unfortunately be presumed. I refer the reader to the relevant sections in 'Sein und Zeit'.

10 See George Lichtheim's Introduction to the Torchbook edition of the 'Phenomenology', xxi-xxii.

11 See Cleve on Heraclitus' word 'Logos'; cf. K.H. Ilting, esp. pp. 100-3.

12 See Walter Kaufmann (1959) and (1965).

13 See Ivan Soll (1969).

14 Jean Hyppolite (1969).

15 Cf. Nicolaus's discussion in his Foreword to the Penguin edition
    of the 'Grundrisse'; Marx's theoretic 'praxis' of standing Hegel
    on his feet would, from my reading, require a reading in which
    Marx's writing itself should be stood on its feet (cf. Nicolaus's
    formulation in relation to Althusser's reading of Marx, footnote
    36, p.40; cf. footnote 37, p.40).

16 'In his Preface, he (Hegel) begins by saying that he cannot allow
    us to gain even a partial understanding of his philosophy before
    we have seen it worked out; he insists that truth lies in the
    concrete development of his system, not in its plan or in the
    'naked result'.   In short, Hegel's Preface is, by his own in-
    sistence, not only an inadequate introduction to his work, but
    because it states what he therein states to be unstatable, it
    would have to be considered an impossible introduction.   It is
    a self-refuting statement of the form "Do not believe that this
    is true"' (Solomon, 1969, pp.119-20).
    In the 'In Place of a Preface', above we have tried to formulate
    a similar self-refuting 'Preface'.   A very different, but re-
    lated instance, can be found in the self-refuting method of
    Wittgenstein's 'Tractatus' which, upon the distinction between
    what can be said and what can only be shown, faces a similar
    internal collapse, and, like Hegel's work and our own, disinte-
    grates as a text in its very success: in asking that it be cor-
    responded to in a thoughtful mood of re-writing; in asking that
    the reader begin to engage in the work of doing social theory
    socially himself.

17 See Palmer (1969).

18 Marx's 'Heidegger and the Tradition' (1971).

19 For instance Seidel (1964).

20 Magnus (1970).

21 Rosen (1969).

Chapter 2

MARX, ALIENATION AND SPEECH
Barry Sandywell

Dixi et salvavi animam meam

Probably there is a complex correlation between the trust
in logical abstraction and the new abstraction of commodity
value, represented by coined money. (1)

Stated concretely this might well form a working hypothesis for his-
toriography and concrete sociology. Let me use this as a hint and
occasion to see Marx's version of this thesis as his way of referring
to the conditions of authentic speech and writing.

A commitment to speech that is perfectly and internally controlled
in terms of abstract and logical properties like the calculi and
algorithms of symbolic logic would be a commitment to a mercantile
form of life: the commitment and trust in the exchange value of
one's money, its identity, communal recognition and 'thinginess'
would then be a kind of metaphor for the trust we invest in the exchange value of speech - understood as a derivative type of speech
modelled on the distance and anonymity of monetary relations. It is
upon the auspices of some such form of life that notions like the
'power' of language, the 'technical efficiency' of speech, the 'instrumentality' of language, the 'uses' of talk, language-as-tool,
speaker as 'homo faber', and so forth can be raised. Faith in the
power of an abstract determination of life (the power invested in
money) not unnaturally gives rise to the engine of the abstract conception of the 'relation' between man and man, man and Nature, being
and Being: which is at the centre of the mathematical driving force
inherent in the development of western science and its rationality
interpreted as 'ratio', technical reason. The constructions of
universal Logics rely on this metaphysical way of construing man's
being-in-language. Man as 'homo loquens' is transformed into a
glassy reflection of a wilful syntactics. Language can then deliver
the goods; present the proofs; chase away the mystical ghosts;
define the relevant parameters of the world; and patrol the corridors
of a self-imposed formalism. We have then turned speech into a
Generative System of propositional theorems empowered with a carto-
graphic will-to-isomorphism. In the end human speech can be deleted
altogether, to be replaced by a purely formal definition of

Structural Generation: in certain paradigmatic linguistic texts the computer takes the role of speaker.   The full power of Max Weber's rationalization thesis concerning the fate-ful stratification of the west as this-worldly engaged as opposed to the east's disengaged other-worldly light, is still to be tapped.

Let me refer to a section in Marx's '1844 Manuscripts' which occurs under the general section, The Power of Money in Bourgeois Society; Marx is addressing the mystification and fetished power of the money-form.   Since Marx was given to frequent comparisons between the fetished form of money and the fetished form of language (2) let us take the liberty of performing a thought-experiment and understand Marx's speeches relating to the money-form as explorations of the fetishing process of speech.   My reading will canvass, with all due respect to the great thinker Marx was (and is), the notion that he is speaking of the grounds of Membership and the ever present possibility of losing sight of those grounds in conceiving of speech as an unlimited, anonymous technical power - as being not only an object, but an all-encompassing machine of appropriation.

I would like to draw out of the following extract from the 'Manuscripts' the ruling idea that for Marx the language of class has become Faustian, pretentious and appropriative, and therein has veiled the light that sustains speech:

By possessing the 'property' of buying everything, by possessing the property of appropriating all objects, 'money' is thus the 'object' of eminent possession.   The universality of its property is the omnipotence of its being. It therefore functions as the almighty being.   Money is the 'pimp' between man's need and the object, between his life and his means of life.   But 'that which' mediates 'my' life for me, also 'mediates' the existence of other people 'for' me.   For me it is the 'other' person (127).   (3)

In like manner speech becomes the pimp between man and Being: the word comes to be regarded as a mediating tool or passage to the thing; it is presumed to present and re-present the world, as having the indubitable characteristic of adumbrating worlds, or, finally, as corresponding to a preexistent world.

Paradoxically speech is both (i) reduced and diminished to this mediating role, but also (ii) raised into a force of unlimited power promising its bearer to raise him into a language-neutral view of the world and thereby, give him possession of the earth.   Marx is absolutely clear that this is the speech of alienating Class, of economic exploitation and stratification.   In several places Marx addresses the concrete class-character of speech.   In the 'German Ideology', for instance, Marx writes: 'The very language is a product of the bourgeoisie and therefore, even in language as in reality, commercial relations are placed at the base of all others'.   In other words, speech as commodity grounds all other relationships: it becomes the paradigmatic model of relation as such, from which all others must be measured and evaluated.   Speech as an available commodity then thingifies its proprietor.   Along with the commercial nexus, language removes itself from the true products of its appropriation and of the real grounds it should authentically bespeak.   With money (speech) one can become what one is not; it is magically transformative.   Speech takes upon itself divine powers of

conversion – it becomes a temple and shrine.   In this way the originary Logos of the Greeks has become the Logos of technical rationality, of the feasibility of ends and means (central to early action
theory) and of mathematization as a universal domination of Being.

This derivative and abstract understanding of speech now becomes
the sole bond that binds man to man: it collects concretely.   Yet
in its drive to become the universal form of speech and the universal
mode of human relation (Marx's descriptions of the speech of Capitalism as the universal transformation of the world on an hitherto un-
known scale often seems to carry away even his imagination) it seeks
to overcome and divide all other forms of speech.   It is imperalis-
tic;   it is the 'agent of divorce' ('Manuscripts', 129).   It differentiates.   We rediscover the stratificational dialectic of identity
and difference;   speech is surrendered to a hostile Other, to a
Concept of belonging-together to which man does not deeply belong
(he belongs to belonging-together as such).   Language emerges as a
Conceptual annex.

The very real successes of the abstract technical mode of speech
(which Husserl and Heidegger later called the 'mathematical' form of
life) makes this derivative Concept of speech mysterious and divine:
its true origins and authority are shrouded since it proves to have
boundless resources in objectifying Being, reducing it to a common
measure and 'unit' (the unit of the physical thing, the material
entity) and, in the end, perpetrating a thorough objectification of
the self of the talk.   Man has become a proprietor of his own language.   He controls his language and in that control loses the piety
of cor-responding to the pulse and song of Being.

By coining (quite literally) our being in an alienated notion of
language we enter and further the path for a far-reaching spiritual
and theoretical bankruptcy.   For the ethos of the market is one of
the commercial inter-changeability of all speeches (Free Speech means
the ultimate gradable character of each and every speech).   On the
surface communication as perfect exchange of free individuals re-
sembles a self-evident picture of equality and justice;   but where
the society is totally organized on this principle we gradually perceive the real relations that it obscures.   Where speech breaks down,
for instance, we would have to look toward the conditions of exchange
as being at fault rather than question the framework of 'ersatz'
exchange.   We are led to trust the Concept and those who have carved
a trade out of 'communications'.   In other words the achievement of
this shell of democratic universality is achieved at the price of
ransoming authentic speech which is the togetherness of writing-
selves within the unity of thought and Being: the true labour of
speech as disclosing-community.   In actual practice the 'free' in
'Free speech' must be understood as a heavy irony, just as Marx
speaks of 'free' in the bourgeois use of 'free labourer' and 'free
labour contract' as ironies.   The true essence of this form of life
is solipsistic.   It emerges in the various philosophies of the individual (epitomized by Stirner's Egoism).   Here the Ego and his
appropriative talk stalks like a thief in a night of worldly darkness, venturing from his inner shell only to appropriate objectivities
and to return before the light of an uncertain dawn.   Togetherness
reduces to a competition in world-theft;   the Other becomes material
for appropriation.   Hobbes sketched the essentials, Descartes uses

the imagery, but its consummation is in the 'raison' of Sartre. Unfortunately the members of these thief-societies are never certain of
their booty, which continually turns into powdery sense data, mental
ideas and 'inner' images.

What for Marx, would stand as non-alienated speech and being-
together?   One of the many displays of his notion of community
occurs in the 'Manuscripts':

> Assume man to be 'man' and his relationship to the world
> to be a human one: then you can exchange love only for
> love, trust for trust, etc.   If you want to enjoy art,
> you must be an artistically-cultivated person, if you want
> to exercise influence over other people, you must be a
> person with a stimulating and encouraging effect on other
> people.   Every one of your relations to man and to nature
> must be a 'specific' expression, corresponding to the ob-
> ject of your will, of your real individual life.   If you
> love without evoking love in return - that is, if your
> loving as loving does not produce reciprocal love; if
> through a 'living expression' of yourself as a loving
> person you do not make yourself a 'loved person', then
> your love is impotent - a misfortune (131).

The non-authored, non-reciprocating speech of techne, of the abstract
exchange and the inauthentic writing that makes no attempt to address
its own production must fall into an alienated Collective diametric-
ally opposed to the ethos of the possible society which Marx has in
mind in his many like descriptions, his phenomenology of intersubjectivity.   Where authentic speech is lost and forgotten the
theorist no longer poses his authorship as the recurrent issue, but
simply concerns himself with the logical form of exchange (with
communicative 'bits', Rhetoric, good Grammar, the persuasiveness of
the 'Polis', the chatter of the market-place and the universal rights
and mercenary power of 'ratio').

The forgetfulness is a forgetfulness of man's very dwelling in
speech - in language which is the house of Being; in the end he
stops speaking since he no longer can speak thinkingly (speak by
listening to language) and is alienated from the mystery of being-in-
language.   For Logos we have substituted Mammon; for use value we
have transposed exchange-value; Quantity for Quality, the finite unit
for the infinite Immeasurable (Apeiron).

To be divided (and consequently stratified) from the sense of authorship over one's own speech fulfills all the conditions that Marx
(and others before him) pointed at with the grammar of Alienation -
of a sundered unity, the separation of thought from Being.   Consider
Schiller's display of this loss (lack, emptiness) captured in his
imagery of difference, schism, fragmentation, split (the imagery of
a forced stratification of an originary unit of identity and difference):

> enjoyment is separated from labour, the means from the
> end, exertion from recompense.   Eternally 'fettered'
> only to a single little fragment of the whole, man
> fashions himself only as a fragment; ever hearing only
> the monotonous whirl of the wheel which he turns, he
> never displays the full harmony of his being, and, instead
> of coining the humanity that lies in his nature, he is

content with a mere expression of his occupation, his
science (The Philosophical and Aesthetic Letters and
Essays of Schiller). (4)

Schiller's premonition of the roots of surplus value (exertion from
recompense) and his emancipatory style are noteworthy. His use of
the expression 'coining the humanity...' must be understood as a kind
of ironic deception of the deceivers. Concrete interpretations read
such texts as making-reference to the repressive outcomes of economic
and cultural oppression or stratification as a structural and historical process. Analytically, here, they display notions of speech
and Membership as the conditions for authentic theorizing - authored
writing. They require that the author and his reader enter a Class-
less collective. Speaking means speaking-to-be-understood, as
authoring means expecting to be read and understood. To constitute
a writing-reading community it is necessary to remove the cleavages
set between reading and writing, reader and author: we must de-
stratify theorizing (captured by the imagery of a Hegel, Schiller
and Marx).

Existence ruled by the god Money was for Marx (and Toennies and
Weber) a pure example of the disruption of a spontaneously lived
unity - typified for him in the creative nature of truly human labour
where it is impossible to separate 'means' and 'end'. Rationalised
existence is the domain of separation where a once undifferentiated
unity is split into calculative means and ends. The same phenomenon
is phenomenologically analyzed by Toenniss under the label of 'essential volition' (Unity) as against 'rational/arbitrary volition'
(Difference). The dialectical texture of this Unity and Difference
as it was realized in the structures and stratifications of the rationalized West formed the basic palate from which Max Weber re-read
the genesis of the West as the complex he termed 'bourgeois capitalism'. When we strip away the substantive formulations of these
theorists we find the recurrent 'grammar' of Identify and Difference.
To use Toennies expression the doubleness ('Zweifachheit') which
splits apart complexes of action and thus provides the fundamental
possibilities of rationalization itself arises from the grounds of an
initial unity.

Moreover the dialectic between Unity and Difference is formulated
in non-absolutist terms, thereby facilitating a phenomenological
investigation of the transitions and adumbrations which span the
theoretically idealized concepts of 'means' and 'end'. Both Weber
and Toennies developed their methodologies of 'ideal-types' and
'normal concepts' (Toennies) in order to explore what they considered to be available structures, patterns, rules, stratifications,
and so forth which were (or could be read as) compounded from these
phenomenologically-pure complexes of action (themselves formulated
with the aid of concepts derived from the dialectic of Identify and
Difference - for example, Weber's famous typology of action upon
which 'layers' of more ramified articulations were constructed).
It remains a rich vein of future work to pose more strictly the
question of the underlying 'grammar' which made a sociology of the
Weberian or Toennesian kind possible. Whatever the outcome of such
an inquiry we are certainly on the right track in exploring their
use of the dialectical relationships founded on the tension between
Identity and Difference.

In the famous analysis of commodities and exchange value in
'Capital' we recall how the genesis of exchange-value itself is
linked to its common denominator in the money-form, and how important money was for the emergence of bourgeois economy.   Indeed Marx
speaks of the money-form as a riddle holding the key to bourgeois
economy: the explication of its formation as a universal expression
of value (speechful relations) 'from its simplest, almost impercept-
ible outline, to the dazzling money-form' constitutes a major part of
the task which Marx set himself in 'Capital'.   In 'Capital' Marx
also speaks of the dominant language as the 'language of commodities'
which is the social form taken by human relations under bourgeois
economy; furthermore all commodities know the syntax and semantics
of this language for it is perfectly simple.   The exchange of words
which occurs when one commodity exchanges with another is measured by
one criterion - whether or not the commodity is valuable - whether or
not it contains accumulated labour.   Where this is the dominant
language-game alternate modes of speech are almost impossible.   Yet
even the abstract language of commodities is still intersubjective -
and to that extent contains the seeds of its own transformation.
That is, it is undergirded by some long-forgotten sense of social
relationality.   Money itself is the universal standard of exchange-
ability by which the value of commodities are measured.   And the
money-form itself is, as Marx makes clear, derived itself from commodity production.   Gold, for example, was originally a simple commodity.   The commodity-form in general gives rise to the specific
commodity-form which Marx calls the money-form.   Like the commodity-
form in general the language of money appears 'a very trivial thing,
and easily understood.   Its analysis shows that it is, in reality, a
very queer thing, abounding in metaphysical subtleties and theological
niceties' ('Capital').   Like the commodity upon which it is molded,
commodity-speech is an intersubjective human relation, a social relation which is disclosed for its speakers in the 'fantastic form' of
the object.   Where commodity-speech talks about the world it is as
if an object were referring to an object.   Speech takes the fetished
form of a relation between things.   Speech is thingified alongside a
fetished world of commodities.   The production of fetished speech
expresses the speechful fetish (forgetfulness) of production.
Speechful production forgets the human grounds of all value - over-
looks the labouring-power which invests the world with meaning and
value.   The fetished commodity and its language are thus icons of
forgetfulness.   Under the regime of fetished speech the community of
labouring speakers takes on the surreal form of an 'intersubjectivity'
between things (which is strictly speaking contradictory or impossible) while the commodity product of labouring speakers takes the
form of social intersubjectivity between things.
The critical unmasking of these fetished relations then constitutes an attempt to recollect the essential beneath the apparent
surface.   Criticism is in many ways a kind of unveiling or 'hermeneutics' - a linguistic model which Marx himself uses when he declares
that the commodity world is like a vast system of social hieroglyphics which require deciphering.   Furthermore that this critical
deciphering is a remembering where we 'get behind the secret of our
own social products'.   The whole process is compared to language:
'for to stamp an object of utility as a value, is just as much a

social product as language'.   However far removed market speech
(money) is from sociality it never loses the communicative character
of exchange; in its purest form money in fact represents the play-
form of universal exchange, the purest idealization of exchange into
which all other forms are convertible.   If, under bourgeois economy
sociality is realized in the fetished mathematics of circulating
commodities, the algebra of the process is found in the money-form.
Money is the idealized algebraic structure - the deep structure as it
were - of discursive exchanges.   In money we find an absolutist
model of speech - a fetished simulation of dialogue, a dialectic
without partners.

In the 'Grundrisse' the four essential properties of money are
outlined as (1) measure of commodity exchange; (2) medium of exchange; (3) representative of commodities (hence object of contracts);
and (4) general commodity alongside all particular commodities.
These relational features are said to follow from money's character
as universal exchange value divorced from commodities themselves and
objectified.   Money is the realized and always realizable form of
capital - the mode of being of capital, its 'appearance'.   In a historical scenario capital phenomenologically appears only in the
money-form.   As capital develops all exchange relations are sucked
into the dominant 'transcendental' power of the money-form, the monetary exchange.   There is, according to Marx, an inexorable movement
(a growth in the immanent contradictions) from production to commodity production, from commodity to exchange value; money-property as
the exchange value of the commodity; the separation of this exchange
value in the pure form of money which 'achieves a general social
existence separated from all particular commodities and their natural
mode of existence'.   Money becomes an object of desire only for the
potential exchange-values it commands, 'stands for', or symbolizes.
Exchange-value as exchange-value is brought to perfection in money.
Commerce is realized within this social form as an insatiable desire
for the transcendental power of money; for command over the symbols
of exchange-value: exchange for exchange.   Money has become, to
recall Marx's aphorism, the imperishable commodity which symbolizes
the purely imperishable exchange.   Human relations have become
purest exchange - and to this extent inhuman.   Where we develop a
condition of discourse in the direction of extreme caricature or
parody it becomes inhuman.   Marx is master of such ironical invers-
ions: originally money appeared as the representative of all values
yet in practice all production and all labour have become the abstract representatives of money - money as the transcendental eminence behind bourgeois economy.

...'it is an inherent property of money to fulfil its
purposes by simultaneously negating them; to achieve
independence from commodities; to be a means which
becomes an end; to realize the exchange value of commodities by separating them from it; to facilitate exchange
by splitting it; to overcome the difficulties of the
direct exchange of commodities by generalizing them; to
make exchange independent of the producers in the same
measure as the producers become dependent on exchange'
('Grundrisse', 1973, p. 151).

Throughout the dialectic (Product-Activity into Commodity; Commodity

into Exchange-Value; Exchange-Value into Money) however Marx emphasizes that the process is not a 'mere' dialectic of categories;
that the analysis attempts the disclosure of modes of being even
where the presentation is 'idealist'.

Continuing the metaphor Marx grounds his dialectical analysis of
reified ('secret') social forms as an enormous attempt both to re-
trieve configurations and also to recollect the meaning of these
configurations as forms of life:

> Man's reflections on the forms of social life, and con-
> sequently, also, his scientifis analysis of those forms,
> take a course directly opposite to that of their actual
> historical development. He begins, post festum, with
> the result of the process of development ready to hand
> before him. The characters that stamp products as commod-
> ities, and whose establishment is a necessary preliminary
> to the circulation of commodities, have already acquired
> the stability of natural, self-understood forms of social
> life, before man seeks to decipher, not their historical
> character, for in his eyes they are immutable, but their
> meaning.

And the ultimately mystifying and concealing form of life is that re-
presented by the language of money, a form of life built about the
money-form.

> Could commodities themselves speak, they would say:
> Our use-value may be a thing that interests men.   It is
> no part of us as objects.   What, however, does belong to
> us as objects, is our value.   Our natural intercourse as
> commodities proves it.   In the eyes of each other we are
> nothing but exchange-values. ('Capital')

The translator between these conversations is, of course, the universal speech of money - the general social equivalent which adjudicates
between the claims of different commodities. Marx associates money
with alienability - to be a general social equivalent means to have
the fundamental property of moveability, handleability, exchange-
ability.   In this sense the social equivalent criterion of money
emerges within 'alienated' groups.   According to Marx nomad-groups
are originary centres for the development of the money-form.   It is
also groups which travel in order to trade that develop some minimally alienable 'lingua franca' to facilitate exchange.   The evolution of the money-form and commodity speech goes hand in hand.
Perhaps a sense of language itself derives from the experience of
alienability linked with commercial exchange - itself linked with the
contact between foreign communities.   Such speculations have been
concretely followed up by Marxist scholars.

Marx takes the metaphor of market speech seriously.   Where there
is a 'language of commodities' we might think of affecting a direct
and unmediated translation of this voice into the discourses of theoretical science.   Such a translation would require a neutral transformation rule or technique.   In this manner Marx could locate the
deep structure of bourgeois economic theory - of the Political Economy of men like Adam Smith, David Ricardo, Say, and the like.

Political economy as a scientific discipline described itself as
a one-to-one reflection of the self-subsisting laws of market existence.   Here the Market itself spoke to the texts of liberal economy

without the mediation of their own voices.   The 'language of commodities' was translated directly into the scientific discourses of
political science, economic science, statistical analysis, and so
forth.   The transformation rule or method was simply that of the
physical sciences: to know the laws of any social formation is,
structurally the same as grasping the laws of a physical formation -
and as in the latter it is thought that the voice of Nature speaks
truly and honestly, so it is thought that the voices of sociality
are likewise direct and without dissimulation.   Following the scho-
lastic rule of 'adequatio rei et intellectus' Political Economy
construes its enterprise as simply objectively re-presenting, 'mapping' and thus 'charting' (with all its predictive-control promise)
the underlying laws of social complexes and stratifications.

Furthermore this very project of translation was only possible
upon the auspices of a notion like the 'language of commodities' and
an unmediated notion of theoretical discourse not as a 'praxis' but
as a neutral mirror within which the real is isomorphically captured.
The place of the theorist himself - his textuality/intertextuality,
his Subjectivity - remains a theoretical enigma for this kind of
writing.

The theoretical discourses of such 'science' act like rules or
techniques for constituting a notion of theoretical Self;   such
rules are then self-formulations - directives to the actor which
inform him of the intelligibility of his programme and constitute
the sense of the enterprise.   These rules (such as 'Regard your
Object as a language to be perfectly deciphered and known', 'Act as
though the social were a thing' (Durkheim), etc.) may now be formulated as a rhetoric of positivistic inquiry, a rhetoric which stratifies the speaker away from other speakers (everyday discourse, for
example), and gathers him in a community of other like-minded speakers (members of the project of Political Economy) as well as providing him-them with a stratified object open to the investigative
techniques and orderings which are themselves bound up with these
auto-stratifications.   Stratification is thus to be regarded as a
discursive method of auto-situating before it is the topic of
autonomously situated theoretical pursuits.   And this is one of the
things Marx teaches about the self-situating speeches of political
economists: they are auto-theorized by the 'grammar' and rhetoric of
their own categories and formulations.   The same 'logic' naturally
applied to Marx's theoretical corpus.   It too is essentially self-
situating, auto-theorized, self disclosive.   As we noted at the
outset, language is characterized by the deep feature of disclosure
and self-disclosure.   We are yet to understand how deep these
stratifications actually are.

The languaged formulation of the social is regarded by Marx as
itself a product of historicity, a product of a specific configur-
ation of relations.   In this manner the language of these relations
and stratifications which Marx speaks of as the 'categories' which
express these relations, comprehend their structure, and so forth are
like archaelogical formations giving us access to the 'structure and
relations of production of all the vanished social formations but of
whose ruins and elements it built itself up'.   In this way the
language of commodities - bourgeois economy - is auto-theorized as
an arche-ological clue to the language of domination characterizing

feudal and ancient economy. As Marx notes in the 'Grundrisse' these
categories, although in an often confused, partial and inverted historical order, express the forms of being of specific determinations
of the social. Marx's own method of dialectical analysis in fact
inverts the ur-archeological 'evolution' of these categorial relations.
He does not begin with the historically most primitive category,
rather the textual sequence is determined by interests which the
totality requires - by the systematic categorial relations characterizing modern bourgeois society - a radical inversion of their
'natural order'. In this way the category of primitive agricultural
or agrarian accumulation does not take textual first place; rather,
it is the 'all-dominating economic power' of capital itself which
occurs first in the categorial dialectic of Marx's writing: it is
capital, the commodity form and the emergent money-form which takes
the abstract role of categorial beginning and which also occurs as
the categorial 'end' in the analysis. In accordance with this
notion of totality or dialectic Marx stratifies his object:
1. the dynamic categories constituting the inner structure of
bourgeois society, sustaining the Class relations characterizing this
order: Capital, wage labour, landed property. The dialectical
interconnections of these categories. The derivative formulation of
'the three great social classes' Exchange. The nature of the Credit
System, the money-form.
2. the concentration of bourgeois society in the form of the state.
Viewed in relation to itself. The 'unproductive' classes. Taxes,
State debt. Public credit. The population. The colonies.
Emigration.
3. the international relation of production. International division of labour. International exchange. Export and import.
Rate of exchange.
4. the world market and crises.
Money has the fundamental feature of being essentially alienable.
It is fluid, abstract, divorceable from its possessor. Its antithesis would be inalienable land. Where land is an icon for rootedness, money is an icon of deracination. It not only symbolizes
ungroundedness but implements the dislocation of rootedness. Money
- the instigation of a money economy - provided a disruptive wedge
which revolutionized and subverted landed tradition. Money is the
symbol of The City, the destroyer of inalienable landed rights.
For Marx the principle of Money deepened this dissolution and extended it to the very base of all right; money has overturned the
very notion of Right. As a universal measure of right and wrong
money provides a universally immoral calculus. Built on money, the
City of Man is in principle 'deracine'.
Speech under the Rule of Money is likewise radically alienable,
uprooted. The human Voice becomes a futile vapour. Like Money
it is 'here today and gone tomorrow' - speaking becomes 'deracine'.
Language can no longer take itself seriously. Speech under the
auspices of the Market takes on all the characteristics of radical
conventionality: Man (Money) is the Measure of all Things, of the
Things that are that they are, and of the Things that are not that
they are not. Speech which had power, relevance and 'truth' yester-
day now rings hollow and leaden like a handful of coins from an in-
flated economy. Speech is temporally 'deracine'. It belongs to

the 'Gesellschaft'.   In his 'Philosophie des Geldes', Georg Simmel
also brought out the connection between money as a principle of mutability within forms of relationship.   Here the money-form disrupts
the hegemony of communally held land giving rise to the development
of individualism and ego-centricity.

A Myth of 'venal' (one of Marx's favourite adjectives) Money is
opposed to a myth of 'virtuous' Land.   Stratifications built upon
the stolid identity of public and private interests of landed power -
communal ownership of land and the productive apparatus - typifies
the good 'polis' in which all stratification will gradually wither
away removing the need for any form of state violence.   Against this
community of virtue stands a political community constituted upon the
power invested in money.   The monetary 'Gesellschaft' typifies the
corrupt 'polis'.   Here political virtue is bought and sold;   offices
of the state are formed and dissolved with the opening of purses;
monetary power purchaess political stability through an exchequer
permanently pouring wealth into mercenary armies;   the scenario of
political life shifts to the chess-board of banking, finance and
international solvencies.   The ideal 'polis' is replaced by the City
state concretely realized in Italy under the Borgias;   moral life
becomes Machiavellian 'virtu'.   Money becomes a secular divinity.

In money one part of the whole has subjugated the whole to its
ordering hegemony;   where everything is alienable nothing is of any
value.   In destroying the myth of inalienable landed property money
began to deify itself: everything is alienable but the form of money
itself through which everything must pass.   Like time itself everything is subject to decay and dissolution except the form of temporality;   so with money, everything can be rendered into money terms,
dissolved into one denominational base - but the form of money itself.
Money - not truth - becomes the whole ('das Ganze').

Money facilitates the ramified processes of circulation which are
essential to an exchange economy.   Marx speaks of the 'magical' properties of transformation invested in the money-form.   Money is the
'metamorphosed shape of all other commodities', it is the result of
their general condition of alienation and like commodities it too is
'alienable without restriction or condition'.

It reads all prices backwards, and thus, so to say, depicts
itself in the bodies of all other commodities, which offer
to it the material for the realisation of its own use-value.
At the same time the prices, wooing glances cast at money
by commodities, define the limits of its convertibility, by
pointing to its quantity.   Since every commodity, on becoming money, disappears as a commodity, it is impossible to
tell from the money itself, how it got into the hands of its
possessor ....   Representing on the one hand a sold commodity,
it represents on the other a commodity to be bought ('Capital').
The circuitry of Money (itself a commodity) and Commodities Marx
terms the circulation of commodities.   For the seller money is pure
potential, the alienated form of the commodity, for the purchaser
money is the absolutely alienable form of the commodity.

'Not even are the bones of saints, and still less are more
delicate res sacrosanctae, extra commercium honinum able
to withstand this alchemy.   Just as every qualitative
difference between commodities is extinguished in money,

so money, on its side, like the radical levver that it is,
does away with all distinctions' ('Capital').
Where money realizes more money – where it leads to capital accumulation (the circuit M–C–M – capital circulation) as an independent
social process we are at the heart of bourgeois economics.   Here
money and commodities are but forms of the process of capitalization
itself.   All value is in process;   money becomes pure process,
transformation, circulation: it becomes capital, endlessly circulating where it multiplies.   The formula for the circulation of
capital is, according to Marx, the general formula of capital itself
as it appears in the sphere of circulation.

In his 'Philosophie des Geldes' and other works relating to the
money-form Georg Simmel follows – almost word for word in many instances – Marx's discussion of money in 'Das Capital'.   Simmel
connects the exchange economy with the disruptive medium of money;
the money-form is intimately connected with the discourses of individualism;   the possession of money brings almost unlimited power;
money enables men to 'split' their personality from functional or
instrumental roles, performance of significance – all roles can be
purchased outside of one's personality with the instrument of money;
money facilitates the functional atomicity of cosmopolitan existence;
money is the perfect symbol of generalized anonymity;   the icon of a
generalized standard of exchange by which all things are measured and
reduced;   money as a generalized criterion is constitutively incapable of expressing the unique, the individual, the qualitative in
things;   money advances the mathematization of social relations;
money encourages abstract mathematical-intellectual attitudes – it
leads to the universal spirit of calculation, quantitative and statistical reasoning (Simmel regards it as a chicken-and-egg problem of
tracing whether the intellectualistic mentality first promoted the
money economy or whether the latter determined the former – whatever
is the 'casuality' the City is the fertile ground for deepening
commodity speech and abstraction);   the calculative attitude linked
to money provides an ideal atmosphere for the numerical determinations of natural science – the world is transformed into a mathematical problem;   money is the universal leveller of things;   and so
forth.   A characteristic description from Simmel might illustrate
his indebtedness to Marx's phenomenology of money.   In his essay,
'The Metropolis and Mental Life', Simmel describes the levelling in-
fluence of money in the following manner:

For money expresses all qualitative differences of things
in terms of 'how much?'.   Money, with all its colourless-
ness and indifference, becomes the common denominator of
all values;   irreparably it hollows out the core of things,
their individuality, their specific value, and their in-
comparability.   All things float with equal specific
gravity in the constantly moving stream of money.   All
things lie on the same level and differ from one another
only in the size of the area which they cover.

It is one of the Simmelian ironies concerning money that the instrumental commodity of money – as means often replaces the goal
which its possessor sought in the first place.   Money which is
sought as an end in itself adumbrates the social phenomenon of the
miser – the hoarding Self.   Here money which originally served

desire has become the intrinsic satisfaction itself.   Money begins
to chase itself for itself.   The miser loves money not for what it
might achieve in circulation - as goods or capital accumulation - but
as an abstract end in itself.   Here we have a pure desire which cannot be satisfied.   Where money aimed to liberate an object in a concrete commodity exchange here money functions as the abstract promise
of such a liberation, as the abstract potentiality of satisfying unlimited and anonymous desires.   The love of wealth becomes a self-
satisfying abstract desire.

A parallel inversion can be constructed for the domain of discourse.   Language is ground in the face-to-face dialectics of the
dialogue situation where speech enters the scene with the promise of
speechful exchange.   Words are consummated in the living arena of
dialogue, in the 'dramatistic' setting of the I-Thou betweenness.
Wherever words are drawn out of this betweeness and regarded as abstract 'elements' intrinsically valuable outside of all possible
context, then we are moving toward the fetishism of discourse para-
lleled by the fetish of money analysed above.   The 'word-hoarder'
might then be concretized as the writer who lives merely for the
abstract desire of writing, where the horizon of the 'for whom' has
been removed from his 'praxis' - where the intersubjective context of
a Thou and a Tradition have been lost, forgotten, abandoned.   Needless to say there are a manifold different types and degrees of word-
hoarding - all of which are available for phenomenological explication.

As commanding power money is the object of greed, which, as Marx
describes in the 'Grundrisse', places its possessor in precisely the
same relationship toward social wealth as the philosophers' stone
would toward the sciences.   Greed as a phenomenal appearance is
treated as a specific historical emergence of the desire to master
and overpower.   Greed is only possible when all value is concent-
rated into a generalized measure.   In this way money is the 'fount-
ainhead' of greed as a historically specific phenomenological form
of human being:

The mania for possessions is possible without money; but
greed itself is the product of a definite social development,
not natural, as opposed to historical.   Hence the wailing of
the ancients about money as the source of all evil.   Hedonism ('Genussucht') in its general form and miserliness ('Geiz')
are the two particular forms of monetary greed.   Hedonism
in the abstract presupposes an object which possesses all
pleasures in potentiality.   Abstract hedonism realizes that
function of money in which it is the 'material representative of wealth; miserliness, in so far as it is only the
general form of wealth as against its particular substances,
the commodities ... Monetary greed, or mania for wealth,
necessarily brings with it the decline and fall of the
ancient communities ('Gemeinwesen').   Hence it is the
antithesis to them.   It is itself the community ('Gemeinwesen'), and can tolerate none other standing above it
('Grundrisse', 1973, pp. 221-3).

Money is the 'common being', the 'common system', a social system in
itself - a language, the real community ('Gemeinwesen') and all other
communities become spurious and insubstantial; yet the community of

money is an abstract community for it represents merely a means of satisfaction. Money smashes the 'Gemeinschaft' thereby instituting the alienated objectification of relations which are external to the individual. Yet perfectly developed money contains all the contradictions which characterize bourgeois economy. In the money-form contradiction itself becomes pure (see Marx's description in 'Grundrisse', 1973, pp. 233-8).

Money is Protagorean. If truth is the human value, the ultimate Good which all men seek, then truth under the Market can be assigned and withdrawn by human will. It is the City of Men, the 'Gesellschaft', which assigns to objects the status as being valuable, beautiful, truthful - just as they assign to metals and paper the value of embodied power over things and men. Unlike truth Money is valued not as an intrinsic end, but as a means to power over things thought eminent in the City. Money is valuable only to the extent that it can be cashed for a thing. Its principle is fluidity or exchange: thus Money is internally connected with the Thing over which it brings magical power.

Thus Money exists only within the fluidity of a system of Things, abstracted from their truth (as the out-standing of being within Being) and regarded merely as exchangeable commodities. In the domain of the Market truthfulness has become a relational function within a System. In contemporary philosophical terms, truth is defined as Coherence within a System.

Here we have the secret connection between the conventionalism of Science and conventionalism in the dominance of the Money-form. Both are ground within the same form of life. Science as radical conventionalism: man uncovers the Voice of Nature - and Monetary speech are rooted in the same disclosure of Being.

Money symbolizes abstraction and the abstract intellect. If the commodity is an abstraction which exists only in an abstract Community - the City, Capitalism - then money takes this abstraction to its logical conclusion. Money represents the pure form of potential exchange. As Ferdinand Toennies said, after Marx, money is absolute commodity, a commodity in perfection. Money retains a magical youth, for discounting physical deterioration it resists even time itself, remaining 'always young and a living source, as it were, of regularly repeated equal quantities of enjoyment'.

One can hardly re-create the revolution which occurred when men began to regard the ground beneath their feet - the Earth - as itself simply another form of Money, an abstract commodity. Yet that day dawned - inaugurating an age of 'brass'. The absurd eventuated: the Earth itself became another coin which, like money, tried to disappear in circulation. But land cannot disappear - it disappears abstractly, analytically: 'Land must first by a mental process be transformed into money or money equivalent; it is then considered nothing but a means, and the rent becomes an end in itself, just as capital is only the means of the moneylender and the merchant, interest or profit their ultimate purpose' (Toennies, 'Community and Society', p. 86). 'It marks great progress in thinking ....
when the individual and society begin to handle land as a special kind of property and capital' (ibid., p. 86). If the very Earth upon which we raise our bodies to speak can be transformed into a commodity, then Money will be present to purchase it. Money is the

incarnation of the rational will, the Will to power over Earth and Heaven.

Writers like George Thomson view the emergence of an exchange economy divided into complex stratifications of producers and consumers as the revolutionary kernel which destroyed the tribally stratified society of ancient Greece. Correlative with this revolutionary change in economic stratification – symbolized by a monetary economy – went a division in the forms of social consciousness; within the contradictory structure of the whole a leisured class became possible, an aristocracy developed within the separation of theory and practice. Abstract thinking, the capacity of objectifying Nature and disclosing it as subject to mathematical determination, prediction and, ultimately, control became a material reality. The ties which dissolved in the transformation of the economic infrastructure of Greek society were replaced by the abstract links necessary for commodity production. Pythagoras and Anaximenes are but expressions of the newly risen merchant class typifying a society whose whole orientation was directed towards the production of exchange values. Production for use and production for exchange de-stratified and re-stratified the ancient world. In this way the Parmenidean thought on the Unity of Being is regarded as a 'reflection' or a 'false consciousness' of the abstract turn which social relationships had taken in the founding of an exchange economy. At the dawn of western philosophy we, if we follow Thomson, find the money-form of abstract value. Through abstract thought the money form dominates thinking by imposing its categories upon the world, categories such as Unity, Good, Substance which are regarded as a reflex or projection of the 'substance' of exchange value. Self-consciousness ('Selbstbewusstsein') is indebteded to the social form of money: 'Das Bewusstsein ist ein gesellschaftliches Produkt' – 'Nicht das Bewusstsein bestimmt das Leben, sondern das Leben bestimmt das Bewusstsein'.

This Marxist 'Wissenssoziologie' reads the Platonic apotheosis of the Idea as an internal necessity of Greek 'Produktionsgeschichte'; Aristotelian logic as a static logic of fixed classes is simply a reflex of the social relations and stratifications generated by the abstract process (Class) required in commodity production and exchange. The rules of logic – Aristotelian logic – articulate historically specific social 'truths' not eternal verities. Truth itself is linked to the dialectic of stratification. Truth is internally tied to the violence of contingent series of 'Produktionsgeschichte'. A Marxist scholar like Lucien Goldmann makes a similar point in his discussion of Kant's philosophy. Here – as Toennies also argues – it is monetary exchange derived from trade which generated the birth of philosophical thought on the Asiatic coast of Ionia, later in the Greek city states and Magna Graecia:

> not, of course, in the sense that philosophy is a product
> of trade, but because in a society based upon buying and
> selling the concrete features and relations of the particular individual give way to the general and abstract
> features of buyer and seller. Thus thought too could be
> directed towards the general and abstract features of
> 'man'. (Lucien Goldman, 'Immanuel Kant', 1971, p. 150).

Money represents a reduced sense of the promise of language. Where it deeply mediates the relations between man and man it

acquires a 'logic' of its own. Labour sells its potential to produce use-value (realized under Capital as exchange-value) in order to
acquire the conventional tokens of money in order that a specific
subsistence be maintained so that more labour-power can enter the
circulation of money and commodity. The Labour-power itself becomes
both for seller and buyer a vast instrumental pool, a pure 'means'.
Money reduces all to 'means'; by its inherent 'logic' the seller of
labour-power requires tokens in order to purchase objects of immediate
use-value which can only be maintained through further alienation of
labour; likewise money is instrumental in the acquisition of more
money - from money accumulates capital. In both cases money is the
embodied promise of an instrumental 'more'. Only through the form
of money can speechful existence be realized. In speechful terms
Capital in all its vast forms and processes is simply the promise of
'more-money' ('Mehr-Geld' as Toennies notes). This promissory
attitude is also basic not only to the accumulation of capital
through the exploitation of labour, but also through the exploitation
of credit and finance markets which are themselves built on a promissory notion of 'security of expectations', 'expectations of returns', and the like. Money purchases the future as a time of
monetary loss or gain. Purely formulated, futurity becomes a field
of pure financial speculation; the promise of language has been reduced to the promise of one of its objects - the promise of 'Mehr-
Geld'.

Failure to respond to this instrumental future, this dehumanized
promise means falling outside this community's sense of normalcy,
humanity, reasonableness. Thus in English and German whoever dis-
poses of money is thought of as a man with a promised future, not a
'man of property', but a 'man of means' ('bemittelt'); the man without the promise of money is literally 'without means' ('mittellos')
and where ends are instrumentally connected with monetary means, the
expression 'without means' literally means 'without purpose', without promise (Toennies).

Where the human sense and project of futurity - our out-standing-
ness toward the future is disclosed through the monetary form of
speechfulness the Interest in the future becomes a function of possible 'interest' in a monetary sense. The engines of this form of
life channel all human instituting into the services of this one infinite end. Given this transcendental goal of all our activities
the 'logic' of that end defines a systematic change in means. To
further this notion of futurity social forms are instituted which
perfect the means - thus technology, machine methodology, pro-
gramming, labour-saving instrumentation, rationalization of the productive process, revolutionizing the instruments of production, and
so forth follow inexorably as necessary processes. Perfecting the
means also transforms language. Language - long since instrument-
ized as simply another tool in the sequence which leads to profit-
making - is tailored into a persuasive net: the speeches and discourses of advertising are born. And we tend to forget the link
between these complicated discourses and the underlying notion of
futurity which the money-form requires. It is a consequence of the
monetary sense of futurity that all advertising constitutes a sense
of 'the future' for its consumer. Advertising discourses are
actually selling transformations of the future which are contingent

upon the purchase of a specific object - about which the discourse
speaks.   In the artful anarchy of the advertising word and picture
we begin to glimpse the violence which the money form has perpetrated
upon speechfulness.   Here the Word is a pure tool which would ideally
obligerate its humanity for the sake of the end it serves - money
making.   In a sense the abstract reason ('Verstand') of advertising
received its epistemological warrant in the pragmatist thought of
early American philosophy, in the 'instrumentalism' of a Dewey;
advertising 'Verstand' receives its philosophical expression in the
equation of language with the tool in Anglo-American thought.   In
whatever way we formulate it, advertising as a vast institutional
system of monetary consciousness or desire is the very face of our
modernity - the site of language in which we moderns disclose Being.
The money-form (and all that this implicates) is the site where the
human passion for intelligibility paradoxically realizes itself as
the being of modernity.

A commodity exchange, credit markets, the 'cash nexus', and so
forth all require the contractual obligations of the market.   Even
with the 'Gesellschaft' the market is touched with the 'promise'.
Money can only facilitate commodity exchanges in an atmosphere of
contractual promises.   Men have to be ob-lig-ated, tied to one another and a common realm of things before even abstract exchange can
take place.   Accepting this ob-lig-ation is a precondition of Civil
Society.   Thus the ob-lig-ation which grounds contract (which sociology theorizes as the pre-contractual element in contract) sustains
monetary exchanges.   However monetary exchange denies its own pre-
conditions and takes 'exchange' as an empirical matter of concrete
selves, rather than as the coming together of reflexive speakers.
Contractual notions of community are oblivious to the social grounds
of their own possibility.   Where their theorists theorize their
grounds they discover their principle in a contractual realm (the
Hidden Hand, a Fictitious Contract, the Identity of mutually opposing
self-interest, and so forth).   As Political Economists they theorize
the grounds of the social in an abstract notion of freedom which
Marx and Toennies ridiculed as the freedom to choose one's captors.
'Money as obligation and obligations as money are the perfect abstract expressions of Gesellschaft-like wealth.   Wealth thus represents well-founded power over alien rational wills which, although
free by nature, are bound' (Toennies, p. 181).   Society as a market
for the sale and purchase of labour-power is as Marx ironically notes
a 'very Eden of the innate rights of man'.   Here alone rule Freedom,
Equality, Property and Bentham: 'Each looks to himself only, and no
one troubles himself about the rest, and just because they do so, do
they all, in accordance with the pre-established harmony of things,
or under the auspices of an all-shrewd providence, work together to
their mutual advantage, for the common weal and in the interest of
all'.

This present essay is devoted to the resuscitation of certain
Marxist themes.   Given the living dialectics of Ferdinand Toennies
work we are not deviating from our aim in referring the reader to the
rich work of Toennies - for Toennies discussion critically extends
the spirit of Marx's reflexive analysis.

For Toennies 'Gesellschaft' found its typifying icon in alienable
paper money.   'Gesellschaft' as he tells us 'reproduces its own

Idea' in the Money form.   'Gesellschaft' is phenomenologically expressed in the willfulness ('Kuerwille') of monetary exchange.
Moreover 'Gesellschaft' finds expression in abstract reason, reason
conceived of as 'ratio' rather than 'logos'.   Willful 'Gesselschaft'
enacts 'ratio'-nally through the embodiment of its members.   If this
is the case then there is a direct parallelism between Scientific
'ratio' and the Money-form of 'Gesellschaft'.
.   Toennies follows where his argument leads:
   Abstract reason in a special investigation is scientific
   reason, and endowed with it is man who discerns objective
   relationships, i.e., who thinks abstractly.   Scientific
   concepts are, with regard to their usual origin and to their
   objective quality, judgments by which complexes of per-
   ceptions are given a name.   Consequently, scientific concepts assume the same position in a scientific system as
   commodities do in the Gesellschaft.   In the scientific
   system they come together in much the same way as commodities do on the market.   A supreme scientific concept
   that no longer denotes something real, e.g., the concept of
   the atom or the concept of energy, is similar to the concept
   of money (Toennies, 'Community and Society', p. 71).
Abstract Science is then a 'contract' with Nature;   the abstract
rules of Science are constitutive of man's side of the agreement,
Nature's Promise to speak truthfully to man, the other side of the
agreement.   Scientific concepts have 'reality' only within the auspices of this contract, just as the Commodity is meaningful only
within the auspices of a Market society, 'Gesellschaft'.   Conventionalism is the principle or Rule of Science only because it is also the
Rule of Contractual Society within whose inauguration Science becomes
possible in the first place.   Science - like 'Gesellschaft' - is a
display of a community's form of life, its 'raison d'etre'.
   In his later work Toennies spoke of the universal drive for wealth
as linked with the striving for dominion and political power as a
means to gain honor ('Ehre') and for the absolute drive to acquire
knowledge.   Upon this triad he constructed three ideal-types of goal
direction.   The first being the prince of money ('Geldfuerst') or
'homo oeconomicus' typified in the merchant who has become an in-
dustrialist, a trust magnate, finance capitalist.   The second -
related - type is 'homo politicus' for whom Being becomes a world to
be dominated.   The Caesarism of absolute monarchy or totalitarian
violence presents the perfect type.   Finally, there is the absolute
egoist - the 'homo scientificus' - who seeks knowledge at all costs.
Like the capitalist the man of knowledge has become all 'means'.
Where the machine is the means for accumulation in the former case,
the scientific method is the means for the accumulation of theoret-
ical-empirical knowledge.   Method - like the 'logic' of the money-
form itself likewise comes to live a life of its own and eventually
to cannibalize the very pursuit of knowledge.   Where Machiavellian-
ism is the speechful expression of 'homo politicus', method-olatory
which develops its own logic and lawfulness exhibits the deeper meaning of 'homo scientificus'.   Toennies in order words - in good dialectical fashion - points to the germ of irrationality, of un-reason
within what is considered to be paradigmatically reason-able.   However even with Toennies (like Weber) rationality is conceptualized

within the framework of means and ends.   The radical question of
Reason-able speech is merely grazed.   However, Toennies's sense of
dialectic contains important elements for radical theorizing in the
field of modernity and its promissory languages.   As he declares
toward the end of his essay, 'End and Means in Social Life', from
which I have drawn the above themes: 'The power of the isolated
means over human thoughts and actions is the hallmark of the spirit
of modernity'.   As Marx ironically notes in 'Capital' modernity
after its birth 'pulled Plutus by the hair of his head from the
bowels of the earth, greets gold as its Holy Grail, as the glitter-
ing incarnation of the very principle of its own life'.   Language
gives birth to money which then cannibalizes and transforms its pro-
genitor according to its own intrinsic 'logic'.   Language becomes
subservient to the powers of wealth and monetary accumulation;
speech becomes an instrument of money, becomes market speech -
speech characterizing modernity.

Speaking metaphorically of money as a part which had monopolized
the Whole enabled Marx to think a de-Classed community as the re-
instatement of the Whole over its abstract parts.   Drawing his
imagery from classical German Philosophy and German romanticism Marx
can now speak of the Whole man as the ultimate aim of his inquiries.
Surely we have to read Marx metaphorically where he speaks of the
restoration of man's Universal being after the sublation of Capital
(Stratification)?   Here Marx uses an icon of wholeness - the total,
undifferentiated social being who hunts in the morning and fishes
before noon in order to be a critic in the evening.   Here, like
Hegel before him, Marx had grasped that truth was the Whole, but
only by metaphor can we speak of Wholeness when living and breathing
within a social grammar of fragmentation and concrete separation.
We are reminded of Rosa Luxemburg's words: the economic overturn
can be accomplished only if the process is carried out by proletarian mass action.   Only the working class, through its own activity,
can make the word flesh.

We can put questions to Nature (hypotheses) and expect her to
dutifully respond with a confirmation or a disconfirmation only within the auspices of our prior contract.   Nature 'promises' to speak
to man not in the primordial sense in which the Logos promises, but
in which promises are made and unmade in Civil Society.   The Contract which flows from 'Gesellschaft' into Science has a performative logic, to use John Austin's term.   Like any performative there
are a multitude of possible ways of its breach or infelicitous performance.   In a similar manner Nature may break her contract in a
limitless number of ways - many of which are covered by terms like
'bias', 'imprecision', 'failure of objectivity', 'breakdown of instruments', 'human error', and so forth.

Only when Nature's Voice can be heard clearly and distinctly can
we learn her laws;   only then can we master and possess her, just as
we would master and possess commodities which are themselves disclosed under a contractual rule.   Clarity of language is a prerequisite for world mastery.   But with the same logic, the masters and
possessors of Nature have incurred a contractual 'debt' - we have
taken without giving as the terms of our contract clearly define.
Here we are just beginning to gather what would count as 're-payment'
to balance our account with that which grants.   Man, so to say, is

labouring under the shadow of an outstanding debt for he has usurped
absolute ownership over Nature under the cover of contractualism.
We are beginning to learn the meaning of absolute possession - which
leads directly from Science to the age of Technology and the Technological seizure of Being - Being disclosed as Technological Violence.

Money reduces Being to a Protagorean principle: money is the
common denominator of all truth and value. In terms of 'telos' its
form of life realizes itself in the Platonic Thrasymachus. Here
Virtue is Power and Money holds the key to power and the means of its
implementation. Money means power over men and things. Money is
the 'general commodity' which facilitates the 'abstract' commodity of
Pleasure (Toennies). Money can realize self-interest by buying the
Other as a tool; it can realize vanity by buying the Other as one's
Mirror; it can satisfy ambition by purchasing its requisites and
paraphenalia; it can even control and possess Nature.

Toennies discusses these themes and draws them together in the
connection between Thrasymachian power and Science. In Science and
its technological application men can realize dominion over both
Nature and their fellow men. This 'superiority' derives from knowledge of nature in its functional relations. Even in the purest
reaches of scientific research, however, Toennies would regard
science as a development and a type of vanity - where man masters
and possesses Nature as his own Mirror. The technological omnipotence of man may then be likened to a cosmic vanity.

If man's labouring under the class-permeated conditions of the
historically unique capitalist mode of production leads to alienated
cleavages which cut man away from authentic Self, authentic relations
with Nature ('physis', being), from authentic relations with the product (remembering the 'poetizing' origins of 'making' - the derivation of 'technique' and 'technology' from the human creativeness
of various 'technai' - 'arts'), from authentic Communion with his
fellow-men - these separations, in true Hegelian style also contain
the seeds of Identity. It was precisely this dialectical problem
of Classing and the immanent Unclassing of social co-existence that
led Marx to do violence with the rhetorics he found available when he
came forth to speak. Only the fluid 'Logik', the 'methodos' of
'Dialektik' sufficed to give form and articulation to the 'coincidentia oppositorum' Marx theorized about.

If conventional analysis fell far beneath the tasks of analytic
thought - then it was imperative that thinking be plunged through the
rigours of dialectical speaking. We can analyse Class, differentiate ourselves from Class speech (World) and prepare the tools for
the Unclassing of Class only through the fires of Dialectic. The
'brook of Fire' (Feuerbach) is to be regarded as a stage along the
way to this ultimate achievement of dialectical speechfulness.

In his commitment to Dialectical Reason Marx exemplifies the many-
sided problematic of his 'object' - and the 'futurity' of his theorizing. Theorizing here is not primarily oriented to the past as
past, but rather to the past as generator of creative or uncreative
modes of existence for the present; springboard into speechful human
community for the future. Marx's dialectically comprehensive
'Begriffe' are thus essentially futural; essentially dynamic. He
speaks of Class; he inquires into the material process of the

formation of Class not for the ultimate end of clarifying Class
Speech and Society - but for the end of Transcending Class Speech
(chatter), and liberating man into the domain of Freedom (Dialectical
speech, Reason, 'Logos', Communism).

Hence the massive difficulties placed in the way of understanding
Marx's work. His corpus was 'not of his time'. His corpus was
deeply and literally 'transcendent', even though it took for its object a historically saturated present. Marx wrote for a future.
He wrote for a notion of Self and Society which would make his kind
of struggles and concrete strains redundant. His surface object is
Class; his 'real' object is Unclassed, de-stratified sociation - and
in this sense it is a perfectly accurate description to say that Marx
theorizes u-topia. The incarnation of critical reason ('logos') as
speechful community, the reconciliation of Subject and Object knows
no concrete 'existence' - functions as a desire, a way of estimating
- in perhaps the only possible human way - what one speaks for and
why one speaks. Marx's re-laying of tradition is both a denial of
the Speculative intellectual 'Logos' of Hegel's Science of Wisdom,
and a re-instatement of the revolutionary Word of Criticism whose
precondition is the unity of theory and practice - a unity which is
not only displayed in political-economic struggle, but also in the
theoretical unity of one's commitment to the tradition of inquiry,
reflexivity, reason as a tradition of liberation. Recognizing these
severe necessities is - as Hegel and Engels knew, recognizing that
freedom moves through not against knowledge of necessities.

To 'write' here, then, means staking a commitment to the unclassing of men. (5) The writer, committed to the 'elan' of emancipatory-
transcendence writes to the Whole man (hence the recurrent image of
the 'whole' man in the writing of Hegel and Marx as in the writing of
Schiller and Goethe). The Whole man is, of course, the Reader: he
is the Unclassed, unstratified 'Dasein'-being-in-transcendence.
The All, the One then becomes the audience as a readership. It is
well known that Marx could never fully articulate the instrument of
this transcendence - the instrument for the radical termination of
human alienation, the unclassing moment. The unsayable was simply
named, the name being 'Proletariat'. (6)

Historically the great disrupters of the abstract, stratified
interpretation of Membership have been theorists and thinkers like
Socrates, Plato, Marx, Nietzsche, and many other minor figures.
Socratic irony directed toward the prosaic speech of his opponents
(the Sophists) intends to transform their state of non-ignorance into
his sense of ignorance: to re-awaken by ironic means the wonder of
inquiry lost by sophistry. Socrates' disdain for political power
and worldly wealth and his outright condemnation of the fetish
effects money has on the attitude of thinking the Good (and his heavy
parodies of those who identified the Good with the pursuit of wealth)
are well known.

His life as a quest for the Good through the prisms of face-to-
face conversation and his gentle dialectic of irony is also part of
our tradition. In the Christian tradition the nearest equivalent is
the absolutely concrete imagery and face-to-face encounter of the
religious genius, embodied in the figure of Christ; we have the icon
of Christ ('Logos', the Word, the Light, the Way) overthrowing the
money lenders who had defiled the very heart of the temple with the

fetished abstraction of commodity exchange - defiled the godhead as
Logos.   Similar considerations hold for Marx, and, above all, for
Kierkegaard.   In Kierkegaard's works (of love) it is impossible to
read in any straightforward way.   Works like the 'Point of View' or
the 'Concluding Unscientific Postscript' are labyrinths of turns and
duplicities designed to shatter the presuppositions of a fixed exchange rate of words and a 'straight' reading.   Unfortunately most
readings of Kierkegaard dwell solely on his phenomenology of faith,
anguish, dread and death, and refuse to delve into the deeper themes
that lie waiting in the ironies of his texts.   We are never really
sure whether, when we have read a work of Kierkegaard's, we have held
hands with 'Kierkegaard' or some persons he has taken up for the duplicity of a naive audience.   His use of the irony of multiple
authorship (and perhaps ultimately none?) forces the reader to become
a re-writing and co-participating self, rather than the usual passive
'tabula rasa' cemented into a market relation of supply and demand.
    Kierkegaard's irony displays his way of letting the reader carry
out the liberating leap: to destroy 'Systems' of philosophy and
System-thinking; to restore the reader as co-participating thinker;
to 'edify' (hence they are 'edifying discourses'); to deceive the
deceivers; to force the reader into the responsibility of Existence;
to convert Christendom to Christianity.   Writing and reading are
thus bound together by a movement that aims to shatter the literal
linearity of alienated speech - ultimately it is directed (as is
Marx's work) to the possibility of a ground transformation of the
self.   The letter killeth, but the spirit giveth life.
    Irony, then, becomes a theorists' grounds for making reference to
deep-seated topics: the auspices of literalness, exchange, the
objectification of speech and membership.   One the surface resides
the appearance of Identity; beneath rages contradiction and non-
Identity (the forgetfulness of language).   The whole is the 'identity
of identity and non-identity' (7) - by experiencing and overcoming
this totality we move into the circle for thinking identity and
difference per se; the name for such thinking is dia-logos; at the
centre of dia-logos - the play of identity and difference - is irony.
    It might be regarded as one way of making reference to alternate
beginnings.   Consider Marx's distinction between 'communication' and
'exchange':

    there came a time when everything that men had considered
    as inalionable became an object of exchange, of traffic
    and could be alienated.   This is the time when the very
    things which till then had been 'communicated, but never
    exchanged; given, but never sold; acquired, but never
    bought - virtue, love, conviction, conscience, etc. -
    when everything, in short, passed into commerce.   It is
    the time of general corruption, of universal venality,
    or, to speak more in terms of political economy, the time
    when everything, moral or physical, having become market-
    able, is brought to the market to be assessed at its
    truest value ('The Poverty of Philosophy', p. 32).

To grasp this estrangement requires an understanding that this loss
is not only a renunciation but a 'making external to oneself' which
results in a subject-object duality permeating the whole of life
(the sundering of author from writing, his method (authority) from

his accomplishments, and so forth. (8) To reclaim a 'new beginning/
alternate form of life' for authorship means to overcome and abolish
the passage of the Good (virtue, love, knowledge, conscience, con-
viction, etc.) into commerce by combating a degenerate form of human
authorship that is Commerce's praxis.

It is not strange that the textual instruments by which Marx formulated the Unclassing of man - his 'fall' from authentic speech and
authentic social co-existence - his phenomenology of human being, as
it were - are also ironically derived. What do we man by this
notion of 'irony'?

In the introduction to this collection of readings I spoke about
the deep sense of Tradition which theorizing both requires and -
like it or not - is tied to. In circumstances of almost total
forgetfulness - re-laying (in its dual sense of re-founding and trans-
mitting) a critical sense of tradition is often carried out under the
banner of biting irony. Thus Hegel claimed to ground his Dialectic
upon the founding sages of the Greek tradition. He claimed to concretely use every sentence of the Heraclitean fragments: 'Es ist
kein Satz des Heraklit, den ich nicht in meine Logik aufgenommen'.
In turn Marx's retrieving transformation of the Hegelian dialectic
re-instates in a deep ironical fashion the Heraclitean dialectical
'Logos'; likewise Engels's Dialectics of Nature attempts to found
dialectics as the one true Science - Voice of Nature - through which
truth itself pours. In similar vein Ferdinand Lasalle in the
middle of the nineteenth century - leader of the largest worker's
Party in Germany - has recourse to comparable theorical analysis.

It is not accidental that the Marxist formulation of our tradition
is in principle Heraclitean - nor that a Lasalle should write 'Die
Philosophie Herakleitos des Dunkelin von Ephesos' in 1858, or that
Engels's natural dialectic traces its genesis to the simple father of
Contradiction. Here there is a collective sense that theory and
practice can only be unified from within the deepest sources of our
tradition - and that the central element of this re-collection would
consist in both the actual and the speechful overthrow of human
forgetfulness - concretely expressed in the absolute internal destruction of the capitalist mode of production.

In a similar manner this deep theme has fed much of conventional
sociological inquiry - although it has been largely emasculated in
the process. The rich tradition of 'Gemeinschaft-Gesellschaft'
thought for instance might be re-interpreted in the light of our
above remarks. Incidentally it has taken almost one hundred years
before conventional sociology has recognized that next to Marx it is
Ferdinand Toennies who is the greatest dialectician in the sociological pantheon.

Again should we not ask the question - why is the theorist of the
demise of 'Gemeinschaft' also a pure dialectician reflexively concerned with the kind of talk that is possible about social formations,
stratifications and transformations?

The answer would be very similar to our analysis of this fragment
of Marx's work: Toennies's work is rich and vital only to the extent
that Toennies began to realize sociology as a reflexive discipline.
Central to this discipline was the notion of Unclassing (whose expression in the latter's work occurs on the theory of 'Gemeinschaft').
Linked to the retrieval of a rational, critical human community - is

Toennies's critique of all 'Gesellschaft' formations – the perfect
expression of which is market speech, speech which categorically
divides means from ends – and treats both speech and speaker as an
inconsequential means – never as an inquisitive theorizer of ends.
Likewise market speech for Toennies (as for Marx) was the realm of
the divorce between public and private – which was itself grafted onto a material base dominated by economic class considerations.   The
realization of community – the politicization (in the sense of
'polis') of alienated social existence meant the dissolution of the
realms of private and public.   Here the dialectical tradition was
absolutely necessary before this kind of problematic could even be
thought – let alone realized in 'Praxis'.

Toennies's sociology – like Marx's – grounds its inquiry critically and has as its ultimate aim the moral futurity of man – the
possibility of another beginning.   This I have called critical tradition – or speech – throughout.   Much work needs to be done in the
domain of traditional sociological theorizers.   First we have to
dialectically supercede ('Aufgeholben') conventional Sociology.   A
start has been made.

The Hegel–Marx term 'Aufheben' (sublation, overcoming) has both a
positive and negative meaning.   For Hegel it depicted the positive-
negative dialectic by which a higher logical category, form of nature
or Spirit, in superceding a lower, both 'annuls' it and 'incorporates
its partial truth'.   In this sense the reversal of speech-qua-
commerce requires that the mathematical speech of commerce be grasped,
understood and accounted before it can be sublated.   Marx's method
is to begin with the abstract and move, by successive approximations,
to the concrete, in order to grasp and understand, and then to
present an account of what is to be overcome.   Marx's writing exemplifies this method: he selects his discourse-categories very
carefully by playing upon the irony of analyzing Political Economy
(his abstract starting point) in terms of the very self-conceptions
of political economy, that is, through the categorical spectacles of
their speeches in order that they be overcome internally in the text
and thereby allow Marx to return to the question of where to begin
authentic dialectical analysis – a question which always puzzled him
(as the beginnings of the 'Grundrisse' will attest).   Irony plays
a central role in this method by means of which Marx transformed the
'material' he worked upon (the works of classical Political Economy,
the statistics, tabulations and government reports from the British
Museum).   Let us read the following extract in this context:

> The alienation of the worker in his object finds expression
> as follows according to the principles of political economy:
> the more the worker produces the less there is for him to
> consume; the more values he creates, the more he loses
> value and dignity; the more his product is shaped, the
> more misshapen the worker; the more civilized his object,
> the more barbarous the worker; the more powerful the work
> is, the more powerless the worker; the more spirit there is
> in the work, the more devoid of spirit and a slave of nature
> the worker (1844 Manuscripts: the section on estranged
> labour must be consulted).

As Marx repeatedly points out the talk of Political Economy expresses
the abstract relations extant in Capitalist society (their 'laws',

and not God-given regularities); but they do not provide for or
comprehend their own texts: they fail to demonstrate how their
writings can depict these things.   Unlike Marx they can neither
understand the problem of demonstrability nor appreciate the great
problems of beginning analysis; Marx's commitment is one to the
provision of the grounds which elude Political Economy; he attempts
to provide for the historicity and mutability of every writing (including his own).   What for him symbolized fetished writing was the
static categories of Political Economy and the empty dance of categories that he read as Idealist dialectics.   Continually Marx
resorts to biting irony in order to overcome the repressive consequences of non-inscribed, non-authored theory:

> Political economy, this science of 'wealth', is therefore
> simultaneously the science of denial, of want, of 'thrift',
> of 'saving' - and it actually reaches the point where it
> 'spares' man the need of either fresh 'air' or physical
> exercise.   This science of marvellous industry is simul-
> taneously the science of 'asceticism', and its true ideal
> is the 'ascetic' but 'extortionate' miser and the 'ascetic'
> but 'productive' slave.   Its moral ideal is the 'worker'
> who takes part of his wages to the savings-bank, and it has
> even found ready-made an object 'art' which to clothe this
> its pet idea: they have presented it, bathed in sentiment-
> ality, on the stage.   Thus political economy - despite its
> worldly and wanton appearance - is a true moral science,
> the most moral of all the sciences.   Self-denial, the
> denial of life and of all human needs, is its cardinal
> doctrine.   The less you eat, drink, and read books; the
> less you go to the theatre, the dance hall, the public-
> house; the less you think, love, theorize, sing, paint,
> fence, etc., the more you save - the 'greater' becomes
> your treasure which neither moths nor dust will devour:
> your 'capital'.   The less you 'are', the more you 'have';
> the less you express your own life, the greater is your
> 'alienated' life - the greater is the store of your es-
> tranged being.   Everything which the political economist
> takes from you in life and in humanity, he replaces for
> you in 'money' and in 'wealth'; and all the things which
> you cannot do your money can do.   It can eat and drink,
> go to the theatre and the dance hall; it can travel, it
> can appropriate art, learning, the treasures of the past,
> political power - all this it 'can' appropriate for you
> ... it is the true endowment ('Manuscripts, 110) (9)

In examples of irony like this, Marx requires that his reader formulate and display what goes unsaid in the speeches of political
economy - their 'essence'.   Economists 'explain how production
takes place in the above-mentioned relations, but what they do not
explain is how these relations themselves are produced, that is, the
historical movement which gave them birth' ('Poverty of Philosophy',
100).
    With the same irony in 'Capital' Marx formulates in basic outlines
what sociologists would call the 'Weber thesis':

> In order that gold may be held as money, and made to form
> a hoard, it must be prevented from circulating, or from

transforming itself into a means of enjoyment. The
hoarder, therefore, makes a sacrifice of the lusts of the
flesh to his gold fetish. He acts in earnest up to the
Gospel of abstention. On the other hand, he can with-
draw from circulation no more than he has thrown into it
in the shape of commodities. The more he produces, the
more he is able to sell. Hard working, saving, and
avarice, are, therefore, his three cardinal virtues, and
to sell much and buy little the sum of his political
economy.

Marx requires of the theorist that he provide for his own theoretical praxis; his main critique against the categories of Political
Economy is that they are thoroughly unreflexive (and thereby inhuman).
On the concrete level of history, Marx admits the relativity of his
own work (in admitting that economic categories are but the theoretical expressions, the abstractions of the social relations of production - 'Poverty of Philosophy', p. 105). He is an iconoclast
against the reification or to use his term 'deification' of speech
and the forms of life which tacitly sustain those speeches. Theorists perennially confuse the Profane with the Sacred by misinterpret-
ing the profane history of categories as the sacred well-springs of
'Logos' (cf. 'Poverty of Philosophy', p. 183). Consequently Marx
had to begin by addressing the texts of Political Economy since it
was those texts that had become 'material forces' by taking root in
the world. In uncovering the textuality of worlds (his theory of
Ideology and false consciousness) Marx has also discovered the world-
liness of texts. Thus he often asks his readership to do violence
with the texts of the established sociology of the day. He directs
us to regard sociologists and philosophers as telling stories. The
sociologist unconcerned with the grounds of his writing is merely
producing adventure stories or documentary fictions without realizing
it. The sociologist will then speak about anything at any time
rather than question the intelligibility of his own speech. The
following extract from the 'Grundrisse' is illuminating:

The individual and isolated hunter or fisher who forms the
starting point with Smith and Ricardo belongs to the in-
sipid illusions of the eighteenth century. They are
adventure stories which do not by any means represent, as
students of the history of civilization imagine, a re-
action against the over-refinement and a return to the
misunderstood natural life. They are no more based on
such naturalism than is Rousseau's 'contrat social', which
makes naturally independent individuals come in contact
and have mutual intercourse by contract. They are the
fiction and only the aesthetic fiction of the small and
great adventure stories. They are, rather, the anticipation of 'civil society', which had been in course of
development since the sixteenth century and made gigantic
strides towards maturity in the eighteenth (McLellan's
translation, pp. 16-17).

Are we to understand Marx here as asking that we relocate the texts
of sociology as works of fiction from which the author absents himself? In which case we find support in those contemporaries who
regard the disciplines of social science and linguistics as our own

self-conceptions and Myth (Levi-Strauss explicitly asks that we regard his text about myth as another such myth - he also adheres to
the belief that the ultimate goal of the human sciences (as socio-
logics) is not to constitute but rather to dissolve man; we might
regard Chomsky's imagery as mythopoetic; Functionalism as the mythology of conservative America; and so forth).   By regarding these
works as 'edifying works of fictitious discourse' (sociology 'telling
it as it is') we sensitize the reader to the fabrication that such a
text is.   For instance at the core of transformational grammer is an
absence which rests on the puzzle of beginning language analysis and
the vacuum puzzle over the notion of 'sentence'.

Marx's suggestion that sociology be read as adverture stories or
poetry can be only taken as a joke or insult given a presupposition
about the nature of 'story' and 'poetry'.   That is, they are taken
as terms of condemnation or ridicule.   But what goes as ridicule for
one theorist may read as positive praise for another: the way we
read Marx's suggestion illustrates how the reader understands the
Poetic, and the form of life of that interpretation.   For most sociologists this would be read as a term of derogation.   But this simply
means that we need to revaluate our terms of evaluation (of 'story',
'poetry', 'aphorism', 'account', 'argument', 'demonstration' and the
like).   As I have tried to show in the introductions the bonds that
unite theoria may also tie into poetry.   A convenient starting point
for this re-valuation of values would centre on the sociological
self-conceptions and commonsensical notions of 'story' and 'poetry'
to be found in conventional works.   This would, however, take us out
of the prolegomenon.

Perhaps the estrangement of man from the poetic, from speech is a
cause rather than an effect of the omnipotence of abstraction and
mathematization in the west?   It might be the case that language is
both the sustaining togetherness of subject and object as well as the
principle of their separation: that it is the community of language
where the individual both meets the reciprocity of perspectives and
overarching unity of things as well as the beginnings of division and
individuation.   This would make language per se appropriative: as
working in accord with the ruling principle of the Negative.

Hegel may have had something like this in mind (cf. Marcuse, 75).
However, for Marx - in his reading of Hegel - there is something
static about the identification of reason as the Negatively appropr-
riative power of language: it tends to raise a possibly contingent
forgetfulness into an ontological niche, thereby introducing an even
deeper - since it is articulated and rationalized - forgetfulness.
Heidegger expresses this as the irony that we have not only forgotten,
but we have forgotten we have forgotten.   This discovery crops up in
the writing of all the ironic philosophers who have taken up a fundamental 'Kritik' of speech (such as Nietzsche and Fritz Mauthner).
The lapidary style of Nietzsche is not composed of hammered words but
with chiselled concepts designed to pierce complacencies.   His style
must be compared to that of the Horatian ode rather than to the Greek.
Nietzsche is Roman.   (10)   It is not accidental that in overthrowing
the idols of the market-place, recasting and revaluating values,
overcoming the writing of professional philosophy, requires from
Nietzsche (as it did for Schopenhauer and as it would for Wittgenstein) an absolute purity from the contamination of unthinking jargon

and the hollowness of the empty ringing phrase.   Hence, as essay-
ists and reviewers, as writers of 'investigations' and aphorisms,
Schopenhauer, Nietzsche and Wittgenstein are the great German styl-
ists in the languages of philosophy.   (11) Both Nietzsche and Schopenhauer, as with Wittgenstein and Mauthner, traced man's bondage to
the grammar of the language.   Language becomes the rock to which
Prometheus is chained.   The hubris of man rests in his belief that
he grasps the correspondent form of the world and its limits through
the grammar of his tribe; but there lies the deception of all deceptions: rather the logic of his language seizes him in its iron-
cage.   Man becomes the fool of his own language.

The infinite positivist task of a disinterested mathematical description of the world enters the ground floor of epistemology as
Scientific Method, a normative notion whose culmination is the correspondence notion of truth as a total isomorphic depiction of reality (or part of reality).   This is why Wittgenstein was deeply
shaken by the crisis in speech and felt the deepest need to set out
the limits of sense and nonsense - speech and silence.   Just as with
the Humian sceptical crisis Kant had attempted to preserve the
antonomy of Newtonian science by setting forth the 'a priori' limits
to knowledge, so the early Wittgenstein is obsessed with what can be
known and what must fall into the domain of the unutterable.   History had almost repeated itself; yet in both cases, by closing shop
to thought we exclude almost every significant philosophical question
and the arbitration of the limits of sense is itself questionable (as
Wittgenstein taught: its essence is metaphysical).

We can see this particular contortion within metaphysics as an
eschatological consequence of the fate-ful forgetfulness of the
question of the meaning of Being.   Nietzsche and Wittgenstein are
great grandchildren of this forgetfulness, in their metaphysical
moods.   Now we can understand the subversive irony of a Socrates who
is trying continually to address his own authorship (what makes his
speech speak) and to give voice to the unspeakable.   The election is
a resort to irony as a way of saying something in the only way in
which it can be said, if it can be said at all (cf. Engels, pp.60-79):

> Incompleteness is indeed 'completed' by its own intellig-
> ibility; to complete the uncompletable is to destroy it
> or render it invisible.   In different terms, philosophy
> is 'completed' by its own possibility, and this possib-
> ility depends upon the actual intelligibility of the whole.
> The whole is in principle the knowable, without which we
> could know nothing.   Or again, whatever we know is made
> knowable by the intelligibility of what it would be to be
> wise.   It is this, and this alone, which enables us to
> distinguish between true and false prophets, or sophists
> and philosophers.   And so, no speech is philosophical
> which denies intelligibility, or the intelligibility of
> the whole as the heterogeneously articulated structure in
> and through which each part is intelligible.   Philosophers
> have always disagreed ... but they cannot disagree on the
> intelligibility of their disagreements without ceasing to
> philosophize.   In this sense, disagreement, alienation,
> and negation, are tokens of the good.   And so, strange as
> it seems, one must in a sense first be wise before one can
> be a lover of wisdom (Rosen, p. 230).

Understanding even the underlying dialectic of identify and difference as bespeaking intelligibility means entering the listening-
retrieval which defines the work of thought as 'dia-logos', as
'philaletheia'.

In a time which has lost the sense of inquisitive language and
replaced it with arrogant pre-determinations and reductions any mode
of speaking which radically contests these idols will appear as out-
landish, un-orthodox, sarcastic, perhaps ironic. Irony may be the
only access to concrete speakers we have. For do we not intend a
'meaningful' dialogue; do we not claim to be speaking 'meaning-
fully'?

But 'meaning' - with all due respects to our analytic friends is
not an object to be depicted or generated in the regimented forms of
'grammar' and 'forms of life'. 'Meaning' is what language promises;
meaning is the reason why we speak - the possibilities of intelligible speaking promised in the hyphen of language. This is both the
stimulus and the 'telos' of our inquiry.

That speech is, is indubitable; that it is meaningful is the
axiomatic starting point of all - not only this - inquiry. Yet how
is speech both meaningful and promissory of meaning? It is as if
'meaning' had been adumbratedly given while leaving that which concerned us most unsaid, to-be-disclosed, to-be-rediscovered, re-
instated, instituted.

If all speech formulates being in one way or another thereby con-
straining the prose of the world into the limits dictated by the
paramaters of that speaking, then we are obliged as speakers to know
the paramaters of our own speaking? To formulate a sense of language and tradition and know it as such a formulation.

We are ob-lig-ated to facilitate the Prose of the World and to
know it as such a facilitation. To repeatedly ask: What face of
being comes to pre-eminence in language's many possible rhetorical
formulations? In what manner is the world disclosed as eminent,
fore-standing in the manifold speech-ways of tradition? How does
the World possibilize through speechful activity? What are the
consequences for the disclosing actualization, this possibilization
of the World?

In the light of these extremely difficult questions, the ironic
self-question: How are we, then, to continue speaking?

If we are saying that Marx critiqued Capitalism - whose watchword
is Class - by formulating a sense of the Unclassed and that this is
realized in his talk about man's Infinite potentials, then we might
look for future research activities toward senses of language which
embody the Infinite as a focal concern. The Critical tradition
might then be regarded as a series of reflections on this problem
which ranges from the Pre-socratic 'Logos' through Socratic 'Logos',
the Platonic tradition through Hegel and Marx to the present. Perhaps even transformational generative grammar realizes this concern
for the Whole and the Infinite in a whispered form. Is it not true
that in Creativity Chomsky - in this a follower of von Humboldt -
perceives the essencing of man? Language - like the Heraclitean
'Logos' - is the infinite. Heraclitus, we might say, grasped the
intrinsic connection between Language and creativity as the site
where a definition of man was to be sought. Chomsky - friend of
'Logos' and liberation (Unclassed 'Gemeinschaft') has also grappled

with the infinite potentials latent in language.   However it would
seem that the Chomskyan 'logos', bound as it is to categorial objects
- deep structural generative rules - has concretized the notion of
the Infinite, thereby restricting it to a purely formal mode.
Chomsky certainly praises the Creative Infinity of speech, using it
deftly as a stick to beat empiricists and positivists - yet in the
end concretizes infinity as a topic of his work rather than as its
tradition and resource.   Infinity becomes the infinite source of
formal reason (Generation) rather than the infinite potentials for
human being and community within the field of Language, construed as
'Logos'.

Chomsky is, perhaps, symptomatic of a tendency to touch upon the
classical problems of Language only to dissipate them for the attra-
ctions of Formal axiomatics, mathematics and other formal 'matheses'
- the omnipotence of Rule and Method.   Analysis then becomes a
Science of the finite Rules behind this Infinite Potential, rather
than a logology of tradition, a form of inquiry which might provide
for the sense of transformational generative grammar - itself as one
possibility among possibilities.

Chomsky may have been given a clue to the Infinity of language if
he read from one of the greatest ironists of our tradition - J.G.
Hamann - where in his 'Miscellaneous Remarks concerning Word Order in
the French Language' he declares:

'Money' and 'language' are two subjects whose investigation
is as profound and abstract as their use is universal.
Both stand in a closer relationship than one might presume.
The theory of one explains the theory of the other;   there-
for they seem to flow from common sources.   The wealth of
all human knowledge rests on the exchange of words;   and it
was a theologian of keen wit who declared theology - this
oldest syster of the higher sciences - to be a 'grammar of
the language of the Holy Scriptures'.   On the other hand,
all the goods of civil or social life have reference to
money as their universal standard... (12)

To terminate these reflections, let me collect my remarks about
the concept of Irony.   Irony (F. 'ironie';   L. 'ironia', Gr. 'eir-
oneai') is bound up with the experience of duplicity and the figure
of the dissembler ('eiron'):   it is speech intended to convey the
antithesis of its literal surface.   Undoubtedly a conceptual in-
ventory might come up with all kinds of irony (the tragic, the
comic, satirical, the cynical, etc.), but here I take it that irony
represents a commitment to a notion of the theoretic of disalien-
ation - of a project towards thinking language.   To be ironic
(minimally) is to differentiate oneself from the object of the irony:
to distance it, to throw it in an opening there, as an ob-ject.
However, the irony that differentiates (as the philosopher's dis-
agreement above) also collects, for it is but a first movement in a
concert toward the serious and the non-ironic.   The 'telos' is dis-
alienation, to the thought of a path, to thinking the belonging-
together of thought and Being, and thereby to think ourselves out of
robotomized speech.   The 'work' of Marx's theoretic 'praxis' involves a recognition of alienated authorship and then its transcendence ('Aufgehoben');   for his this meant the practice of re-
writing history dialectically (cf. Nicolaus, 42).   To be ironic

does not necessarily mean to be cynical.   Just the opposite: not to
suffer the irony of speech is an incipient cynicism (the arrogance of
positivism and naturalism based on the idea of a photographic reflection of reality).   A Socratic simulation of ignorance might be
used to confute an adversary, or just confuse him.   Yet Socrates'
ignorance is hardly simulated - it is truly felt and very real.

   To presume Genius - to presume that one is not ignorant (that one
has a perfect control of one's language) displays a greater depth of
ignorance than to openly admit that one is ignorant.   Hence Socrates,
the self-claimed historical ignoramus, in search of enlightenment
about the forces that move men's souls, becomes in the act of con-
fession the wisest of men.   The cynicism of claiming Genius is part
and parcel of the forgetfulness of language which the ironic gesture
aims to combat as a first orchestration of a total movement into the
sphere of the reflexive text.   At the kernel of the irony of
Socrates, Kierkegaard and Marx is the low burning flame, the element
of faith, which opens the space for irony and the possibility of hope
for another beginning.   Irony might be likened to a preliminary
catharsis which opens upon another notion of writing and speech.
Irony is the art of dialogue where dialogue is understood as the
preservation of the soul.   To speak in the voice of Kierkegaard:
the simulated adoption of another's point of view is not for the
purposes of put down or ridicule (think of the seriousness which inspired Marx's reading of Classical political economy), but for the
purposes of 'edification' and transcendence.   It is known that after
completing the 'Grundrisse' Marx busied himself with the work of
Lassalle already noted where the latter attempted to reconstruct the
thought of Heraclitus from the cosmic fragments; it is also known
that he felt great resonance with Greek philosophy; his early
doctoral work was devoted to themes from Greek philosophy; but it
is less well known that Marx completed his extremely pragmatic comm-
entary on the Gotha programme with the rather amazing maxim: 'Dixi
et salvavi animam meam'.   I have spoken and saved my soul !

NOTES

1 Van der Will (1969), p.214.   The concrete importance of the
   rise of commodity production and its grounding in monetary relations in the economy of the Greek city states with specific
   relation to the problems of 'abstraction' and 'mathematization'
   has long been a subject for Marxist sociologies of knowledge.
   Most recently it can be found in the work of (1) Thomson (1955),
   esp. ch.1; (2) Alfred Sohn-Rethel (1970) and (1972).   Sohn-
   Rethel's earlier work attempts to derive the 'basic categories
   of the abstract intellect, one by one, from the exchange abstraction'.
2 Cf. Marx's comparison in the 'Grundrisse' (McLellan's 'Marx's
   Grundrisse'): 'It is no less false to compare money with language.   It is not the case that ideas are transmuted in language in such a way that their particular nature disappears and
   their social character exists along-side them in language, as
   prices exist alongside goods.   Ideas do not exist apart from
   language.   Ideas that have first to be translated from their

native language into a foreign language in order to circulate, in order to be exchangeable, constitute a slightly closer analogy; but the analogy here lies not in the language, but in their being in a "foreign" language'. (71)

3   In the passage immediately following this section Marx goes on to quote from Goethe's 'Faust' and Shakespeare's 'Timon of Athens' on the power of money (pp.127-8).   It is there where we find Shakespeare's vivid image of money as the 'common whore of mankind'.   Hegel's concept of alienation rooted in the medium of money was developed in the 'Phenomenology' which Marx knew inside out.   His description of the moral disintegration of the 'Ancien Regime' caused by the universal Desire for wealth and money (echoing Diderot's 'Money is everything, but we should not say so') is well known.   See Jean Hyppolite, ch.3 (1969).

4   From an early 1845 edition;   Schiller has been called the father of alienation (Deric Regin, 1 (1965)); we might call him the father (within the Romantic period) of the Classless writing. For further details on Schiller see Wilkinson and Willoughby (1969).

5   Cf. Kaelin's discussion of Sartre's concept of 'total literature' pp.113-16 (1962).

6   See Jean Hyppolite, p.123 (1969).

7   Cf. Nicholaus's formulation, in relation to Hegel, p.32.

8   Cf. the translator's note on terminology at the beginning of the '1844 Manuscripts', pp.12-14.

9   Max Weber, another great ironist, is also puzzled that an 'ideal typical' representative of the Calvinist ethos like Benjamin Franklin should spend his life struggling after pecuniary gain and yet get 'nothing out of his wealth for himself, except the irrational sense of having done his job well';   or his question: How anyone should be able to make it the sole purpose of his life-work, to sink into the grave weighted down with a great material load of money and goods (1968, pp.71-2).

10   See Nietzsche's own statement, What I Owe to the Ancients in 'Twilight of the Idols', pp.105-11, 1968.

11   Cf. Wittgenstein's 'Notebooks' with the 'Prototractatus' and the 'Tractatus';   See Engel (1969), Janik (1966), Collins (236-42) (1972), and Schopenhauer (1970).

12   Quoted by O'Flaherty, 1952, p.30 who comments:
     Language and money, economics and theology – for Hamann these things are not separate, but must be seen and understood in their togetherness.   If natural language is the key to revelation and reason, money is the key to trade.   Thus the visible is the gateway to the invisible, and through it one must pass, if he would reach the invisible.

BIBLIOGRAPHY

BLUM, A., 'Theorizing' in Jack Douglas (ed.), pp.301-19, 'Understanding Everyday Life', 1971, Routledge & Kegan Paul, London.
CLEVE, Felix M., 'The Giants of Pre-Sophistic Greek Philosophy',
1969, Martinus Nijhoff, The Hague.
COLLINS, J.,'Interpreting Modern Philosophy',1972, Princeton Univers-
ity Press, Princeton, New Jersey.
DEELY, John N., 'The Tradition via Heidegger, An Essay on the Meaning
of Being in the Philosophy of Martin Heidegger¦ 1971, Martinus Nij-
hoff, The Hague.
ENGEL, Morris S., 'Language and Illumination, Studies in the History
of Philosophy', 1969, Martinus Nijhoff, The Hague.
GADAMER, Hans-Georg, 'Wahrheit und Methode', 1960, Mohr, Tuebingen.
GOLDMANN, Lucien, 'Immanuel Kant', 1971, New Left Books, London.
HEIDEGGER, M., 'Existence and Being', 1949, Henry Regnery Company,
New York.
HEIDEGGER, M., 'Erlaeuterungen zu Hoelderlins Dichtung', 1963,
Vittorio Klosterman, Frankfurt.
HEIDEGGER, M., 'What is Philosophy?', 1956, Vision Press Limited,
London.
HEIDEGGER, M., 'Being and Time', 1967, Basil Blackwell, Oxford.
HEIDEGGER, M., 'Kant and the Problem of Metaphysics', 1969, Indiana
University Press, Bloomington, Ind.
HEIDEGGER, M., 'Discourse on Thinking', 1969, Harper Torchbooks,
New York.
HEIDEGGER, M., 'Identity and Difference', 1969, Harper & Row, New
York.
HEIDEGGER, M., 'Poetry Language Thought', 1971, Harper & Row, New
York.
HEIDEGGER, M., 'On the Way to Language', 1971, Harper & Row, New
York.
HYPPOLITE, J., 'Studies on Marx and Hegel', 1969, Heinemann, London.
ILTING, K.H., The structure of Hegel's 'Philosophy of Right',
pp.90-110 in Z.A. Pelczynski (ed.), 'Hegel's Political Philosophy',
1971, University Press, Cambridge.
JANIK, S.A., Schopenhauer and Early Wittgenstein, 'Philosophical
Studies', 15, pp.76-95, 1966.
KAELIN, Eugene F., 'An Existentialist Aesthetic', 1962, University
of Wisconsin Press, Madison.
KAUFMANN, W., 'The Owl and the Nightingale, From Shakespeare to
Existentialism', 1959, Faber & Faber, London.
KAUFMANN, W., 'Hegel: A reinterpretation', 1965, Doubleday, New York.
KISIEL, T., The Language of the Event: The Event of Language, in
John Sallis (ed.), 'Heidegger and the Path of Thinking', 1970,
Duquesne University Press, Pittsburgh, pp.85-104.
LANGAN, Thomas D., 'The Meaning of Heidegger, A Critical Study of
an Existentialist Phenomenology', 1959, Routledge & Kegan Paul,
London.
LICHTHEIM, G., Introduction to the Torchbook edition of Hegel's
'Phenomenology of Mind', 1967, Harper Torchbooks, New York.
LOBKOWICZ, N., 'Theory and Practice: History of a Concept from
Aristotle to Marx', 1967, University of Notre Dame Press, Notre Dame,
Ind.

MARCUSE, H., 'Reason and Revolution', 1968, Routledge & Kegan Paul, London.

MARX, K., 'Economic and Philosophical Manuscripts of 1844', 1844 (1959), Progress Publishers, Moscow.

MARX, K., 'The Poverty of Philosophy', 1847, Foreign Languages Publishing House, Moscow.

MARX, W., 'Heidegger and the Tradition', 1971, North Western University Press, Evanston.

MCLELLAN, D., 'Marx's Grundrisse', 1971, Macmillan, London.

MEHTA, J.L., 'The Philosophy of Martin Heidegger', 1971, Harper Torch-books, New York.

NICOLAUS, M., Forward to K. Marx's 'Grundrisse', pp.7-63, 1973, Pelican Books, London.

NIETZSCHE, F., 'Twilight of the Idols' and 'The Anti-Christ', 1968, Penguin Books, London.

O'FLAHERTY, James C., 'Unity and Language: A Study in the Philosophy of Johann Georg Hamann', 1952, University of North Carolina, Chapel Hill.

PALMER, Richard E., 'Hermeneutics, Interpretation Theory in Schleiermacher, Dilthey, Heidegger, and Gadamer', 1969, North Western University Press, Evanston.

PRAWER, S.S., Hinton Thomas R., and Leonard Forster, 'Essays in German Language, Culture and Society', 1969, University of London, Institute of Germanic Studies.

REGIN, D., 'Freedom and Dignity, The Historical and Philosophical Thought of Schiller', 1965, Martinus Nijhoff, The Hague.

ROSEN, S., 'Nihilism, A Philosophical Essay', 1969, Yale University Press, New Haven.

SOHN-RETHEL, A., Mental and Manual Labour in Marxism   pp.44-71, in Walton and Hall (eds.) 'Situating Marx', 1972.   Human Context Books

SCHOPENHAUER, A., 'Essays and Aphorisms', 1970, Penguin Books, London.

SOLL, Ivan, 'An Introduction to Hegel's Metaphysics', 1969, University of Chicago Press, Chicago.

SOLOMON, R.C., Approaching Hegel's 'Phenomenology', in 'Philosophy Today', pp.115-25, vol. XIII, no. 2/4, 1969.

THOMSON, George, 'Studies in Ancient Greek Society', vol. II, The First Philosophers, 1955, Lawrence & Wishart, London.

TOENNIES, Ferdinand, 'Community and Society', 1957, Harper & Row, New York.

VAN DER WILL, W., Name, Semeion, Energeia: Notes on the Permutations of Language Theories, in S.S. Prawer, Thomas R. Hinton, and Leonard Forster (eds.) 'Essays in German Language, Culture and Society, 1969, University of London Institute of Germanic Studies, London.

WALTON, P., and Stuart Hall (eds.) 'Situating Marx', 1972, Human Context Books, London.

WILKINSON, W., and Willoughby, The 'Whole Man' in Schiller's Theory of Culture and Society, in Prawer, Hinton and Forster (eds.), 1969.

WEBER, M., 'The Protestant Ethic and the Spirit of Capitalism', 1968, Unwin University Books, London.

WYLLER, E., The Architectonic of Plato's Later Dialogues, pp.381-92, in Raymond E. Olson and Anthony M. Paul (eds.), 'Contemporary Philosophy in Scandinavia, 1972, Johns Hopkins Press, London.

Chapter 3

DAVIS AND MOORE, MARKET SPEECH AND COMMUNITY
David Silverman

This begins with an analysis of the theory of social stratification
first proposed by Kingsley Davis and Wilbert Moore almost thirty
years ago (Some Principles of Stratification, 'American Soc. Review',
1945, pp. 242-9). It locates a reading of the grounds of that
theory in what I call market speech. However, as will become clear,
this is not offered as a conventional critique - for that would be to
criticize their form of life and, as I conclude, their form of life
is ultimately my own. Instead, I address Davis and Moore's text as
an occasion to make reference to my own speech (its commitments, its
community, its author). So one unfamiliar thing about this paper
is that it makès no claim to get you (or me) 'closer' to that about
which it speaks. It derives its authority not as an accurate (insightful, unbiased) interpretation of Davis and Moore's theory but
from that which provides for any text's intelligibility (ourselves,
our community).

Yet this is not to be solipsistic. We cannot choose any interpretation we like, for this would be to choose our form of life. In
recognizing this, our project becomes dependent on the joint work of
writer and audience in their attempt to address the mode of existence
which unites them.

Perhaps the other unfamiliar thing about my paper is that it is
not one, but two. Further, the second part does not 'advance' the
argument (in the sense of providing additional information, points of
criticism, etc.) but 'goes back' in order to address the intelligibility of what has already been said. This second part has only been
possible because of the violent readings which colleagues have made
of the first part. For, in writing one necessarily glosses over
what makes one's text possible and must call upon others to formulate
that which the writing relies upon but cannot say. But further
violent readings are not only possible but required. In this sense,
this paper cannot possibly be 'about' Davis and Moore's theory or
'about' market speech. In my production of it and through your
reading of it we affirm our community (form of life) and use that as
an occasion to re-view ourselves.

So to interpret a text is to enter a dialogue with it. Yet to
address simply what is said is to gloss over that which provides for
the intelligibility of both what is written and what is offered as

its interpretation.   Dialogue thus expresses itself by an involvement with its own animating grounds - the unsaid.   As Heidegger has
put it, the 'soul' of dialogue is thus 'unspoken':
> Every interpretation is a dialogue with the work, and with
> the saying.   However, every dialogue becomes halting and
> fruitless if it confines itself obdurately to nothing but
> what is directly said - rather than that the speakers in
> the dialogue involve each other in that realm and abode about
> which they are speaking and lead each other to it.   Such
> involvement is the soul of dialogue.   It leads the speakers
> into the unspoken (M. Heidegger, 'What is Called Thinking?),
> Harper Torchbooks, New York, 1968, p. 178).   (1)

I

I want to show, as a beginning, that there are grounds for finding
Davis and Moore more convincing than their critics.   More specifically, Davis and Moore, unlike their critics, locate their mode of
discourse (the vocabulary of structural-functionalism) and address
(in their terms) analytic rather than concrete issues.   In contra-
distinction, their critics, in failing to attend to their own
grounds, provide a fine display of commonsense accounting in which
the practices involved in providing for the world and displaying 'its'
rule-governed properties are necessarily uninteresting.   That is to
say, they engage in 'constructive theorizing' where that is understood as the character of any enterprise claiming to formulate the
sense of a socially located occasion without engaging the grounds of
its own sense.   (2)
    Davis's reply to Tumin explicitly rejects the latter's 'concrete'
reading of the original paper:
> Tumin confuses abstract, or theoretical reasoning on the
> one hand, with raw empirical generalizations of the other.
> Much of his critique accordingly rests on the fallacy of
> misplaced concreteness.   Our article dealt with stratified
> inequality as a general property of social systems (1953, 394).
By providing for a reading of his account as a treatment of social
stratification 'as a general property of social systems', Davis displays what he takes to be the analytic character of his discourse.
By analytic, or what he calls 'abstract or theoretical', reasoning,
I take him to mean a deduction of the relations between a body of
concepts in terms of the functionalist conceptualisation of a possible society.   The status of these concepts and of the deductions
offered about their relations, exists, then, solely by reference to
the functionalist system;   likewise the status of the system exists
solely by reference to its concepts and their possible relations.
    In doing his criticism, for instance by referring to the dys-
functions of stratification and suggesting other 'possible motiv-
ations' for occupational choice, Tumin, however, is not concerned to
locate his analytic grounds.   His auspices seem to consist simply of
'what-every-educated-social-scientist-knows' and he makes no attempt
to address the grounds which provide for the recognizable 'sense' of
his account.   (3)   Further, in calling for empirical test of the
Davis/Moore 'propositions' (as does Stinchcombe), Tumin treats as

'raw empirical generalizations' (Davis) what Davis and Moore display
as a deduction of the relations between a body of concepts which both
provide for and are provided for by the functionalist version of
'society'.

But this is not, of course, to imply that the Davis/Moore paper
resists any other treatment than that provided for within the space
of functionalist grand theory. Rather it is to maintain that that
treatment (within our mode of discourse) should concern itself with
the analytic rather than the concrete level. One way of addressing
this is to ask about the discursive formation which their paper displays and thus to treat their discourse as an occasion to display my
discourse. (4) The rest of what follows is generated by these concerns.

My way of providing for the sense of the Davis/Moore account, i.e.
in seeing its grounds, is to locate it within the frame of political
economy. Their analysis resonates with notions of 'supply' and
'demand', of 'cost' and 'price' and of the 'market' in which 'commodities' (in this case persons and skills) are bought and sold. Indeed, where the vocabulary of Adam Smith occasionally competes with
the newer terms of system theory, it is the latter, albeit reluctant-
ly, with which Davis and Moore are prepared to dispense.

To be sure, in a general statement of their argument, more than
the market seems to be involved:

> In general those positions convey the best reward, and hence
> have the highest ranks, which (a) have the greatest im-
> portance for the society and (b) require the greatest train-
> ing or talent. The first factor concerns function and is a
> matter of relative significance; the second concerns means
> and is a matter of scarcity (1945, p. 244)

However, in the subsequent paragraph, 'functional importance' (point
(a)) immediately has most of its explanatory significance removed:
'Actually a society does not need to reward positions in proportion
to their functional importance ... If a position is easily filled, it
need not be heavily rewarded, even though important'.

For Davis and Moore, then, the concept of function ('a matter of
relative significance') largely gives way to the concept of means
('a matter of scarcity'). The 'market' thus provides the crucial
way of making sense of the 'prices' of 'commodities' (rewards for
talents). The 'functional importance of a position' - a notion
which has no place in the vocabulary of political economy - is to be
made subordinate to the market mechanism. What really counts is the
fixing of a price which calls forth a 'proper' supply of the commodity. At best, then, 'functional importance' simply becomes a metaphor for 'market demand' (for which read 'what society demands', for
which read 'what society needs').

I want to argue, however, that the market model provides more than
a vocabulary for Davis and Moore and more than an analogy for seeing
the sense of their viewpoint. It makes available (in Foucault's
sense) the discursive space in which that viewpoint is expressible
and recognizable.

Within the market metaphor, not only goods and talents but language itself becomes a commodity, a medium of exchange. Hence, language is to be attended to as inherently neutral (a medium) through
which our concrete projects in the world can be accomplished.

Indeed, let us see three propositions as being made available in this mode of discourse:

1. Language is distinct from the world, i.e. there are words and there is the world;
2. The world is the reality, it alone has a self-constituting on-tological status;
3. Language is a convention used as a tool to apprehend the world and to exert our control over it.

These propositions run as a kind of silent thread through the text, affirming the good sense of what we read - affirming that it is indeed speech of some-thing (some commodity).

This commodity form of language (language as a medium of exchange, language as money), by divorcing language from the world (mens' activities and the social structures they produce), divorces also morality from the grounds of speech.   From the market position, there is not more point in engaging with the moral grounds of a discourse than there is in asking what is the morality of money.   For, since both are commodities, and inherently neutral in themselves, the only issue can be how they are used, not that they are used.

If language is a tool, then the activity of doing science requires of it that it be an efficient tool.   Hence language must be got into shape, must be made into an efficient instrument with which to do description and explanation.   In the market place (which is the world), terms, like the prices of commodities, must be clearly defined and publicly available so that 'hidden' meanings are 'avoided' and the real business of this project (reporting on Nature/ making decisions about investment, production and consumption) can be accomplished 'without distortion'.   Heidegger catches this 'market' treatment of language:

> The characteristic of positivism, wherein we have stood
> for decades and today more than ever, is ... that it
> thinks one can sufficiently manage with facts or other
> and new facts, while concepts are merely expedients which
> one somehow needs but should not get too involved with,
> since that would be philosophy (M. Heidegger, 'What is a
> Thing', Regnery, 1967, p. 67).

His analysis of concepts as expedients provides for the sense of the scientific paper which establishes its notion of a phenomenon by an 'operational definition' so that its real project, the accumulation of knowledge (facts), can commence.   Seen in this light, the scientific paper resonates with economic notions of price-fixing so that the accumulation of capital can proceed.   In this way, we can come to grasp both capitalist activity and positivist science as features of alienated labour in which language/profit seen as the Slave of man becomes his Captor - since the ways of seeing provided by a market discourse are never located or challenged.

If the world (Nature) is the true reality within such discourse, it follows that language is simply the mechanism by means of which the properties of Nature are to be displayed by the observer. Nature thus becomes the Hidden Hand which authors speech.   Speech becomes merely the surface appearance underlying which there is the deeper reality of Nature.   Once again, this discourse resonates with the market speech of political economy: the surface appearance (price, exchange rates, costs) are located as mere features of

deeper structures (market forces).   This Hidden Hand of market
forces, while it is unseeable and can only be recognized in its surface displays, is to be viewed as the undoubted author of such displays.

Translated from its setting in the economic market, the notion of
a Hidden Hand opens up a discursive field in which it becomes possible to speak of objects (which language reports upon) which exert
forces, contain potentialities and make demands.   This personalization of Nature provides the space in which Davis and Moore can write
of Social Stratification 'calling forth ...', of the means by which
'societies ensure ...', and even to report that 'it therefore becomes
convenient for the society ...'   The pervasiveness of this mode of
discourse is all the more apparent in that Tumin, in doing criticism,
asserts exactly the same type of speech, e.g. 'Social stratification
system', he writes, 'function to limit ...'.

I ought to point out, however, that these comments are not meant
to serve as a criticism of Tumin or of Davis/Moore.   The critique of
functionalism that it 'illegitimately' concretizes social phenomena,
i.e. it reifies, is well-established.   Yet these assertions draw on
exactly the same mode of discourse whose products they criticize.
For to claim that social phenomena are 'really' of one character or
another (i.e. in this case, social products rather than reified objects) is only recognizable as criticism within market speech.
Within our mode of speech, such criticism merely reaffirms a discursive space in which it becomes possible to speak of the 'real'
character of phenomena and to ground that claim in the Hidden Hand
of Nature as both the producer and judge of speech.   Doing criticism, then, is doing confirmation of the market mode of discourse;   it
is to attack what we see while confirming our ways of seeing.

The Hidden Hand character of market discourse provides for not
only the personalization of Nature but for the depersonalisation of
authorship, for a denial of the act of writing as a commitment to the
animating grounds of one's discourse.   The indirect mode of speech
routinely used in doing scientific descriptions is then not simply a
matter of convenience or style, but a feature of the very mode of
discourse within which the speech is articulated and through which
its recognizable sense is provided for.   Under the auspices of
market speech, then, Davis and Moore can sensibly write, 'It can be
maintained that ...', or 'Such ownership should be distinguished
from ...', for it is not them but Nature which authors the speech.

How does market discourse permit men to produce speech and then
deny their production of it?   How does it allow them to miss the
paradox that, if Nature authors speech, they cannot account for
themselves?   In answering these questions, I can summarize my analysis.

The possibility of such speech is provided for within a discourse
which separates language from Nature, while allocating to language
an instrumental or commodity role.   Using scientific language and
scientific procedures, Anyman can view the properties of Nature.

Thus his text will not be a report of the accounter, as using
(being used by) the mode of discourse which his account inhabits,
but (providing he can bring off an adequate display of his scientific project) his account will stand as a report on Nature.

So Davis and Moore can say 'It can be maintained that ...'

because this is what any competent social scientist could be expected to see in Nature.   Nature speaks through the account-giver, Nature is the Hidden Hand which authors the account.   To suggest otherwise is to do criticism - by implying that the account illegitimately reports upon the account-giver.   The implication is ever present in Tumin's critique that the Davis/Moore account is a product of Davis and Moore's (conservative) values, rather than the message which Nature is relaying about itself.   His claim is not that Davis and Moore's speech is a feature of their commitment to the moral grounds of their discourse, but that they are (but need not be) bad messengers.   Equally, he wants us to treat his speech not at all as a display of his commitments (and method), but simply as the product of a good messenger.

Davis/Moore have provided me with an occasion to analyse the market metaphor which, by locating language as a commodity that expresses the Hidden Hand of Nature, provides the grounds for the depersonalization of authorship.   Market discourse makes possible not only functionalism but positivism in general; its analysis permits the grasping of both as features of alienating market economics, and the location of their products as products of alienated labour.

II

Market discourse makes possible not only functionalism but positivism in general; its analysis permits the grasping of both as features of alienating market economics, and the location of their products as products of alienated labour.

But what permits 'its analysis'?   What authority provides for the intelligibility of this speech, the speech of the speech of market discourse?   Who can be the theorist who can write: 'I want to show' and 'I want to argue'?   Can this paper possibly be 'about' Davis and Moore's theory?   Or must it necessarily be 'about' the tradition of good speech that provides for the possibility of its project?   And, if the latter, then so far has it not sought to conceal the authority which its speech covers over?

For we have been presented with 'intelligible' speech which does not address the grounds of its intelligibility; with an apparently 'self-contained' argument which does not consider that which contains it; with an analysis that ties up the separate pieces and cust off the unshapely corners without recognizing the irony in its formulations.   Faced with this 'finished' text, the reader must feel obliged either to take it or leave it.   His option is only that of acceptance of its concrete arguments ('so be it') or rejection of them ('I see things differently').   This, then, has not been a text which addresses that which makes it possible.

What are we to make of the apparently libertarian claims of 'I want to show' or 'I want to argue'.   This conjures up a vision of the author who chooses what he wants to say about any topic.   You (the reader) don't have to agree with his arguments or even his choice of topic but, after all, he is a free man, exercising the right of free speech.   Yet my grounding of the authority of my speech in what people choose to say (i.e. in usage) is itself self-defeating for it provides no basis for choosing speech over silence:

if everything is conventional (i.e. could have been otherwise) so is
speech — then why speak it?

Of course, usage has its standards.   Certain formulations are im-
proper and would not be warranted by its rules.   So the author cannot 'want to argue' anything, if that 'thing', in context, is not in
accord with the language-game he is playing (sociology, physics,
commonsense).   But, of course, the rules of the game are entirely
conventional.   Men have made them; whatever games men have not made
are meaningless.   And even this assertion is itself a human construction — it is merely 'a contingent arbitrary fact engulfed in the
silence of nothingness' (S. Rosen 'Nihilism').   Usage fails, then,
as an author's authority since, while it formulates correct usage as
that usage which obeys the rules of the game, it can provide no
grounds for playing the game: 'To the question what good is reason?
reason would have nothing to say' (ibid.). (5)

If usage is addressed as conventional, then everything is permitted as long as it is permitted (by the conventions of the language-
game).   Then it makes no difference what we do (as long as it is
done).   So nothing is worth anything, and anything is worth nothing.
Hence nihilism.   The author's claim to know turns out to be more
chatter, his free will becomes arbitrary and worthless — 'What poses
as the creative freedom of human autonomy may then be described with
equal justice as the absurd chatter of self-deception' (Rosen, p.47).
Because 'I want to show' trades upon such a notion of 'creative freedom', it does indeed begin to look like the 'absurd chatter of self-
deception'.   In its display of casual mastery over language, it is
mastered by language.

However, the production and intelligibility of a text ultimately
rest on something other than grammar (i.e. usage).   Or rather that
grammar rests on our lives together and thus on the nature of our
selves and of our world (form of life).   So the author's text is
non-conventional in the sense that to change its intelligibility we
would have to change what we do and how we live.   Ways of seeing are
thus not conventional (and hence arbitrary), they are features of how
we act together: 'Our concepts rest not on a kind of seeing on our
part, it is our acting which lies at the bottom of the language-game'
(Wittgenstein, 'On Certainty', para. 204).

So the author's differentiation of himself through his text, his
claim to 'see beyond' what appears, is possible only from within a
way of being-in-the-world (he and you as members of a community)
upon which rests his authorial claim to know, his Authority.   His
very claim to difference thus shows his deference to some mode of
production (of sense, of social relations).

So we recognize the sense of Davis and Moore's market speech (of
their use of language as a commodity) because we too live in a market
society.   Their version of good speech is speech that does ruling
through its (commodity) use of language.   Through a claim to correspondence between its definitions and what-any-educated-social-
scientist-could-see-in-the-world, they provide themselves with a
secure topic to address, with a secure beginning.   This subject
(social stratification as defined by Davis/Moore) will then be their
authority and their speech will speak about this subject (and not
about how its subject is possible).   They will proceed to show us
the organized character of their subject and we will grasp that

social stratification is indeed in-accord-with-rule (i.e. intelligible, reasonable (?) through our grasp of arguments which are themselves displayed as in-accord-with-a-rule (of doing scientific ex-
planations).   Differences of opinion about this subject will then be
synthesized or replaced by conclusions that are held to be correct
because they are founded in facts which we all can recognize.   Thus
their task is the creation of a community who see the same way
because they have heard speech which addresses its subject in a rule-
governed manner.   Such a community will arise because rational men
can be trusted to ask proper questions of a text and to avoid im-
proper questions.   For instance, they will enquire as to what the
speech says but not address what the speech covers over.   They will
ask is the speech correct? but avoid asking what makes the speech
possible?   They will enquire whether the speech creates communal
agreement but not address the community that is made available when
we speak.   Finally, they will ask does the speech convince? but
avoid asking what convictions does the speech show?

Indeed, this last pair of alternate questions emphasizes the standards of good speech which science provides.   Good speech is that
speech which convinces because it follows the communal rules of
science in generating propositions about some-thing which Anyman,
were he to follow such rules, would be able to replicate.   Thus
good speech for science is de-authored speech – speech whose authority is grounded in the properties of that thing which it addresses
(which Anyman could see were he to adopt the proper methods).   Bad
speech arises under the auspices of special interests and commitments
which make the observer see what he would not otherwise see and define his speech as ideology but not as science.   The public character of speech (the presumed interchangeability of any two observers) is thus undermineded by speech which is seen to report on the
private world of the ideologist (note that this is not at all to
subscribe to science's dichotomy nor to elect its version of bad
speech as my mode of discourse).

This standard of good speech is equally a feature of Davis and
Moore's speech and of that of their critics.   Thus Tumin wants to
imply that Davis and Moore's argument (regrettably) reports on their
(convervative) values rather than upon that thing (social stratification) which their speech claims to be 'about'.   Davis and Moore,
on the other hand, maintain that their account of the thing is indeed
a reflection of that thing's character (and hence could be replicated
by any other observer) when one reasons in accord with the rules of
'abstract or theoretical reasoning'.

But what provides for the sense of labelling speech as ideological
and hence private?   How can speech be private when to characterize
it presumes that it is intelligible?   Must not its intelligibility
be made available within a tradition and a mode of existence?   Let
us then see the sense of the criticism of speech (as mere ideology)
as arising within a market discourse which itself is an icon of the
relations of a capitalist mode of life.   The speech of commitments
understood here as the speech of the author's discourse then becomes
recognizable as bad speech.   'Bad' because it distorts the market,
it is an imperfection in the market mechanism through which the
hidden hand of nature (the price system) writes texts about itself
(dictates the prices of commodities in terms of market demands)

through a neutral language.   'Good' speech is speech in which the
author's text (the supplier's price) reflects not his commitments to
a tradition (his quest for a high price) but the impersonal voice of
nature (the balance of supply and demand) in which the individual
voices of persons are submerged in a public voice, the voice of
science (the voice of the market).   Good speech (for Davis/Moore/
Tumin;   for science) thus resonates with the speech of the market-
place in a dual sense: not only should it reflect market forces
(the voice of Nature) working through the texts of individual authors
but its authority will rest upon the views of the marketplace, i.e.
what everyone knows about the subject-at-hand.

But what standard of good speech does my formulation of Davis/
Moore make reference to?   If 'I want to argue' glosses over that
standard, does not 'let us see' do the same?

I wanted to use 'let us see' to point towards the irony of the
ease with which, under the auspices of free speech, such invitations
are offered and can be accepted (and the security which that acceptance provides).   Let us then see the irony in the invitation 'let us
see'.   Such an invitation resonates with the activity of a free man
using free speech for his purposes, where his purposes provide the
authority for his speech.   Yet to speak in this way, to use language
'as one pleases', is to display the kind of empty mastery of which
Heidegger writes:

the language in general is worn out and used up – an
indispensable but masterless means of communication that
may be used as one pleases, as indifferent as a means of
public transport, as a street car which everyone rides in.
Everyone rides in.   Everyone speaks and writes away in
the language, without hindrance and above all without
danger (M. Heidegger, 'An Introduction to Metaphysics,
Anchor, 1961, p.42).

Such users of language speak without danger because their speech
addresses some-thing and not themselves.   They want to tell us more
about the world and not to recover themselves as the maker of fate-
ful elections as members of a community of speaker/hearers.   To
accept the invitation 'let us see' in order to see more is to trade
cavalierly on that which we see already, and thus is to see nothing
at all – this is the irony.   Let us not accept such an invitation in
order to see more (further, deeper, more extensively), so as to
accumulate more knowledge (capital) but in order to address that which
the invitation makes reference to, points towards – our community,
our tradition.

But this is not the only irony.   My use of the language of
political economy in speaking about texts may present itself as intending to give a 'deeper' insight into them (telling us what we did
not know already, allowing us to see the real grounds of their
speech).   But such a reading fails to grasp the irony in such a
formulation.   For speech which claims to capture underlying patterns
in things-out-there (a deep structure under a surface structure, a
market discourse underlying sociological texts) replicates the
speech of Davis/Moore.   Like them, it proposes that the standard by
which speech is to judged is whether it produces an accurate (insightful, unbiased) account of its subject.   The accuracy of our
reports of this subject (social stratification, Davis/Moore's text)

of which our texts concretely speak is to be our authority.   Our
speech is then to be 'of this subject' and our task is to be the
display of 'its' intelligible, organized character.   So our authority is to be science which instructs us to speak of our subject as
some-thing.

Let us instead see our authority as residing in that mode of production which is our text.   The use of the language of economics is
then an ironic way of making reference to my-self and my community.
Yet to formulate one-self and one's community is itself to do irony.
For in formulating my-self I must stand outside my-self, I must use
science as my authority, I must deny my-self as the author of what I
write (by objectifying my-self, by turning my-self into a commodity).
So in such formulations we employ what is being formulated as a resource and turn both the grounds of our speech and our speech itself
into commodities.   I use an ironic style, then, to point towards the
ironic character of the enterprise and yet towards its ultimately
serious intent - the attempt to speak dangerously (to re-collect my-
self in my speaking) rather than securely.

I elect to see Davis/Moore's speech as market speech so as to
collect myself around the idea of the speech of our common humanity
(the speech of our community) in order to differentiate myself from
the speech of the market.   The speech of this paper then does stratification but not for the sake of that act (status, assertion of
genius, superiority), nor in order to gain benefit from the consequences of that act (profit, proven findings).   Rather my speech
stratifies as a way of re-collecting the commitments which give it
life.   In theorizing a version of stratification as those activities
of collection and differentiation which occur under the auspices of
the market form of life (capitalism, science), I point towards my
commitments to an alternative mode of speech - hence to an alternative form of life.   A mode of speech which speaks not in order to go
on (accumulate capital/knowledge) but in order to go back - to engage with that mode of existence which provides for the possibility
of its collection and differentiation.

I use market speech, then, as a way of making reference to my
theorizing and community (form of life).   A community which provides
for the recognition of market speech as speech which stratifies in
order to go on, by turning speech into a commodity used for instrumental purposes.   By denying the human activities which his speech
covers over, the market speaker not only produces commodities but
produces himself and his community as a commodity.   In electing to
formulate market speech as an icon of the capitalist form of life, I
point towards my commitments to another community.   A community in
which speech is no longer a commodity bought (read) and sold
(written) for instrumental purposes as the masterless means of communication of which Heidegger writes - the mode of existence which is
enslaved by what it seeks to enslave.   Instead, a community which
replaces the standard of the marketplace by the standard of our
common humanity as persons who are also (necessarily) members.

I want to address that humanity, yet I find difficulty, even embarrassment, in going back for that purpose.   I feel I cannot use
language to do it.   What kind of alienated existence is it that
recognizes language as the expression of our common humanity yet cannot address that humanity through language? (6) Curiously, this

allows me to make negative statements (as in the last few pages)
more freely than positive ones: to be able to address what I am
only through what I am not.   Yet the security (for oneself) that
this negative mode of speech provides must itself be addresses.
What is the form of life of negation?

It seems that we can do things with language (use it as a commodity) yet it fails us in expressing our common humanity.   Think of
how, when faced with acts of inhumanity, we are rendered speech-less;
or when words 'fail us' when we are confronted by extreme grief.
Perhaps at such times we are brought face to face with our commodity
use of language, we feel for ourselves that language is 'worn out and
used up'.   We recoil, when we want to make reference to our common
humanity to be grieving person, at expressing ourselves through a
commodity (language), for in doing so we turn ourselves and our relationships into commodities. And so we express ourselves through
touch, gesture and expression.

Speaking to another's humanity, addressing one's own humanity
thus become double (and inseparable) embarrassments in our form of
life - a market form of life in which words can do everything, except to engage that which makes them possible.   So if, as a theorist,
I experience embarrassment in confronting my own humanity, it must be
because that market form of life is my own - it is my society, it is
my language, it is me.

NOTES

1 In this context, the translation of Heidegger's text as the
   'realm and abode about which they are speaking' seems to imply
   that Heidegger means that speakers define their subject for themselves and thus that what is directly said should be the concern
   of dialogue.   Yet he expressly denies this a few words earlier.
   Perhaps a way of retrieving Heidegger's thrust is to note that,
   in the book from which this quotation is drawn, he addresses
   'What is called Thinking?' in terms of 'What calls us to Think?'.
   This part of his text can then be read as making reference to the
   'realm and abode which calls us to speak', or, to use the language of the latter part of this chapter, the 'tradition which
   calls us to speak'.

2 Garfinkel provides an example of constructive theorising in the
   form of the coroner who has to formulate accounts as courses-of-
   action.   He has noted:

      In short, what we have is the temporal ordering of a
      coroner who, knowing the ways in which the society is
      organized, sees in the beginning as his problem the
      state of the corpse as a problematic matter.   From
      the various ways available, he is to formulate the
      sight as a phase of the action that the sight is also
      a report on.   He is now to conduct an inquiry so as
      to elaborate the alternative courses that would in-
      corporate some set of these features as intelligible
      reports of the same actions that they are part of
      (Purdue Symposium on Ethnomethodology, 1967, ms. 152).

3 Although Tumin's reasoning is equally (with Davis/Moore) sensible within the possible society of structural-functionalism,
   concretely, it serves to re-affirm Merton's argument that functionalism can be both conservative (Davis/Moore) and radical
   (Tumin) in its implications.   Analytically, I argue later that
   Tumin's paper re-affirms the market discourse exemplified by
   Davis/Moore.

4 The notions of discourse and discursive space which are traded
   upon in the first part of this paper are provided by Michael
   Foucault in his 'Archaeology of Knowledge', Tavistock, 1972.
   The following statement gives some idea of his project:
     But what we are concerned with here is not to neutralize
     discourse, to make it the sign of something else, and to
     pierce through its density in order to reach what re-
     mains silently anterior to it, but, on the contrary, to
     maintain it in its consistency, to make it emerge in its
     own complexity.   What, in short, we wish to do is to
     dispense with 'things'.   To 'depresentify' them ... To
     substitute for the enigmatic treasure of 'things' anterior
     to discourse, the regular formation of objects that
     emerge only in discourse.   To define these objects
     without reference to the ground, the foundation of
     things, but by relating them to the body of rules that
     enable them to form as objects of a discourse and thus
     constitute the conditions of their historical appearance
     (pp. 47-8).

5 Although it might conceal this behind the aesthetic appeal of a
   mathematical project which mirrored the mathematical structure
   of the world (see Blum, 1974, ch. 5).

6 A Heideggerian reading of this question might see its quest for
   a perfect, complete speech as part of the tradition of commodity
   speech.   No doubt both Marx and Heidegger would also resist the
   'humanistic' thrust that it implies.

Chapter 4

CLASS AND DIFFERENCE [1]
Maurice Roche

> It is all one to me where I begin: for I shall come back
> again there.
> It is the same thing that can be thought and that can be.
>
> Parmenides [2]

A. BEGINNING: SOCIOLOGY AND DIFFERENCE

It is conventional for thinking, and the writings it generates, to
unwittingly recapitulate the history of Western civilization (no
less).   That is, just as civilization is supposed to have developed
from tribalism, myth and magic to industrialization, science and
logic, so thinking recapitulates this Progress, this Enlightenment,
by moving from belief to knowledge, from questions to answers, from
introductions to conclusions.   The historical movement, and the
movement of thought, occur between and in terms of two poles, two
moments securely taken in hand, the beginning and the end.   The
rationality of history and the rationality of argument conventionally confidently announces itself as the necessity of progress;
progress is secure as a teleological synthesis, the end ('telos') is
co-present with the beginning in the beginning, the beginning is the
inauguration of the end required by the end.
    It is at least a preliminary requirement for the project of re-
flexive and dialectical analysis which this collection of papers ack-
nowledges, to find a way of achieving a sight of, and therefore a
distance from (within), the secure social organization of history
and thought, the conventional character of progress and enlightenment as the thoughtless standards of thought.   A sight of conventional social organization, and more important, of a deeper notion of
sociality than that, can be achieved by affirming dialectic and
circularity as standards of the mode and movement of thought; the
question as a form of theoretic life and community.   To affirm dialectic and circularity means not only that every display of reflexive
and dialectical analysis is ultimately a display of what it is to do
such analysis; it is also and further a display of the question of
what it is to do such analysis.   So, while it might appear to say
what it has to say assertively and confidently, - that is, as writ-

ing it has to seek to stand and be heard – this is in order to open itself, through its reading, to be held in question, to be held by its own question.   If the speech demands attention, it is not for its Self that it does so, but rather it is for its Sake, its reason, its ground.   Reflexive and dialectical analysis does not question the progress of thought in order to implicitly critique society and history: Rather its unconventionality, its restless circling, its questioning assertiveness, is its critique, and its attempted re-appropriation of society, sociality and history.   It is its commit-ment to the possibility of thoughtful community, of sociality as answering to the responsibility and the desire to think.

Progress, as the teleological synthesizing of beginning-end, or-anizes thoughtlessness in history and in attempts to think, speak and write (together we may understand history and these attempts as constituting 'tradition') by organizing security, a sense of what can be taken for granted, a sense of what it would be irrelevant and meaningless to question, concretely formulated in the positivist logico-empirical demarcation criteria and verification principle. Progress organizes security by appealing to the unthought ration-ality of science, which is powerful and therefore (!) prestigious and valuable and therefore unquestionable.   The progress of society and of thought lie encapsulated within the progress of science, the paradoxical 'telos' of which is the simultaneous humanization of the world, through the practical will to control, and the de-humaniz-ation of man, through the theoretic denial of the will.

Progress demanded and called forth a 'logos' of the social, a sociology, but one which was to be encapsulated within the progress of science; progress called forth sociology as the science of society.   In contrast to this, if reflexive and dialectical analysis situates itself in relation to sociology it does so as a critique of sociological reason. (3) It strives to remember what has been, and had to be, forgotten in the founding of the new science with the neologism 'sociology'.   It strives to remember what it is to listen to and hear 'logos' originarily, not as artifically constructable and re-constructable new speech ('neo-logos'). (4) This remember-ing of 'logos' is its sociology, its 'logos' of the social; and indeed 'logos' may be seen as the social, in so far as it names togetherness (of things, of thought and being) and the groundedness of speech. (5) Sociality and community is the phenomenon that 'logos' shows in its rememberance and that which claims the atten-tion and concern of any true socio-logy.   Reflexive and dialectical analysis calls sociology to stand philosophically and not to run busily at the work of science.   It calls sociology to consider the character of the notion of society, sociality and community that it serves, and that it constitutes itself as in its work, and then to think beyond and back to gather other notions of society and social-ity as other ways of being in language, in order to re-experience sociality as possibility and as that which grounds, displays itself through, and shows its difference from any actuality and any present presence (any thing, whether called 'social' or 'natural').

Reflexive and dialectical analysis or theorizing is a sociology which circles the beginning of progressive scientific sociology, which is its unthought and allegedly 'irrelevant' placement, always already secure in progress and science as forms of life and as ways

of speaking or being in language.   In questioning its Other, that
is, conventional sociology, it comes back to question itself and its
difference; it uses its re-think of sociology as an occasion, and
perhaps as a means to rethink itself.   It renders sociology's beginning insecure in order to regain the insecurity of true inquiry
as its own, to regain its belongingness to beginning.

Conventional sociology begins in difference and gives its thought
to difference.   Like the members it purports to describe, explain
and differentiate itself from, sociology recognizes and utilizes
such dichotomies, polarities, and continua, as male-female, black-
white, rich-poor, rural-urban, undeveloped-developed (regarding
'individual actors' e.g. child-adult and 'socialization process'),
undeveloped-developed (regarding 'societies', e.g. traditional-
modern and the 'modernization process').   Sociology differentiates
itself over these differentiations according, for instance, as to
whether it totalizes them (that is, whether it regards them as all
overlapping with and dependent upon one major differentiation), or
whether it fragments them, (that is, whether it regards them all as
independent of each other).   Another line of sociological differentiation concerns its politico-moral understanding of its togetherness
with progress, whether as conservation-reform on the one hand
('committed' structural functionalism and 'uncommitted' empiricism
respectively) or revolution on the other (the 'committed' 'science'
of historical materialism).

The notion of class appears differently when it is turned in the
'light' of these differentiations in the sociological tradition
(which, needless to say, are peremptory and crude simplifications of
a form of life which has rarely been deep but has always been complex).   Reformist empiricism, by taking class as status, and status
as the prestige allocated to different roles, and roles as predomin-
antly performed by individual actors or act units, de-constitutes the
notion of class by individualizing and fragmenting it.   Conserving
structural functionalism retains a notion of class as dichotomous
differentiation in the economic sub-system of the social system.
Class is then one of a threesome (e.g. class/economy, status/society,
power/politics) or of a foursome (e.g. class/economy/adjustment
function, politics/goal-orientation, family/pattern-maintenance
function, law/integration function), or an aspect of a foursome
(e.g. cybernetic hierarchy of controlling systems, from human biology,
personality, society (class), culture (underlying moral consensus)).
In whatever formation it is paraded, as part of an attempt at theoretical and analytical totalization, class is derogated as either
relatively autonomous, or as relatively subject to the control of
politics or culture, or as progressively disintegrating into roles
under the impact of structural differentiation in the social system;
apparently the end, the 'telos', the destiny, the fatality of social
life in the eyes of structural functionalism's historicism is a
meritocratic liberal-conservative atomized 'consensus' which concretely is either upon us or near at hand (embourgeoisement, the end
of ideology, etc.)

By contrast, historical materialism's revolutionary totalization
theorizes the historicity of class (as in the series, primitive
communalism, slavery, estates, classes, classless communism), and
the diffuse primacy, dominance or hegemony of class (in some

versions as the political over the economic, in other versions as
the economic over the political) in the modern period.   From the
point of view of historical materialism the functionalist-empiricist
dero gation or deconstitution of class is a feature of the class-
character of empiricist-functionalist sociology.   And to round the
circle out, historical materialism is itself on its own account, a
feature, indeed a product, of the class struggle it theorizes, what-
evever other claims it might also make to 'scientificity'.

A re-think of sociology as reflexive and dialectical analysis is
better served, it seems to me, by taking class as its occasion than
by taking other versions of stratification and social difference, at
least initially.   Class is more fruitful than status stratification,
it is lodged in a less thoughtless and more accessible zone of the
sociological tradition, a zone where the claims of politics and
morality on thought are not ignored, where the dialectic of theory
and practice is at least seen, and where the social rootedness of
thought in the project of community creation gets some recognition,
however concretely, as a grounding of the practices of inquiry, description and explanation.   Less accessible zones of the sociological
tradition, but also including historical materialism to a large extent, begin from difference, encounter and lose themselves among the
dispersal of concrete differentiations through ungrounded and unthought commitments to the theoretical practices of differentiating,
categorizing, marking off and so forth.   What can be said of that
form of life, which shows itself in a specific way in the sociological tradition, which takes difference as its first word, its
rule?

Perhaps we can schematically formulate such a form of life through
the forms of its speeches, as a world in which there are many things
to speak about; where there is no unity to be listened for among
the many, but where unification is an exclusively theoretical project,
an artificial after-thought calling on the will to control and not
the openness of a waiting and hearing.   It is a world where there
are many things to speak about, many speeches to be made, and many
things to use in the speaking of them.   It is a world of progress,
news and names, of possessions and individuals; where politics,
money, utility and mathematics are the standards and criteria of
speech and of the theoretic life.   It is a world which further ex-
empts speech from the responsibility to that which authors and provides for it, where the reason or meaning of speech is subjected to
transformation into what are the objects of purely and abstractly
practical interests, the reasons or meanings of speakers.   It is a
life-world which renounces life in favour of world, in that it ex-
empts itself from its sociality, its theoretic responsibilities and
community.   It is a life which finds life through the world, and
thus through mortality;   and just as its speech waits on silence as
its resource, so its life waits on death as its resource, and its
relief.

Finding the thoughtlessness of the sociological tradition in a
form of life which takes difference as its first word and rule,
however requires some reflexive consideration of the form of life
within which the finding is practised, and where thoughtfulness is
the standard or at least the responsibility.   Later we shall speak
of morality as metaphor for this form of life, pointing up its

difference from politics.   But for the moment, could art be a metaphor for this form of life?   Where that invokes a notion of art as
a concrete object, produced as different from all other such objects
by an author or genius who as such is an individual authority different from all other 'producers' and speakers then the world of art
merely replicates in various ways the features of world of difference
we have just been looking at.   However, as a world where the speaker,
artist, is the work, and where the work is conceived as showing its
difference from tradition (the creative reconstitution of tradition)
and its togetherness with tradition (the educative and moral 'telos'
of community building with its audience-readership through its display of its call for and its call to some notion of authoritativeness and rationality grounding the speech-production) then art could
well qualify as a candidate at least for further consideration as the
kind of form of life in terms of which the restless thoughtfulness of
the reflexive and dialectical analytic project could situate itself.

We make this suggestion tentatively in order to inscribe one of
the thematic differences which underlies this paper as oriented to
the authority of reflexive and dialectical speech, and that is the
difference that such analytic orientation makes, the difference between progressive scientific speech, secure in its unthought ground
of difference, and a form of analysis which takes the difference it
is and it makes, as its theme.   Reflexive and dialectical analysis
does not contrast with forms of thought thoughtlessly founded on
difference in that it is thoughtfully founded on what is undifferentiated on unity, identity, sameness or relationship.   Rather,
that is the contrast it is in search of;   in the (enduring) meantime
it must reach for a sense of the undifferentiated through the foundational reflexive and dialectical analytic difference, which is best
formulated as that between speech and tradition/language/logos.
Art could conceivably stand as the icon of this difference, in so
far as art lies in the standing-apart-from-but-together-with of the
work and the tradition, of 'it' and 'its' ground.   And the difference between speech and tradition, a difference which stands within
the occasion of speaking, just as the occasion of speaking stands
within tradition/language, is one (crucial) way of talking about
what in recent philosophy has been identified as the 'ontological
difference', between things or beings and thingness or Being in terms
of which they are.   (6)   The elusive meaning of this difference is
the 'answer' to the insecure and restless questioning that is reflexive and dialectical analysis as a sociology, and as an ontological as opposed to an epistemological philosophizing.

In sections C, D and E we will look at various ways in which the
topic of class opens up and requires us to think of difference.   In
section C we note how Marxism, for instance, requires us to think
difference as between thing and practice on the one hand and theorizing on the other.   In section D we take further another version of
difference suggested by Marxism's class-think, that between morality
and politics, in the direction of a self-understanding of reflexive
and dialectical theorizing as, ideally, being moral and educational
in its speech, as against the condition that threatens much theoretic
and mundane speech, of taking politics and power as its standard and
ideal.   In section E we re-think the thing/practice - theorizing
version of difference in terms of Heidegger's notion of the Ontolog-

ical difference between beings and Being, and between speech and
Language as the ground of speech.   That brings us back to some of
the issues raised in the next section concerning speech, language
and meaning.   Drawing at this stage more on Wittgenstein's philosophy, rather than Heidegger's hermeneutic of man and speech, which is
stressed more later, we look at the difference between the positivist
form of conventional sociological theorizing and reflexive-dialect-
ical theorizing as a difference between ways of speaking, ways of
implicitly theorizing language, ways of showing the grounding play of
man's being-in-language.

B.   LANGUAGE AND DIFFERENCE: REFLEXIVITY AND DIALECTIC

My discussion is (to become) situated in terms of a reflexive and
dialectical theoretic problematic.   (7) This requires us to appreciate an immediate difference between ways of understanding the
nature of speech, language and meaning, which, almost in order to be
put at all, needs to be put somewhat blandly, schematically, and
crudely.   Dialectical and reflexive theorizing, in remembering
'logos', shows its hearing of language in its speech about language,
or about anything else as topic.   It speaks, shows and affirms what
may be called, in an initial and crude fashion a multi-dimensional
paradigm (8) of language.   As against that, positivism, the theorizing of science (in particular scientism in the social and human
sciences), and also (in some of its modes), of commonsense, speaks,
shows and affirms a one-dimensional paradigm of language.   (9)
   Before we look at this further, first let me draw attention to
some related and equally grounding and unavoidable senses of difference in relation to language.   There is the difference between what
can be said and what cannot be said, which is not the same as that
between what is said and currently present and what is unsaid, and
currently absent, but yet sayable, a potential present.   The difference between the sayable and the unsayable, in so far as, following
Heidegger we acknowledge language as the dimension of the disclosure
of Being for man, is equivalent to the difference between what speech
says (or speaks, about whatever its topic is) and what speech shows
(about why, how and what it is to speak about anything at all).
Wittgenstein (10) reminds us that a picture cannot (although some
modern art raises a question to this 'cannot') picture, or refer to,
its character as a picture, its pictorial form;   yet none the less
it unavoidably must use this form, and thus show it through whatever
it pictures.   And he draws an analogy between this and the fact
that in so far as we theorize the basic nature of language as propositional, it is the case that propositions cannot propose or refer
to their propositional form - which has interesting consequences for
the speech of this particular kind of theorizing - yet none the less
unavoidably using and thus showing such form.
   Reflexive and dialectical analysis makes the Heideggerian difference between speech and the grounds of speech, unsayable in speech,
and also the not unrelated Wittgensteinian difference between speech
and its form, what speech says and what it shows, central and enduring concerns.   Which is to say that it remembers the ontological
centrality (horizonality) of language or discourse;   it re-members

speech's standing out-from and within language or discourse.   It
takes note, as a version of sociology, of what Auden once characterized as the duty of the poet - to preserve the language.   Immanent-
ly for sociology this injunction could be taken to mean the duty -
and we will look further at its moral character later - to resist the
dehydration, decomposition and mystification of our's and anybody's
(that is, everybody's) language, which is what happens when it is
treated as mainly or exclusively referential in a descriptive way,
that is as one-dimensional.

Language and meaning are not to be understood, as they might well
be according to this paradigm, as engendered within us by a radically external world/reality for the purpose of giving voice to it in
description.   Alternatively, but equally over-emphatically it might
be said that the world does not form speech, but speech forms the
world, or gives form to the world.   Even if this way of putting it
is accepted, it must at least be added that speech does more than
form the world as merely describable.   It forms sharability of the
world in more than just the mere sharing of descriptions.   To preserve the language is to preserve its possibilities, its multi-
dimensional and poetic character, its power to evoke; it is to preserve ourselves as speakers.

Describing, ascribing predicates to some subject, referring,
pointing, indicating, are indeed basic features of speaking.   But
such speaking hardly makes itself available as one set of possible
forms of discourse.   Such speech says nothing about what it shows,
for instance the context, the discourse within which the utterance
has its life.   It fails to acknowledge what it shows in the course
of its referring; it says nothing about its actual use as an activity, that is, what it does or enacts.   And no foreclosure is possible concerning its possible uses, the possible contexts in which it
could be called upon to do work.

Describing pretends to report upon a world unaffected by the
describing.   But description of the social world of actions and
action contexts and situations, is itself a describable action and
action context.   Given that most men most of the time are hearers of
a described world of specific actions to which they are not original
witnesses or participants, then the world comes to be its description.
Its description is all that we have got.   But description of an
action is an action that purports to present us with something without presenting us with itself as a showing of one form of action.
It pretends to be one-dimensional and referential to an actuality
when it is, on the contrary multi-dimensional and self-reflexive
upon possibilities of intelligibility.   Thus describing hides its
question 'why describe?', 'describe for what purpose and context?'.
Describing hides its possible character as dramatic re-enactment, re-
living the moment; it hides its possible character as aesthetic
appreciation; or as a call to action, or as a condemnation; it
hides its possible character as a further elaboration of the situation it describes, etc.   The described action has its light, its
being for us through an activity upon which no light is cast, and
which remains hidden.   The phenomenon has its being for us through
a descriptive activity within a discourse, the character of which the
descriptive activity does not address or even recognize.   Describing
strives to become a non-situated, extra-linguistic transcendence;

while denying transcendence within language through its one-dimensional levelling out of the life and possibilities of discourse; that is its pretence and its pathos.

Thus as 'initially' described action is, exists as, the possible forms and uses of its 'subsequent' descriptions, whether by the agent or by others. (Consider the day to day world of 'public affairs' or politics in this respect, the interpretive flux concerning what counts as an action, how 'it' is to be described, when 'it' 'happened', how 'its effects' have reverberated over time, etc., etc.). That is to say, the doing is in the form of the telling, and the telling is that which can itself be told in many ways. To recognize language is to recognize that we live within the dialectic light and shadow, showing and hiding and in terms of the reflexive problem of the hand that cannot grasp itself, of the eye that cannot find itself as an object within the world it sees, (11) and of the man who cannot step over his own shadow.

A one-dimensional paradigm of language use might have it that language and meaning are of one basic kind (perhaps modified to include logic and tautology) and that is descriptive of or referential to an objective world, pre-given beyond language and beyond the describing.

A multi-dimensional paradigm of language might have it that language and meaning have many different forms, and indeed that meaning is in use. (12) Language evokes, produces and constitutes for speakers and hearers the variety and complexity of the experienced world in its variety and complexity. Speech acts and speech constitutes world in the most demonstrable way when it is used poetically. But it works the same way in the hidden poetizing that is everyday speech and conversation.

The one-dimensional paradigm, positivist and objectivist as it is, gives birth, of necessity, to the reflexive and dialectical problematic, but in such a viciously regressive way that it destroys itself in the process. In this respect consider the necessity of the movement of Wittgenstein's thought. His picture theory of meaning (that meaning in any natural language is ultimately analysable as founded upon and reducible to atomic propositions which picture the world of facts) could not itself be analysed as a picture. (13) In subsequent empiricist modifications of this positivist atomism the one foundational form of meaning was held to be the possible empirical verifiability of any proposition; (14) and once again the reflexive problem, which is vicious in these circumstances, announced itself; what is the verification of the verification principle?

Wittgenstein's later thought was, as he himself acknowledged, (15) dialectically related to his earlier thought. It proposed a multi-dimensional paradigm of language and meaning, seeing it now as tool-box containing words, concepts, grammatical forms, and so on which performed many functions in the life of natural language use, but which performed no overall unitary function. And the theory/ metaphor which substituted tool-using for picturing as the character of language was itself not intended as a testable general theory, but as a specific and active intervention in academic philosophy to redirect it from the aspiration to produce knowledge to a view of itself as analytical and clarificatory activity.

Positivism (or the speech of one-dimensional picturing) and re-

flexivity/dialectic (or initially the speech of multi-dimensional
tool-using and meaning-enacting) are the two main paradigms of language which sociology has to take seriously if it is to take language
seriously at all.   If it is said that the latter is obscure and that
the former is logical and clear, it can also be said that the former
is spuriously and superficially clear, that it raises its own reflexive problem as to the very intelligibility of its own speech,
that it is ultimately deeply unintelligible and that it collapses
into the undoubted difficulties of the multi-dimensional paradigm of
its own accord.   Sociology, which is at the moment wedded to and
bedded by scientism and the one-dimensional paradigm, has had and
can have no more than a totally sterile and unproductive relationship to it;   better by far to divorce on grounds of non-consummation.

This paradigm difference gets more complicated if we note at this
point that to call one-dimensionality and multi-dimensionality
'paradigms' is only to appear to differentiate them according to a
unitary sense of 'paradigm' which remains unaffected by the differentiation.   Thus, to call multi-dimensional tool-using and meaning-
enacting a paradigm is to formulate paradigm (in the calling) as the
open-ended and ungraspable (reflexive-historical) possibilities of
analogical and metaphorical use of concrete exemplars: On the other
hand to call one-dimensional picturing a paradigm is to formulate
paradigm as a graspable (concrete-historical) and unitary form of
theoretical life or community of beliefs and practices.   (16)

Reflexivity and dialectic involve the notion that the intelligibility of any piece of speech is never self-evident, self-given in
the speaking, although it is also the case that in one sense the
speaking is all that we have got.   Thus to take reflexive and dialectical theorizing seriously is in large part to take seriously the
multi-dimensional, active and poetically constitutive character of
any speech seriously.   It is to be continually attempting to hear
and to provide the grounds of speech;   and it is also the recognition
that the grounds of speech cannot ever be once and for all provided,
grasped or described;   which is to say that life, language and history 'go on';   this is the 'world' of which we speak when we say that
we cannot stop the world and get off.

In trying to understand what something means Wittgenstein often
asks how we come to learn it, how we are taught it.   (17)   Another
way of putting this is to ask by means of what examples and situations do we come to understand a concept as a trans-situational rule
formulable in, and only formulable in terms of, situational speci-
fics, contingencies and exigencies.   Meaning and rule are only formulable in the situated doing, the 'knowing how to go on' which can
never be totally formulated in detail.   (18)   This exemplifies the
reflexive and dialectical problematic in that every formulation of
the grounds of speech, whether or not it aims at presuppositionless
self-evidence (a la Husserl) (19), can never achieve that Heavenly
state;   it is enough that it speaks in time to a community of like-
minded men, who are responsive and responsible hearers to each others'
speech.   The difference between concept/rule and specific situational enactments, between thought/language and the world, between
theory and practice, are forms of difference, even of alienation,
that are to be seen and superceded in the practice of theorizing,
that is, thoughtful speaking to and for the community of thoughtful

speakers, both historic and contemporary, both analytic and existential.

Irrespective of what speech speaks, then, it shows its difference
from that which provides for its intelligibility, its way of being
in language.   This difference provides for the difference between
positivist theorizing, which conventional versions of sociology display, and which in seeking to speak of some object, called class or
society, covers over the possibility of seeking for the social in
speech's ways of being in language.   Reflexive and dialectical
theorizing, on the other hand, lives precisely as this seeking.
Positivist sociology is not grounded in its explicit notion of the
social, for that is something that it seeks to stand apart from and
not together with, in order to describe it accurately and explain it.
Therefore we may hazard that we may find its grounds, its implicit
commitment to and version of the social, in its implicit notion of
'logos'.

The first and last words to be spoken in any self-comprehension of
sociology must address themselves to the fact that it was founded as
a first word, a new word, sociology, a bastard out of 'socius'
(friendship, togetherness)(Latin) and 'logos' (rational speech, the
togetherness of things)(Seidel, p. 89, Greek).   It promised new
knowledge of the social, and was centrally involved in the original
Comtean positivist vision of scientific knowledge as teleologically
oriented to the construction of the rational (here, scientific)
society.   But this new social knowledge and society construction was
implicitly premised upon and formulated in terms of the possibility
of constructing new concepts and new words, that is of speaking in a
new way;   sociology's hidden premise and ground was neology as a way
of being in language.   Neology would allow speech to correspond to
world/reality, and thus convey knowledge and truth about it.

At one level then, new speech, neology, is oriented to the togetherness of speech and world, and this notion of reference or
correspondence is its underlying version of the social which shows
through what it speaks of.   And at another level there is a further
version of the social, togetherness, which also shows through and
that is the presupposition supporting neology as a practice that it
is possible for men to create, ultimately 'ex nihilo', their language
and meanings, and to control them through will and contract, one example of which would be the kind of contracting that stipulative
definition is;   'let us all define X as Y, so that henceforth whenever we speak X we always mean Y'.   There are two notions of togetherness here, firstly the 'us', the sociological scientific community formulated henceforth as methodic and programmed speakers, and
secondly the togetherness of word/speech and action, in that by saying something we are necessarily also doing something.   Sociological
speech thus shows its versions of sociality as the correspondence of
word and world, the identity of speakers and identity of word and act.

Reflexive and dialectical analysis seeks for its difference from
this neological sociology, and its versions of the social embedded in
its versions of 'logos', by affirming at least the presence of these
versions as suppressed within sociological discourse, and by reaffirming them as ways of being in language which are neither new,
nor adequately understood, nor the only possible ways of being in
language.   It must understand possibility of grounding descriptive

speech on performative speech, and performative speech on the constitutive possibilities of language which are best illustrated in
poetry and poetic constitution.   This is at once an original speech
which opens up for an interpretive hearing the depths, movement and
possibilities of what could be called the old language, and which
arranges for the extraordinary to be heard in the reformulation of
what is ordinary speech.

One way of doing reflexive and dialectical analysis is to re-
cover the performative character of apparently descriptive speech,
and my remarks following on Marxist theorizing of and speech about
class are oriented to trying to make that recovery at least visible
in a particular case.   A deeper way to proceed is to listen for the
movement of poetic constitution in any theorist's or speaker's
utilization of what is always inevitably the old language;   it would
be to reopen the question of the grounds of speech, of how speech
shows its being in language, which the speech, and sociological
speech in particular, of neologism implicitly seeks to close to take
in hand as a secure basis from which to proceed and progress, and
to keep unquestioned.   My remarks throughout this paper, while acknowledging this deeper way to proceed, limit themselves in the main
to understanding the former performative character of speech, and
class speech in particular;   and this is to orient in various ways
to the question: What does class speech do?   What difference does
it make?

C.   CLASS AND THE THING-THEORY DIFFERENCE: MARXIST THEORIZING AND REFLEXIVE DIALECTICAL THEORIZING

We can elect class as the occasion of some brief notes on the notion
of re-thinking the sociological tradition;   taking into account the
relatively greater accessibility of class discourse, compared with
other sociological formulations of difference.   Class, and its
formulator Marx/historical materialism, is less secure and less
desirous of becoming secure within the thoughtlessness of the tradition.   Whether or not it may ultimately come to be seen as succ-
umbing to the security of silence about its grounds (and silence in
its own particular way about its grounds, in so far as it conceives
grounds to be practices), is another matter.   However, initially
class and its theoretic formulator (its idea - whether as philosophical anthropology or science), appears accessible to the notion
of a re-think of tradition.   It raises, or allows to be raised, the
thought of the political and moral character of tradition, the dialectic problem of theory and practice, and a recognition of the reflexive and dialectical groundedness of thought.   Ground, in terms
of this formulation, can appear as human, trans-human or both;   it
can appear as a voluntaristically or a deterministically conceived
history, or both.   This either, or and both is also formulated as
the totality of being, or rather as the totalizing of becoming, the
progressive differentiation (contradiction, struggle) and collection
(synthesis, surpassing) of the alienated couple man-world, and the
alienation of its mediation (the process-practice of labour) in the
class-struggle (this latter is less the dichotomy bourgeoisie-
proletariat or capital-labour, than the dichotomy class-classless-
ness or capitalism-communism).

Marxism reaches outside of the mundane scientism and progressive-
ness of the sociological tradition to find and found its own tradition now in philosophic thought of totality and now in science, now in
irony and now in activism. We take this reaching, this think-out of
the sociological tradition, as an occasion to consider the character
of our own reaching in the project of re-thinking the sociological
tradition, and thereby thinking originarily and in a beginning way of
our own tradition.

There are certain prescriptions, methods, and examples of ways of
thinking-out of tradition in, for instance, the way that Marxism has
appropriated its intellectual sources, British-Scottish political
economy, Hegelian idealism and French socialism. That is Marxism
offers for consideration a certain mode of relation to tradition, and
therefore a certain understanding of what tradition could be; it
offers reading, (20) and furthermore it offers its ver:s ion of the
Kantian form of theoretic life, critique, (21) as the method and
purpose of reading. Kantian critique searched for the limits and
bounds of sense, the demaraction of the limits beyond which metaphysics and the arbitrariness of unrestrained speculative rationalism were allowed their head, both in the realms of pure and practical reason. Marxist critique (22) searched for real men beneath
the abstractions of political economy and idealist theories of history and the state; it searched for the humanly historically re-
creatable beneath the reified timeless natural lawfulness 'discovered' by the economist; it searched for practical probabilities
and possibilities beneath utopianism; and it searched for humanity,
as reason and morality, as repressed and abused 'telos', beneath the
unreason and amorality of social life self-restricted to and constituted in the rule and measure of money, commodity, and utility.
Marx taught a way to read, a way to establish relationship and difference with the intellectual inheritance of tradition, a way to
inherit.

The reading relation-difference, regarding tradition, subsists
between two poles, literalism (believing what the papers tell you)
on the one hand, and playfulness ('It means whatever I want it to
mean') on the other. (23) Literalism, at first sight appears as an
attempt at a reading rule and thus superior to playfulness, which is
the absence of any rule at all. But this claim to authority is of
course the poor disguise of an absolute subjection to the authority
of the text. The tradition is constituted (in the reading) as
masterful, and (although only formulable through a slavish reading)
as requiring no other, whether slavish or otherwise. In this
arrogance tradition is formulated unwittingly as supremely un-
reasoning, and unreasonable; and the dialogue that is reading is
supressed beneath a political denial of sociality. Literalism is
the politicization of tradition as domination and mastery; it is
the denial of reason and morality; it is the denial of tradition
as dialogue and discourse, relationship and history.

Literalism then has no reasonable claim as a formulation of the
relation-difference that is the (reading of) tradition. But has
playfulness any more reason, any more authority, for it apparently
has none? It appears to be no rule at all, the arbitrary licence
of any reading at all; it subjects tradition to the wilfulness of
arbitrary reading, and constitutes it as the nihilism of speaking

anything at all, nothing in particular, and nothing at all.   Literalism abolishes morality in establishing a purely political 'society'
(totalitarianism) whereas playfulness abolishes any notion of
society, relationship tradition, whether moral or political in an
arbitrary individualist exercise of will (solipsism).   The moral
life of solipsism is suicide, that is, death.   But perhaps solipsism
is only the degeneration of playfulness;   perhaps it can have its
reason, can seek to preserve what it reads, can think its community
(as play), and can begin to find its morality in the violence of
critique, and the responsibility of interpreting.   On the other
hand, play must be with something, given that it is to transcend
that something;   it must confront a corpus, given that its reason
lies in the transformation of that corpus.   Initially, at least it
must take in hand a writing, with its named writer and named topics,
as a conventional and publicly available thing, in order to show what
such a thing can be turned to.   Within the polarities of literalism-
totalitarianism and playfulness-solipsism reflexive and dialectical
reading searches for itself, for its tradition.   It is within the
totalitarian Party version of Marx, and the solipsistic 'my version'
of Marx that reflexive and dialectical analysis tries to hear Marx
both as an occasion to search for its own tradition, and as itself an
interesting and exemplary way of searching for tradition.   In a
reading the writing is not dispensable;   in the search for tradition
the occasioning encounter with tradition is not only to be understood
as a dispensable occasion but is also comprehensible as an indispensable symbol of the search and perhaps of the grounds also.   Speech
can begin concretely by referring to anything- the reference and the
anything are dispensable, but that from which (and not to which)
speech speaks, that from which speech begins (analytically) is not
in any sense dispensable.   But the interesting and ambivalent issue
which underlies my present discussion is the extent to which and how
the concretely dispensable beginning can stand as a symbol of, or
can show in some way, the analytically indispensable beginning.

This issue does not arise in re-thinking the names (the writers,
the works, the concepts and theories) of the bulk of the sociological
tradition, blinkered in the security of its scientific project.
However, if we enlarge upon this tradition, and include names such as
those of Plato, Nietzsche and Hiedegger, not to mention Marx, then
the issue does arise.   These names (their works, their ideas) cannot
readily be treated as dispensable occasions for analysis, dispensable beginnings of the search for tradition.   Rather, in many
ways, they enable us to conceive of the very project of analysis at
all;   they have some grounding relationship to our project and aspirations;   they constitute the tradition we are searching for, or
perhaps the tradition in terms of which we ground our search for
tradition.   Perhaps our notion of tradition involves, then, the
idea that there exists a corpus of named works and ideas which speak
to the ground of thought at the same time as, or rather through the
(moral) fact of, occasioning thought and reading.

In relation to our concern for Marx, we are allowing for the possibility of the charge of exegetical characterization to be levelled
against it.   We are not reading as totalitarians or solipsists;   we
are not accepting that there is an authoritative version of what
Marxism is which commands assent;   neither are we assuming that Marx

either called for, or can reasonably be turned to the services of,
any reading whatsoever.   Rather we are at least engaging with some
kind of a conventional (that is political) consensus on what the main
features of Marxism are, that Marx said, and should be heard as saying this and not that.   And this particular decision on how to engage a reading stands not for a commitment to Marxism, but rather for
itself and for its own implications as a feature of the reflexive and
dialectical analytic project.   This is more of a principled way to
proceed initially in a reading than to accede to the horizonal polarities of literalism and playfulness.   To proceed in a more principled way is to make available one way of understanding the notion
that - 'it really doesn't matter' (whether we are reading Marx or
Comte or Heidegger).   It really doesn't matter in the sense that we
are not going to read them differently, or rather we are always going
to try to read initially for their own differences.   We are not
going to subject our reading of Marx to a literal version of him,
and then play about with Heidegger nor, conversely are we going to
subject our reading of Heidegger to a literal reading of him (although I have very little idea of what that could possibly mean
anyway), and then play about with Marx.   It really doesn't matter
whether we read Marx or Heidegger or any other name, what matters is
how and why we read.   That is, 'initially', how do we establish the
specificity of the writing; 'subsequently' how do we establish the
traditionality or unity of the writing?   Then 'ultimately' how (and
why) do we seek for unity, reason and tradition in the self-comprehension of a reflexive and dialetcital analytic enterprise?

In relation to Marx, then, we hear and acknowledge that he offers
us, as a possible version of reflexive and dialectical analysis, the
way of reading that is historical materialist critique; but we are
not saying, in saying this that we can accept this offer.   The offer
is made less acceptable by being discovered in the context of, and
related to, other problematics, for instance those of science (where
the reflexivity of reading-critique is made comprehensible as a
method of formulating the 'epistemological break' between science
and ideology) and political action (where the reflexivity of
reading-critique is subject to the pragmatic interests of polemic,
propaganda and de-bunking).

Science sets the standards of progress, enlightenment and determinism for speech; while political action requires the standards of
the proletarian delegate, the struggling militant, and the situated
inspiration as the standards of speech.   The security, the very
comprehensibility of those standards, however, remains unavailable
for questioning.   The situated inspiration, for instance, is a way
to read some of Marx's contemporary political analyses.   They could
be held to stand with the authority of the philosophical haiku, the
aphorism, the minimal statement, pointing beyond what they speak to
requiring (and propagating a certain version of) responsible readership.   The text that appears to report upon the class-struggle in
France in 1848 (24) for instance, can be read as reporting upon
its genesis, the desire to both analyse a situation as an example of
how to analyse any situation, and to locate the analysis as a part
of the situation, an (the) intellectual moment of the historical
situation.   The report about 1848 says that it was written in 1848;
read from 1948 or 2048, it says 'report about 1948 or 2048'; it

stands as a situated call, as an example of the situated formulation
of a situation which calls for situated formulations of situations.
But the paradox of the situated call is that while it appears to
command by commanding emulation, it can provide no method for doing
so, no criteria of emulation.   That is, emulation is a mode of
agreement and consensus, which is the political character of the
community required by science, where method provides for replicab-
ility and for a certain superficial notion of sameness and difference.   However, whether as science or as the situated call to action
Marxism makes little attempt to understand its own political character, where politics is understood as its ground, its form of life.
Partly this is because 'true' politics, politics as morality, human
community in freedom, is segregated, in Marxism, from any given
present as an indefinately postponeable but conceivably concretiz-
able future state of affairs.   We must presume that it is the difficulties in acknowledging statelessness/classlessness as the ground
of Marxism (as the allegedly class-determined and class-committed
theoretic-political practice and intervention of class-analysis) that
has led to it being rendered silent and forgotten.   Perhaps a concrete display of this analytic forgetfulness is the absence in
Marxist texts of what they would derogate as speculation about the
socialist utopia.   One way to awaken a self-critique of Marxism's
involvement with the certainties and commands of science and
political action might be to re-consider the character of its tradition as constituted in the difference that its speech makes, that
is its life in the difference that its critical reading makes.
Here this grounding difference would be understood as the outstanding
of its speech/reading from (that is, within) the (Western intellectual) tradition.

    Let us turn again to class and Marxism as class theorizing to try
to find a dialectic in the concept and the phenomenon which will
allow us to think again the difference-relation it occasions and
inaugurates between thing and theory, action and theory, occasion
and theory.   Initially, surely class is a thing, an object reality
in this our world? (Or, alternatively, depending on your tastes/
your commitments, the 'evidence' or what have you - surely class has
ceased to be an objective reality in modern society?).   Take the
former question and its implied assertion first.   What does it mean
to assert, implicitly or explicitly that class is a thing, an objective reality in this world?.   Does it mean that at any given
moment in history, in any specified community or society that there
exist distinct groups of men doing distinctive things?.   Does it
mean, as it does in organized education, that there exist classes
defined in space and time, such that a man could step into some
place at some point in time and be able to describe himself now as
being 'in class' and now as being 'out of class'?.   But this is too
crude, perhaps class is not a thing, or a number of things, but a
relation between two or more things.

    Thus in Marxist theorizing classes exist in relations founded on
the relations of production, between those who sell their labour-
power and those who buy it.   This is a step away from that treatment of class which makes it equivalent to stratification and hence
ultimately to the differentiation of concrete individual persons.
Class is something offered as equivalent to stratum, a rank, a

grade or a position in the world.   But if it is viewed as founded
in some kind of market relation, then it cannot be spoken of in
isolation from the class which it relates to, and from the process
of relating. (25)

We take a further step away from the reified theorizing and speech
which treats class, or whatever is spoken about, as a thing to be
described, if we can come to see class not only as relation between
two things in the world, but as constitutive of the world.   This
involves the theorizer/speaker/observer of class in what he addresses.
If he holds that all men's speech is always seeable as class speech,
then so also must be the speech which formulates such a possibility
universalistically.   Thus, whatever else is an instance of class,
this theorizing is. Apart from the way in which this raises the
issue of reflexivity, we can say that to step away from thinking
class as a thing is to entertain as intelligible the possibility of
thinking it as no-thing.   I will initially take no-thing in the
sense of non-existent.   To know that God is dead, or that a species
like the dodo is extinct it is necessary for their existence, or
possible existence, to be intelligible.   Reciprocally and conversely, to understand the nature of the existence of things in an objective world it is also necessary to understand their contingency,
the possibility of their non-existence, or so empiricism would tell
us.   And yet the non-existence of God, His death, is a form of his
meaningfulness, his presence and his existence for some.   Similarly
extinct-species live on as 'part of the past'.   Like any form of
memory or history, the past can be used to organize the present.
God and the extinct species exist sociologically in spite of their
apparently demonstrable physical absence.   Indeed they exist
through it, in the sense of possibly organizing social life, and of
possibly being used in the social ordering of thinking and acting.
Dead thinkers live in the thought of their texts, and societies can
organize themselves in terms of their word.

Class, also, can be said to exist in its absence.   Thus, although men sell their labour-power in modern industrial capitalism,
they need not be conscious of themselves as a class in relation to
those who buy their labour-power, and need not constitute the buyers
as a class either.   This is the theatre within which socialist and
revolutionary activism is played; the tragedy of the never-bridged
gap between - 'real' interests and 'false' interests, 'true' consciousness and 'false' consciousness, 'appearance' and 'essence',
(26) 'class in itself' and 'class for itself', 'Ideology' and
'scientific socialism'. (27) Talk of 'the working class', 'the
proletariat' and so on in this theatre, and in the academic, economic and political scenes and situations of which it consists, can
never be only to do description of a thing in the world.   Whatever
else it is, given that it is anything else at all, it is at least
helping within the organization of the project to bridge the gap:
Describing does work within the revolutionary project; describing
class is a contribution to the work of bringing class about as
class-consciousness.   As science it is the project (or in more
Marxist-Leninist terms, it is the political intervention to produce the
confirmation of its own prediction: of the science of historical
materialism in a particular conjuncture through the Party); as
morality and politics it is the project to heed its own rule, to

obey its own commandments; as religion it is the project to enact
its own prophecy.   Class theorizing, however it is viewed, in
describing class as in the world can only be talking to the world's
possibilities; description of class does the work of willing a world
describable as classed.

So, class as absence has been attested to within revolutionary
theatre as the project/drama of bridging, in relation to situations
where men are involved in selling their labour-power.   But it has
also been attested to in situations where the market and indeed the
society has virtually ceased to exist, in the concrete sense that its
membership has been dispersed, and is dying or dead.   If the proletariat ceases to exist - as in the early post-revolutionary period
in Russia, through famine, militarization and de-classing into the
peasantry - contemporary uses of the term could hardly have had a
descriptive rationale; 'dictatorship of the proletariat', the party
as 'vanguard of the proletariat' become expressions of the will to
maintain a certain theoretical practice, a certain organization of
life, in the midst of chaos and threat. (28) They become expressions of a will to keep the present safe for the sake of the future,
when the proletariat would not only be re-established in its original,
minority, place, but would also become the society through industrialization and the proletarianization of the masses.

Class as concrete absence attests to its character as the commitment and will, not to describe the world but to constitute the describable character of the world, that is to theorize.   Class as
absence attests to the practice of theorizing, the decision to see
the world as classed, the commitment to speak the language of class.
And class, as reflexive upon this decision, as constituted in this
decision, is, and could be, no-thing, no object in the world.   It is
no object in the world not in the sense that it has ceased to be one
or has yet to become one, but in the sense that it is in its theoretical practices; that is, it is in and through men's practices of
ordering their thinking and their speaking, their lives, in terms of
it, and in its terms.   To speak of class is not to report upon a
thing in the world but to 'report upon' the speaking of class; it is
to reflexively utilize class as the grounds of speaking at all, as
the reason and resource for speaking, it is to show class. (29)

Before we get further into these issues, and ultimately into the
reflexive character of this piece of writing or showing class let me
say something about the reflexive character of Marx's speech about
class as showing class.   In the final analysis I want to say that
not only is class no-thing for Marx - in that he conceives it as
theoretical practice(s), and as his theoretical practice(s) - but
also that the rationality, the 'telos' of class as no-thing is to
become no-thing. (3) That is, Marx's class-analysis utilizes class
as the grounds for thinking class; it thinks class in order to enact
the class-conscious society, the revolutionary society; and it contributes towards and desires the revolutionized society in order to
provide the possibilities for class-less living, for class-less
theorizing and speaking.

Marx's class-analysis, in so far as it does so at all, formulates
itself as another instance of what it refers to.   That is, unlike
nineteenth-century political economy and twentieth-century

structuralist sociology, which formulated themselves as scientific, objective and neutral, forms of theorizing, ostensibly disconnected from every social order, and unable to see themselves as a social order, Marx's analysis of class presents itself as a class analysis of class; it is the theorizing of the proletariat.   Whatever other claims it also makes about scientificity (31) and objectivity, Marx's analysis of class is presented as being grounded in, made intelligible by, reflexive upon, and a further instance of that about which it theorizes, i.e. class.   We are invited to read Marx this way. What are some ways in which we can take up this invitation?

The world Marx produces in his theorizing is a world in the making, tearing and twisting in its contradictions, forming and reforming, being negating and becoming itself in time, evolving in revolutions towards some kind of fruition, maturity or end. (32) He explicitly conceives of an internally contradictory reality when he describes the class-struggle involving the exploitation of surplus-value.   On the one hand this reality tends towards organizing itself as large-scale production (oligopoly and monopoly), and a labour movement founded on workers' trade unions, while on the other hand it tends towards formulating and theorizing itself in terms of freedom, possessive individualism (33), democracy, and indeed in terms of the abolition of classes and the end of ideology. Marx's class-struggle endures in and through the ongoing struggle between a practical constituting of classes in the sphere of economic production and an ideological deconstituion (into a collection of atomic individuals) in the sphere of theoretical production. But ultimately and strictly speaking the latter sphere is the true locus for Marx's class-struggle;   that is, a class is a class in so far as it becomes conscious of itself as such, and in so far as it organizes itself and acts politically in pursuit of its interests as a class.   Thus, as well as class becoming constituted in the production of use and exchange values, it is crucially constituted in its political consciousness of itself in the relations of production.   Class constitutes itself;   class exists in its conscious class practices;   class is class-ing or class-ifying.

Marx's class-analysis presents itself explicitly as existing in a struggle with bourgeois thought's de-classifying tendencies and purposes.   It exists as a theoretical intervention in political life, in the theoretical sphere, as an attempt to bring about the proletariat as a class-conscious class-for-itself.   Marx classifies analytically in order to bring about a classified world, which in turn constitutes the possibility of engaging in non-class-ifying theorizing (in socialism classes will cease to exist in the sense that it will be unintelligible to think them).

Marx's class-analysis, then, if read as the formulation of a factual and describable world (i.e. if read as 'describing the world') becomes its own positivist revision: it becomes revisable. Rather it is best seen as the formulation of a created/re-creatable world containing possibilities of transformation, and as an attempt to transform that world, to realize its possibilities.   In this sense it is a continual attempt to analytically produce the concrete in the service of analysis;   that is, it is a continual attempt to negate itself in the service of its supercession.

Abbe Sieyes said of the class which made the French Revolution,

that the third estate is 'nothing' but wants to be 'something': (34)
paraphrasing that we may say of Marx that he held that the proletariat is nothing and wants to become nothing. (35) He speaks from a
world in which the proletariat was to become no-thing by transforming itself from being an object, through consciousness and theorizing, and he speaks on behalf of that transformation. Further, he
spoke to a future possible society in which the proletariat would
negate itself through revolutionary universalization; from being
the negating no-thing in relation to the bourgeoisie it would become
the self-negated class-less society in which it would be nothing,
nothing there, concretely, and nothing that could analytically
occasion or ground speech.

Let me now make some remarks about Marx's showing of class before
coming at the problematic of showing in a different and more direct
way.   In what ways could it be said that Marxism shows its class?
In what ways is it a class-ifying practice?   This could be taken as
- How does Marxism show itself, its theorizing as having class, as
being classy, that is to say as good, worthy and authoritative
theorizing?   Or it could be taken as the performative question -
How does Marxism do or enact class, that is by classification, by
class consciousness?   The former is the more intriguing and possibly
deeper question, but I will restrict my remarks to the latter.
Marxism does or enacts class in at least two ways.   First, it
classifies the classes it thinks.   That is, it assigns them super
and sub-ordinate positions in relation to each other in a rank
ordering system which is constituted by the dialectical development
of history.   Thus, while it is true that there have always been
ruling classes (and that there will continue to be so until the
abolition of classes in socialism and arguably until the withering
away of the state in ultimate communism), they get 'better' in many
respects as history unfolds through its stages.   The bourgeoisie,
for instance, are to be seen as economically, technologically,
politically and even morally superior to Asian despotism or feudal
monarchy.   And the revolutionary proletariat are to transform and
transcend bourgeois society and culture in its turn, that is it is
to enact its relative superiority. (36)   Second, Marxism classifies
itself as the articulate expression of that which it has thought as
the highest and most superior class;   the highest class, the best,
expresses itself in the highest class of theorizing, the best way
of living and thinking (or, in 'modern' versions, as the only truly
scientific theorizing of social formations).   Marxism, the class-
ifying thought of class, is 'high class' in the preposterous achieve-
ments answering to its preposterous claims.   Indeed, perhaps its
claims to speak the truth and to speak on behalf of the future, its
will to transform the world, cannot be evaluated, but only grasped
and comprehended in outline, unless heard through an analysis of the
theories and practices concretized under Lenin and Mao, which
analysis cannot be undertaken here.

But what is it for Marx to show no-thing, to show what is absent,
not only in society, but in his concrete speech?   In spite of its
many presences in Marx's texts, his notion of class (like his notions
of party, state, ideology, future communist society and science) is
just as noticeable by its absence.   It is used in a variety of
contexts, but the possibility and the intelligibility of these uses

is rarely explicitly addressed.   However this apparent lack of reflexivity on Marx's part can be read as necessary and as exemplary.
Thus it is possible to see the absence of a theory of class on the
part of Marx as a writer in his call to his readers to think class
from their own historical and social situation.   Class as absence
then becomes intelligible as Marx's recognition of the dialectic of
reading and writing, his recognition of the reader's theoretic responsibilities to provide self-transformative readings.   The self-
transformation of responsible readership is here recognized, then,
as providing for the possibility of the historical and political
constitution of the class, as a self-conscious and transforming
collective agency.

Put in less abstract terms, how could Marx be required to 'spell
it all out' for his reader if he is involved in calling upon the
reader to think and act the revolution, that is, to prop gate a
certain way of seeing the world, and to organize politically and
industrially.   He cannot speak to the reader's concrete historical
situation.   But he can call upon the reader to do so by showing him
how he, Marx, can read a contemporary situation as a class situation.
(37) If Marx's class-analysis is to speak to a readership to transform the world, if it is to transform the world through the word
(above all else), then it must be exemplary.   Marx's 'Eighteenth
Brumaire' is lost to us if we read it as corresponding to, representing, or describing some set of historical events.   It is as well,
and primarily, a call - 'do likewise in your here and now' - and as
such it cannot tell us of its methods, it can only show us and
exemplify its commitments. (38)

What point have we reached in our discussion?   We have turned to
Marxism, and its accessibility in order to help us re-think what re-
thinking the sociological tradition might involve.   The point we
have reached is that of fraternally characterizing some of the
problems that a re-think of Marxism might involve; but such characterization only has weight in so far as it shows another interest,
that of what reflexive and dialectical analysis could be.   Bearing
this in mind, let us look further (but even more briefly) at class.

It is possible to think the intelligibility of class in terms of
the notion of thing on the one hand, and in terms of the notion of
theory on the other.   That is to say, class speaks of alienation
and dichotomy.   It speaks of contradiction as its way of speaking of
dialectic, synthesis and unity.   The dichotomies in terms of which
it can be located are numerous; consider for instance, mind-matter,
subject-object, idealism-materialism, reason-will, theory-practice,
master-slave, besides theory-thing as dichotomous schemas which
have been and can be used to formulate any and every kind of concrete social difference, including class as a concrete difference.
(39) We take class analytically to index such deeper dichotomous
intelligibilities which authorise and make provision for its sense
in the scenes, interests and times of its concrete uses.

In so far as class is the thing (here in the sense of the kind of
society) that contains within it the future of classlessness, then
we may consider the thinghood of class to be different from the
thinghood of things.   Class is the thing grounded in dichotomy
which tends towards classlessness as the transcendence of dichotomy,
and as the self-grounding, the transparently rational and free unity

of men with men and with the physical world, the end (or beginning) of history, the presence of the unity of Being.   Inscribed in the history of the thing, the differentiated being, class, is the destiny of thingness, the undifferentiated, Being; or so it would appear in the class/difference/dichotomy thought of Marx/Hegel.   One way of conceiving of this is as follows; the existent being, the thing present, that is class tends to bring to presence and to the present, the thought of class that is to negate it; that is, the presence of this thing presences the no-thing, the absence that is thought. And class-consciousness (the thing's no-thing, the presencing's absence), itself tends to bring to presence classlessness (the thing's ultimate no-thing, the presencing's ultimate absence).   In this view, the object world progressively unfolds itself as con- taining (inter) subjectivity, and as becoming subject to (inter) subjectivity.   Just as science is the self-conscious moment of nature's progressive development, so socialism is the self-conscious moment of man-nature's progressive unification.   The unconscious induces the conscious, the deterministic induces the voluntaristic. The history of the class-struggle re-enacts the movement of the phenomenology of mind, and that is so not abstractly but on every occasion that the thought of class is taken up.

The thinker initially encounters the sociological externality of class.   Classes are conceived of as realities 'out there' in the 'real world'.   They are themes that are literally readable in the world's text, its significations and meanings.   They are things that passively resist attempts to alter them or to think them away; they are encountered as active in many respects also; they 'rule'; they send certain percentages of the population they structure to university and to prison, to Beethoven and to Rock; their units multiply and die at characteristically different rates; and these units speak with different accents and perform different roles in the economy.   Of course, formulating 'reality' as 'out there' derogates the site and the point of the speech of formulation to the status of a non-situated spectatorship, as does attempting to ground the speech of formulation in literal reading and the world's literal readability.   However, having ventured the thought that classes may be things, it is conceivable that thought may turn itself to the character of the relationships that exist between these different- iated and external entities.   And here it might encounter cause, rule, exploitation, oppression and sufferance.   But the ground of such relationships are consciousness action and speech.   That is, the thinghood of classes may be located through the character of their interrelationships to their consciousness, of themselves as classes, which is to say their consciousness of themselves as an Other to an other, their consciousness of one form of relationship as difference, alienation. (40)   Existence in conscious activity, of which speech might be taken to be both an important constitutive feature and an important model or metaphor, provides for the poss- ible sense of the political existence of classes, as the speeches of a bifurcated 'polis', the speeches of mutual comprehension but mutual antogonism.   But then would class be no more than the political and theoretical organization and commitment which sustains the sense of class and propagates it in a political and politicizing community? Would class then be equivalent to the difference that will and

idea(1) constitute and make, that is the difference between the concrete now and the concrete future, realized by means of the idea(1)
of a classless society, and the will to power to enact the revolutionary transformation. (41)

Initially the thinker of class encountered the presence of an
external fact.   He thus encountered differentiation, the difference
among presences, facts, and also the difference, required by the
notion of externality, between itself, external facticity and the
non-situatedness of theorizing as spectatorship.   That is he encountered the difference among objectivities, and between objectivity and subjectivity.   This introduced him to a set of possible
formulations which also contain (whether or not as culmination as
here presented), class as theorizing (here as idea and will) and
thus the difference between the being of man and of the world as
that between subjectivity and objectivity.

But this way with theorizing provides no model or standard for
reflexive and dialectical theorizing.   The understanding of class
as theorizing implicitly involves a derogation of theorizing in so
far as theorizing is tied to subjectivity and the subjection and
subjectivization, otherwise understood as the humanization, of the
world.   Theorizing is subject to the existence of the object; that
is, it is derogated by being understood merely as a means in relation to the existence of the world, the presence of things, here
their transformation and construction.   Theorizing, by appearing in
this subject - object, mind - matter, dichotomous version of difference, degenerates into technology.   Thus, theorizing is used as the
means, technique or method for constructing a new society, a new
speech and a new world.   That is to say, theorizing is the technique of construction of society as the new stasis, the new status
quo, socialism, during the course of which construction it will exhaust itself and be dispensable; class theorizing anticipates less
the withering away of class and the state, but rather the withering
away of theorizing.   Class theorizing is as well the anticipation
of the forgetting of theorizing as the remembering of grounds, in
the course of the construction of new social knowledge on the basis
of an artificial and constructionist way with language.   And
finally theorizing as class theorizing is the technique, which as
science, services the transformation of the natural world into
energy, produce and supply for the social order.

Class has occasioned our thought of difference as thing-theory
and subject-object, in the following two sections we will look at
how it can occasion thought of difference as that of morality-
politics (D) and beings-Being and speech-Language (E).

D.   CLASS AND THE MORALITY-POLITICS DIFFERENCE

Thinking, in forms of social organization where that is treated as
a special and professional activity, is always threatened with
collapse into the thoughtless.   Theorizing, that which is extraordinary, is always threatened with what it is not, but what it can
become in these forms of social life, that is the mechanical and the
ordinary.   Theories, instead of attesting to theorizing, can become
things to be described, used, unpacked, toyed with, and passed on.

In modern forms of life the accumulation of great numbers of these
things, and the natural selection between them, survival of the
fittest things, is called progress.

In sociology as elsewhere theories can and do become things near
at hand; they become only what is called 'useful' and are no longer
evocative, pointing to and calling for thought.   To decide to re-
think 'theories' is not necessarily to put them out of hand's reach,
rather it is to re-awaken their nearness, to see just how familiar
they are; it is at least not to treat them as a thing.   I have
talked about class theories, particularly Marx's, in the sense of
being no-thing, which is a way of avoiding treating Marx in a forgetful way as familiar.   Another move to avoid forgetting class, to
re-awaken its nearness to hand, to avoid it as a familiar thing, is
to see it in everyday talk.   Everyday talk is not thoughtless as
science is, by doing special theory about special things, but never-
theless it incarnates forgetfulness, the familiar, and utilization
of thinking as a means to hand.   However, in the context of a reflexive analytical interest everyday talk of class can speak to that
interest.

Consider a difference, which I will return to in a moment as a
trouble, between two collections of uses of the term 'class'.
1. 'This/that shows class'; 'That's classy'; 'I'm not up to that
class'; 'We're nowhere near that class'. 2. 'They come from a
different class to us'; 'They are very conscious of their class';
'It is typical of that class to do something like that to us';
'That class always looks after its own'.   Initially we may characterize the former as a set of usages which have a moral character in
so far as they treat class as quality, as an ideal other, a good, an
other to be understood by being valued, an other that shows itself
through a variety of appearances and situations.   And the second
set are political in that they treat class as a concrete other, a
power to be reckoned with and calculatively evaluated an other to be
negotiated with, and thus understood politically, something which
lies fully graspable, quantitatively, in its appearances.   Understood literally and positively Marxist class theorizing helps us to
understand only the second set of political uses of class; but
understood dialectically and reflexively such theorizing helps us to
attend to speech not only as political speech, but as moral speech
also.   I will return to Marxist class theorizing as an occasion to
attend to the grounded character of speech seen as its moral and
educational character later in this section.

First I want to say something about the problematic character of
finding and holding to a difference between what is moral and what
is political at all.   The phenomenon of class makes available at
least the phenomenon of differentiation; my discussion is responsible to its apparent topic, class, in so far as it is responsible for
that which its topic makes available as a theme, that is differentiation.   My discussion can be responsible to this theme by listening for differentiation in the play of speech, for instance between
what speech speaks and what it shows, as we have already argued.
Some class speeches, such as those mentioned above, allow us to see
a differentiation between those which formulate the class phenomenon as that which stands there in the calculable and quantitative
features of its appearances, and those which formulate the class

phenomenon as that which underlies and shows itself through the
qualitative features of appearances.   I have called the differentiation that between moral and political ways of theorizing, of speaking.   But the differentiation, and my/theorizing's appreciation of
it must always of necessity be problematic.

Any use of class in speech, such as 'That shows class' can be
collected under moral or political auspices.   Such speech can
occasion either kind of theorizing and theoretical speech.   The
ambiguity of class, as the differentiation phenomenon, permitting of
moral or political interpretation, is present also with speeches
which formulate any other quantity-quality, might-right, or even
appearance-essence differences and oppositions.   In particular note
here the set 'superiority', 'authority' and 'mastery', and their
respective oppositions of 'inferiority' and 'subjection' (42).   Thus,
the difference that class is and shows, and the difference that
grounds my speech on class, is seeable as the difference between
superiority/authority/mastery and inferiority/subjection taken on the
one hand as political and on the other hand as moral.

It is over-emphatic, but let me call the political 'military' and
the moral 'educational' for a moment.   Thus, political mastery/
authority/superiority is like the command by the commander in an
army, and political inferiority/subjection is like the hearing and
obeying by the commanded soldier.   And on the other hand moral
mastery/authority/superiority is like the showing of a good teacher
(a teacher of the good), while moral inferiority/subjection is like
the seeing (and the showing of the seeing), and like the hearing (and
the speaking), of a good student.

The school of politics is an alienated school, where mastery has
the resource 'Don't do as I do, do as I say', which alienates theory,
thought and language from their togetherness as action with action.
Politics abolishes discourse in abolishing the possibility of
questioning mastery.   Morality equates itself with discourse, the
dialectic of teaching and learning, speaking and hearing;   moral
mastery enacts itself as that which is open to question.   And all
this is not to deny that morality has made an historical appearance
in the degenerate form of moralizing and of the unquestionable
command, whether of God in the Judeo-Christian tradition, or of
Reason's 'Categorical Imperative' in the post-Kantian tradition. (43)

Speech shows its difference from silence, grounds and from the
speaker, his actions and his intentions.   Speech concretely happens
in dialogue where two speakers take turns to address and listen to
each other.   Analytically the only other that speech needs is the
tradition, and the only self that a speaker needs is the self that
theoretic speech provides in its discourse with tradition.   The
self's discourse with tradition should be moral, or in the deepest
sense education;   the other (the tradition) learns and develops and
so does the speaker (i.e. committed speech) who learns more about
the nature of his commitment, the standard of good speech, and notion
of community or sociality that involves.   Community (society)
presupposes communication (speech), and that presupposes the
sociality of self-other dialogue and dialectic (Language and Being
as the dialectic of difference-identity/unity/relatedness).   The
good society is to be understood as grounded in good speech, and in
the good or value of speech, which in turn is grounded in good

sociality and the good of dialectic.   Good sociality can be seen
as educational, and is as much the attended resource of reflexive
and dialectical theorizing as its topic and theme.

We can consider the contrast, the difference, between educational
and political sociality a little further for a moment.   Political
thought, speech and action can be understood as deviation from and
defiance of the standard of good speech and of commitment to it,
where good speech is educative speech which studies and learns of its
groundedness in the ontological difference, between beings and Being,
speech and language.   It is a concretization of self and society and
a conversion of them into concrete entities which can be placed in a
means-ends relation, and in a master-slave relation.   It is a relation of calculation and domination.   The speech of such a relation
formulates the difference between concrete action/self/speaker and
speech in order to dominate: e.g. 'Don't do as I do, do as I say'.
Here speech produces a speaker and a listener, (the explicit 'I' and
the implied 'you') and subjects itself and its standards to the
intentions of its concrete speaker.   The speech subjects itself to
the concrete intention to concretize a 'you'/hearer who doesn't
speak, but only hears and obeys, and furthermore who can differentiate speech from action (in particular the speaker's speech from
the speaker's actions, which, implicitly belie the former).   It is
difficult to see how, in such a political world the command could be
obeyed, for it says, 'make a difference between action and speech,
and subject the former to the rule of the latter'.   However, this
message comes from a source which has its speech belied and under-
mined by its actions, which is hypocritical and in bad faith, which
knows that this will show itself, and which feels that it has to
make explicit reference to this knowing.   Of course, whether it
makes explicit reference to it or not, the hypocrisy of political
domination cannot but show itself.

One rule of politics, 'divide and rule' means 'divide in order to
rule successfully'.   For an analytic of politics this can be understood not as a rule for the treatment of some political objects, or
for the politicizing of some objects, but rather as the standard of
political speech.   It says, 'be forgetful' 'make differences', 'be
hypocritical', 'speak but don't listen', 'divorce intentions from
speech from actions'.   It holds rule, law, the 'polis', to be
dependent upon differentiation, on division, on classing.   The
political world, political speech, begins with and in difference,
and this is a beginning which it does not and cannot re-trieve without changing its character, for its head is turned away from its
speech, in the direction of the efficacy of its actions, particularly
the efficacy of its will to dominate.   Not only men, but speeches
also, are no more than a means.   The differentiation of means-ends
which speech generates and makes comprehensible is used as the
standard against which to judge the 'worth', which is to say the
utility and efficacy of speech;   while speech and language as ground
are ignored and repressed.

The speech, sociality and relation-difference of education is the
opposite.   Here speech provides for the differentiation of speaker
and hearer in order to posit their belonging-togetherness, so speech
if it gathers itself around a speaker-notion, gathers itself around
that of the teacher.   But this teacher is such that he recognizes

the beyond of speech, the unsaid, and the unsayable, so that his
speaking is a showing and a pointing beyond.   He thus utilizes
silence and action as differences and beyonds of speech, as symbols
for the grounding beyond of Being.   Educational speech and sociality generates a teacher which is the unity of thought, speech and
action, and which puts its speaking to the service of this speaker-
identity-unification, as a way of putting speech to the service
of showing Language/Being, the undifferentiated, the identifying-
unifying.   'I do what I say', thus formulates a concrete notion of
integrity, as against the bad faith of the political 'Don't do what
I do, do what I say'; and this stands as a symbol for togetherness,
identity, and the undifferentiated; and its address to the learner
it formulates is a call for the undifferentiated to be seen through
the difference of speech.

There is a further disclosure of notions of morality and education in the following notion, available to an Other for understanding the sociality required by Self's speech.   Other, as dialectical antithesis can say: 'You speak, but actions speak louder
than words'.   Concretely this counsels silence and mute activity.
But this apparent distrust of words/speech shows a deeper trust of
speech.   It shows, 'keep your word', where the threat is that if
Self's word is not kept by him then its communicating (community
showing) character will be threatened - which is to say that the
word he is to keep was always already 'ours', and that as speaker
his duty to keep his word is another way of formulating the commitment of speakers to the possibilities of community sense and intelligibility.   For Self to keep his word is for him to reaffirm
the sharability of speech and thus to reaffirm sociality.

Concretely actions do not speak, they can only be said to express
(using the dubious inside-outside schema implied by ex-press) such
things as intelligible intentions, or better, to display what it is
to follow some social and speakable concept and rule.   But reflexively and dialectically they can be found as already founded meanings, recovered as covered and uncoverable speech possibilities.
Thus 'speaking acts' and enacts the possibility of the acts which
are then and thus able to be heard as speaking.   But speech enacts
more, it puts into play, or releases into time and space, history
and society, the play of language as the ground of speech; speech,
in acting, shows language as ground.   Thus 'language speaks' - and
indeed 'language speaks louder than words', for 'language speaks
louder and more than speaking'.   To hear language we must listen for
more than speech in the occurrences of speech; however it is through
and beyond those occurrences that language comes to be heard.   Actions don't speak louder than words, only as loud as them, for what
speaks louder than both, through both, is language.

The Other, hearing actions speaking louder than words may be
being politicized and be coming to accept the analytic silence of
political speech and sociality.   Or he may be realizing an educational sociality, listening for integrity, and word-keeping, integrity
and the unity beyond and grounding any speech.   We need to be careful in thinking this through not to posit a difference between speech
and act in order to provide for the possibility of a grounding unit
which is purely mathematical, and thus which treats speech and acts
as basically equivalent and identical by equation; speech equals

action: action equals speech.   But the unity, identity and relationship we answer to whenever we speak and theorize, that from
which we have always already learned, cannot be taken in hand mathematically as equation in this way.   We answer to, and have always
already learned from 'logos', not its neutered and stunted (though
currently philosophically charismatic) offspring, logic.   What is
truly social, truly educational, is not to be found in logic which
speaks the power of calculative human will, nor in politics, which
speaks the power of manipulative and dominating human will.   It is
rather to be found in that listening again to that which allows us to
speak and theorize, whether logically, politically or in whatever
fashion.   What is truly social and educational is to be found in
that which educates and socializes man, and that is man's being-open
to Being in his being-in-language.

One way of formulating my organizing problem in this analysis,
then, could be said to be that of the relationship between moral or
political mastery on the one hand and moral studentship or political
slavery on the other.   In collecting my thoughts, in getting it together, in gathering my wits about me, I turn to the voices of the
unruly and unharmonic chorus that make up what I can make out of the
tradition(s) of Western thought.   Some voices I hear louder than
others as speaking to the way difference appears to me, and as speaking to the supercession of difference in the life of discourse and
dialectic.   But those who speak loudest can be heard to speak at
least in the two ways with which I am most concerned.   That is, they
can be heard to speak as moral masters, in which case one can come to
learn, one can come to hear them better.   Or, alternatively, they
can be heard as political masters, in which case one has to think
through the social life their speeches organize.   And here I have to
think the problem that any reader has to face; what is it to be a
master with them, and what is it to be a slave – within their community, but apart from them, an object in their gaze, speechless in
their discourse?.

This is the problem for any hearer of teachers like Plato and the
pre-Socratics, Hegel and Marx, Nietzsche and Heidegger.   In lieu of
unpacking this problem in relation to these teachers any further,
which is beyond the scope of what I can do here, let me offer some
surface remarks.

The Greeks give us the originary unity and togetherness of thought
and being through language;   they teach us to think through and
beyond alienated and dichotomized speech, which we could call the
speech of class.   But they theorize a dichotomous community none
the less, a 'polis' (or class, in the Roman sense of 'classis' or
assembly) in which only some men can speak, and in which only some
men can hear.   We need not say that Plato implicitly presupposed a
slave economy, it is enough that he explicitly proposed a classed,
functional hierarchy as his way of formulating the ideal or the rule
of, philosophy, justice and the vision of the good.   (44)   Parmenides, who envisaged no 'polis', explicitly at least, generated the
bifurcation between those men (-gods) who follow the Way of Truth
and those men (-mortals) who follow the Way of Illusion.   (45)   At
least, unlike Plato, he gave us no hint as to whether or not the
Way of Truth could only ever be open to some elite seers and speakers, whose 'raison d'etre' is to rule the 'polis' for the good of

the whole.   What can be seen in Plato can be seen just as explicitly in that fundamental critic of the dichotomous master-slave
thought of the whole Judeo-Christian tradition, Nietzsche.   His
supercession of dichotomy reinstates and requires a new dichotomy,
between ultimate man and superman.   (46)

We can read Plato, Parmenides and Nietzsche as moral masters,
teachers, whether philosophizing on behalf of Oneness, or whether
excoriating dichotomy and difference.   But to hear them as political
masters is to hear concrete difference and dichotomy speak;   it is to
hear a call for extraordinary speech to differentiate itself, or to
sound in the space of its evident difference, from ordinary speech.
The moral call for superiority as excellence is too easily translat-
able into the political call for superiority as a rule, which destroys the 'polis' as discourse.   Political rule irresponsibly vac-
illates between two contradictory modes of unintelligibility.   That
is, it formulates its groundless, unquestionable character either in
terms of what we may call, borrowing from Weber, traditional or
charismatic authority, respectively, the authority of 'It is written
..... therefore .....', or 'It is written ... but I say unto you'.
(47)

Of course we may choose not to hear great speakers of Western
thought as political speakers but yet still to be political with
them;   that is we may decide to select, to hear them for pragmatic
and utilitarian purposes, as hooks upon which to hang ideas we want
to call our own.   There may be a claim in this that such hearing, in
its apparently active and participatory character, is morally responsible and thoughtful.   But this, to repeat what was suggested in
an earlier context, as arbitrary playfulness reveals itself as only
responsible to will, to the power to ex-press Self and to manipulate
Other or Tradition;   and this is a form of a-moral politicking.
Class in Marxist theorizing offers us an occasion to give thought to
the difference between speech and the grounds of speech as the difference between moral-educational ground-seeking and ground-showing
speech on the one hand and political ground assuming and ground-
forgetting speech on the other.   The understanding of Marxist theorizing as a moral discourse and enterprise is made available reflexively and dialectically when we read Marx as not only not exempting
his speech concerning th e class-groundedness of the tradition's
speech, (German philosophy, English political economy and French
socialism), but as definitely affirming his own class-grounded
character, where this also involves the notion of his class, the
proletariat as the universal class, and of their 'telos', socialism
as classless sociality.

On the other hand the understanding of Marxist theorizing as a
political discourse and enterprise is made available reflexively and
dialectically when Marx is read as founding a new science.   Thus he
may be treated as making a complete 'break', 'epistemological' or
otherwise, with 'ideology' as the tradition of theoretical and
politico-moral discourse.   This reminds us that Marxism, like the
other major modern sociology, conventional scientific sociology, may
be understood as neology.   In this context this is as much a display of political will as it is of epistemological possibility to
found a new discourse, a new way with language.   But this forgets
its own self-proclaimed grounds in dialectic.   Thus there is dia-

lectic in any claim to newness which necessarily already utilizes and requires to be understood its difference from the old; and the newness of the new only persists as long as does its retention of this difference from the old. The revolution, whether in consciousness or in action, is thus only truly conceivable dialectically, as a continuing encounter and engagement with tradition, and thus as a moral and educational enterprise. It is undialectical to conceive the revolution as animated by, and as a propagation of, socialism as political stasis. Revolutionary speech and action would then be grounded only by a political ideal of socialism as the artifically constructable end of (pre-) history. But the end of history (pre- or not) is also the end of the revolution, and the end of the moral and educational possibilities for transforming the social into anything more than the political, that is, as anything more than oriented to the univocal speech of domination and control.

Class and its Marxist theorizing allows us an occasion once again to re-think the difference between political sociality and moral educational sociality as the difference between the theoretic and speech life of monologue and that of dialogue respectively. And it allows us to reaffirm, as sociologists, hearers of the 'logos' of the social, our commitment to dialogue, to that by which we, our speech, any anyman's speech are always already committed.

E.   CLASS AND THE ONTOLOGICAL DIFFERENCE: beings-BEING: speech-LANGUAGE

What difference is class?   What difference does it make?   So far we have thought of, and theorized within, the movement, the dialectic from class as thing to class as theory (section C), and between morality/education and politics. We can now try to think of class in terms of the Ontological Difference in the course of bringing our remarks on class and difference to a close. Ontologically the difference that the thought of classlessness could be interpreted as making would be that of helping to inaugurate the 'step-back' in re-trieval of a sense of the 'ontological difference' between being and Being. (48) Since class can figure as the name of a class or of a universal concept on the one hand, and also as the name of a class member or a particular, on the other, it can be used as a metaphor either for beings or for Being, but we will use it here as a metaphor for the former and for the Difference rather than for Being.

A being, such as class, is. It is something, it exists, it has being, it is present. A being is not is-ness, thingness, presence; it is not Being. On the other hand, Being is not as beings, but it is not apart from them. Only beings are; Being is not; rather Being means the is-ness, the are-ness, the presence of beings. Being is not a lump, a plenitude; neither is it a heap, everything, all things, the totality of things, totality. It is not a fullness, because beings are what are fully and exhaustively there present. But Being is not absent from them in their presence, it is not a negation. Rather it is together with them as their presence, as the thingness-presencing of things. If Being is, then it is as the difference between everything and things, between Being as Totality and beings; Being (thingness) grounds the difference between everything and things, and allows the difference between (every)thing and thingness to show itself in this difference.

Being cannot be dialectic as an (external) process organizing Totality; (49) nor can it be mere will and mere method or mere reason (internally) organizing its speech as a movement from parts to wholes and back again, or as a movement from the abstract to the concrete, and so forth. (50) Tradition and Language/Logos come near to Being (mis) understood as Totality, which would allow for a closer understanding of Being as the withinness of speech in terms of Totality as horizon. But it is closer still, and therefore more difficult to understand, to conceive Being as the happening, the presencing of this withinness. For speech, that is the withinness-ing of speech, is an ex-stasis from the horizonality of the unknow-able (untotalizable) fullness and plenitude of the Totality of the common language, with its etymological and metaphorical depths and play, its historicality, situatedness and openness.

Speech stands out in the light of Being - there - in - Language. It announces its difference from the Totality of Language, the Tradition, or Logos.   I want to formulate this here as the 'within-ness' of speech.   That is, speech speaks its withinness from Language/tradition; speech 'shows' its 'withinness' as its relation to Language/tradition or as its relation to everything sayable, Totality.   We take note, as sociologists, of what Auden said was the duty of the poet - to preserve the language. (51) This I take to mean, for sociology, the duty to show the showing character of speech, the duty to think the withinness of speech in its relation to/difference from Language/Totality as horizonal.   Thinking this withinness of speech in relation to/difference from tradition means to think tradition as partly creativity, development and change, and partly remembering and reaffirming, but not as ritualistic re-petition or exegesis.   It is in this area that difficult problems arise.   As was noted earlier in the paper we must not arbitrarily construct, sport with, and masterfully will, the character of tra-dition when we are explicitly recursive upon it.   Thus, to emphasize the character of a reading of Plato or Marx, as merely 'my version', to present a reader with 'my Marx, my Plato', is to endanger the committed and authoritative character of one's own speech.   On the other hand, to go in for literalist readings is to reify and con-cretely repeat the tradition instead of taking on, as the traditions own duty, the duty to re-think it. (52)

So preserving the language - as the poet (Auden) and the poetiz-ing philosopher (Heidegger) would have us do - is discoursing with tradition creatively, and gathering thought towards its standing-out from its grounds (thought's ex-stasis), the gathered-gathering; it is to gather thought in recognition of its difference from, but to-getherness with what is undifferentiated, the unifying-synthesizing of Being.   Speech, standing out in the light of its difference, its withinness, in relation to Language/Being/Tradition, is the happen-ing of the latter, in that it breaks with silence, nothingness, death.   Being happens as the unsayable horizon of speech when speech breaks the silence of thoughtlessness.   The unsayable shows itself and its superiority to the nihilistic silence of thoughtless-ness when it presences itself in discourse and speech. (59)

To say all of this is to speak at one remove from the consider-

ations normally voiced of speech as usage, such as, does speech
accurately describe and represent what it purports to?   Does speech
only point to things, name and indicate them, leaving much that is
otherwise speakable about them actually unspoken?   This indeed is
inevitable, and has been noted as the indexicality or reflexivity of
speech as usage. (54) However, to debate merely at this level,
between considering speech as representative/descriptive or as
constitutive as a practice of the sense of that which is described,
(55) is to miss those much deeper levels and issues which the phenomenon of speech raise for thoughtful attention, and which have
already been mentioned.

It is not enough , or indeed very enlightening at all, as some
forms of modern sociology such as ethnomethodology do, to critique
the notion of pre-given externality and objectness with which a des-
criptive/representative formulation of speech operates, by invoking
the notion that the existence, reality, of social phenomena are constituted in the linguistic practices which account them.   This is
because the primordial characteristic of thinghood of which social
things partake, must itself be understood.   Existence and thinghood are not humanly constituted, they are what is revealed and what
comes to presence in relation to the horizoning that is Being, thingness.

It would be possible, at the ethnomethodological level to dissolve the experienced reality or existential character of any of the
topics of sociological and everyday interest by demonstrating their
situated linguistic constitution in speech practices, and their
radical indexicality.   However, this makes reality in its Durkheim-
ian aspects as externality and coerciveness, incomprehensible and
unavailable for analysis.   Reality, instead of being analysed in
terms of its rationality and meaningfulness, is rendered irrational
and meaningless under the auspices of a project which derogates
notions of rationality and meaningfulness to those of everyday usage,
while purporting to uphold them at that level of usage.   To show
constitution at this level is to deconstitute the object or topic of
analysis, and it is to provide no grounds for doing so.   The rejection of ethnomethodology as idealistic by Marxists for instance
is not at all incomprehensible or unjustified.   But this is not to
say that class-theory, or Marxist speech, sees much beyond its
version of usage and its commitments to the silence, arbitrariness
and willfulness of masterful politics and politicking.   Reflexive
and dialectical analytical attention to class, on the other hand,
would require an awareness of class as the occasion for thinking
the difference-relation of thought/speech from Being/language; and
it would thus allow us to conceive of class as thing in the context
of a version of alienation;   that is class as a thing is different
from thingness, that in terms of which it is;   the is-ness of class
stands out from any consideration of the ground of that is-ness as
Being.

However, thought which produced class as a thing, and which produced itself as the (no-thing) thing of class, as a class thing
(as ideology), as much Marxism appears to do, cannot be other than
forgetful of the ontological difference.   Marxism, class-theory,
is therefore thinking which is forgetful of (the limits of) itself,
thinking which is radically alienated.   The problem is to see alien-

ated thought and life for what it is and to overcome it;   Marxism, which has often spoken of this problem, has rarely heard it, or listened for it in its own speaking and life.

To sunder, to make a radical difference between, to alienate, action from speech from theory, rather than to understand the need to think their difference as a particular form of belonging-together, is to lose theorizing in the ultimately mystifying pseudo-clarities of an idealist-materialist theoretical problematic.   (The notion that there are separate and distinct materialist and idealist problematics, sometimes propounded by those who formulate their socialist commitment in 'purely' materialist terms, is deeply illusory and illustrative of such pseudo-clarity).   (56)

Reflexive and dialectical theorizing doesn't de-constitute the thing, but commits itself to think the thinghood of the thing.   The thing remains and retains its presence, but what really counts about this remaining and enduring is that it allows us to glimpse Being as thingness or presence itself.   (57)   This remaining-enduring is the way that thingness shows itself in and through its things;   it is the way that presence shows itself in and through presences.   What goes for things goes also for concrete particulars, actions, even self and self and will.   The concrete symbols of the ideal and the material, the subjective and the objective, mystify thought if they allow difference to be formulated as radical separateness, rather than as that which issues from that which differentiates.   If Being or Language is understood as that which differentiates, then the differentiations of concrete particulars, things, actions, speeches have always to be understood as belonging together with the movement of their differentiation.

Things can indeed be understood as the icons of reification: action can indeed be understood as the icon of solipsism, the will to silence and to power.   But this is not to understand what they are, how they partake of whatness and isness, how they or anything can be iconic, and what kind of being that is.   Concretely and practically we take account of things and actions and their persisting coming - going, facilitating - resisting presence in our lives and situation, our world.   Reflexive and dialectical theorizing is answerable to life and death;   it is answerable to the question of the nature and intelligibility of the persisting presence and present which form the situation of theorizing and the theorist.

Our preserving of the language, our remembering of 'logos', requires us to retain some sense of thing and action in order to be able to speak of world as differentiated presences at all.   The historicity and situatedness of our speech, and its intelligibility as morals or politics requires us to retain a sense of the presence and presencing that action is, and even of the unavoidability of acknowledging self and will as dimensions of differentiated presence, often jarringly actualized in the encounters of everyday life, and also in the ideologies of the age.   Reflexive and dialectical theorizing, whether as fundamental ontology, as hermeneutics or in some other guise, as socio-logy and philo-sophy, is a form of theoretic life;   its living, its speaking, is to be understood as a showing of sociality and commitment.   But we would cease to understand that living and speaking if we were to make the thing and the act radically different, from each other and from the thought that

thinks their being.   The act and the thing, as occasions for
thoughtful and ground-seeking and showing speech are not thereby
theoretically denigratable or dispensable.   If we understand difference as the movement of differentiation, and differentiated things
as being together in difference, then we must continually be responsible for thinking not how the occasion, for instance class, is
dispensable to that which it occasions, that is, thought of ground
and being, but rather how the occasion is that which dispenses the
possibility for thought of ground and being.   And this is to think
the togetherness in difference of topic and resource, occasion and
analysis, the concrete and theorizing.

Perhaps here we can learn again from a notion which spoke loudly
in Heidegger's early work, particularly in 'Being and Time', and
which has tended to be muted in his later work, or transformed into
something like poetic speech.   The notion is 'Dasein', Being-there-
in-the-world.   'Dasein' is not Being, but it is inseparable from
Being.   It is that without which Being cannot come to presence and
presence itself.   'Dasein' is the site of the happening of Being in
the early work rather as poetic speech is the site of the happening
of Language or 'Logos' as Being is in the later work.   'Dasein' and
poetic speech is the site of the disclosure of the truth of presences
and presencing.   Philosophy, thoughtfulness ultimately grounded in
and by the Ontological Difference, as that which differentiates, in
a sense is 'Dasein' (and poetic speech) as that to which differences
and the movement of differentiation within and allowing presence,
become manifest.   The earlier existential hermeneutic of 'Dasein'
should be borne in mind when re-organizing thought in terms of
Heidegger's later hermeneutic of Language and Being.

An understanding of both can help us in our attempts to rethink
sociology and its tradition socially, that is as theoretic community
and commitment, in our times, which are those of the degeneration of
societal self-understanding into the rhetoric of public adminis-
tration, of theory into calculation, community into market, and
commitment into political pragmatism.   The thing, the act, the
occasion, which stands there with us, in our situation indispens-
ably dispensing the possibility of ground-seeking thought and speech.
Class stands with us as witness to the degeneration of our social
self-understanding, and as an occasion to remember our theoretic
responsibility in the midst of it.   It stands there as the thing
(the differentiations) and also as a version of the thingness (the
differentiating) that is our modern society and sociality, in the
midst of which ground-seeking thought must show its difference and
in terms of which it searches for the truly differentiating, and
that which gives the differentiating.   Class stands for us as the
midst within which theorizing must begin to inquire after beginning.
Theorizing begins by re-cognizing and re-membering its being-there-
in-the-world as available in its being-in-language, and further by
thinking its being-in-language as available through a re-view of
what speech shows, a re-hearing of that which grounds and provides
for the intelligibility of speech.   It begins to speak by hearing
its and any speech as the conclusion of a performative, and more
deeply a poetic, constitution and differentiation which has always
already begun, beyond and before the speaker, the poet and the
philosopher.   Sociology begins to understand what it is to be a

true 'logos' of the social only when it forsakes its false beginning
in neo-logy and listens instead, poetically and philosophically for
the sake of the movement of language and of the social which has
always already begun in its and every speech.

NOTES

1 The remarks which make up this paper hopefully reflect features
   of most of the other papers in this collection.   The papers as
   a whole arose from collaborative work among ourselves as a group,
   which originally issued in a set of papers entitled 'Stratifying
   Practices', which were presented at the British Sociological
   Association annual conference in 1973.   The inadequacies, naiv-
   eties, inconsistencies and blunders that remain in the paper are
   of course my responsibility alone.   Peter McHugh and Alan Blum
   commented on an earlier draft of this paper and provided the main
   stimulus for me to re-work the material.   But although their
   style of work pervades the paper in many ways I want to make it
   clear that they have not seen or acknowledged this draft and can
   in no way be held responsible for the views expressed here.   I
   would also like to acknowledge, besides the members of the group,
   Mike O'Pray, Brian Torode, Dave Walsh and Stuart Clegg with whom
   I have talked and tangled over parts of this and related work.
2 J. Burnet, 'Early Greek Philosophy', p. 173;   see also Kirk and
   Raven, 'The Presocratic Philosophers', p. 269, 'the same thing
   exists for thinking and for being'.
3 For another understanding of this kind of critique, see
   J. O'Malley, 'Sociology of Meaning'.
4 See below, section B, for an elaboration of this point.   See
   also my Sociology and Moral Language (paper, forthcoming in
   'Theory and Society', 1976).
5 For a discussion of 'logos' in the context of Heidegger's
   thought, see G.J. Seidel, 'Martin Heidegger and the Pre-
   Socratics', ch. 5.
6 See below and also Heidegger, 'Identity and Difference'.   See
   also J. Derrida, Differance, in his 'Speech and Phenomena'.
   Derrida's subtle play on differance as retaining an interpretive ambiguity between notions of deferring and differentiating,
   as relevant and as important as it is in the elaboration of
   Heideggerian phenomenological hermeneutics, does not figure in
   my discussion in this paper for reasons not least of which are
   those of space.
7 What I mean by 'problematic' here is something like 'thematic
   problem', and this bears some relation to Althusser's main
   use of the concept, that is as the ground or site of theoretical
   practice.   However, his associated uses of it – to characterize
   the scientificity and objectivity of theory, Marxism in particular, and to polemicize not only against concretely subject-
   ivist epistemologies, but also against analytic and 'idealist'
   subjectivism (cf. Althusser and Balibar, op.cit., pp. 25-8) –
   have nothing to do with my use.   Analysis concerned with showing dialectic and reflexivity is meant to be equivalent to
   Heidegger's understanding of what 'phenomenology' is, c.f.

M. Heidegger, 'Being and Time', Basil Blackwell, Introduction, particularly section 7, pp. 49-62.   He provides an analysis using the Greek roots of the meaning of phenomenology in 'phenomenon', or 'the-letting-something-be-seen-in-discourse'. Phenomenology, as the 'logos' of phenomena, is therefore to be seen as 'the letting-be-seen-in-discourse of the showing-itself-in-itself'.   'Logos' as discourse 'lets us see something from the very thing which the discourse is about.   In discourse ... so far as it is genuine, what is said is drawn from what the talk is about, so that discursive communication, in what it says, makes manifest what it is talking about, and thus makes this accessible to the other party .... This mode of making manifest in the sense of letting something be seen by pointing it out, does not go with all kinds of "discourse".   Requesting .... for instance, also makes manifest, but in a different way', p. 56.

8   For the concept 'paradigm' see T. Kuhn, 'The Structure of Scientific Revolutions', passim and ch. 5;   and also M. Masterman, The Nature of a Paradigm, and T. Kuhn, Reflections on my Critics, in I. Lakatos and A. Musgrave (eds.), 'Criticism and the Growth of Knowledge'.

9   My use of this term derives from H. Marcuse, 'One Dimensional Man', but somewhat indirectly.   That is to say both of my notions of one - and multi-dimensionality would be one-dimensional in Marcuse's terms, as not transcending 'the established universe of discourse and action', op.cit., p.27.   My uses derive in this instance partly from Heidegger and partly from Wittgenstein's early and late philosophical positions.   Thus they would fall under the (to my mind completely inadequate) criticisms Marcuse makes of the positivist and behaviourist character of Wittgenstein's philosophy, op.cit. ch. 7.   On the other hand, Marcuse suggests the possibly one-dimensional character of his own work, in his own terms, when he writes: 'The terms "transcend" and "transcendence" are used throughout in the empirical, critical sense', p.10.n.

10   See no. 13 below.

11   Cf. L. Wittgenstein, 'Notebooks': 'the subject is not a part of the world but a presupposition of its existence", p. 79, 'The I is not an object.   I objectively confront every object.   But not the I', p.80;   and, 'But really you do not see the eye. And nothing in the visual field allows you to infer that it is seen by an eye', p.117, 'Tractatus Logico-Philosophicus'.   Cf. also, M. Merleau-Ponty, 'The Visible and the Invisible', 'I do not perceive any more than I speak - Perception has me as has language ... What is it that, from my side, comes to animate the perceived world and language?', p.190.

12   Cf. Wittgenstein, 'Philosophical Investigations': 'For a large class of cases - though not for all - in which we employ the word 'meaning' it can be defined thus: the meaning of a word is its use in the language', section 43, p.20.   Also 'It is interesting to compare the multiplicity of the tools in language and the ways they are used, the multiplicity of kinds of word and sentence, with what logicians have said about the structure of language (including the author of the 'Tractatus Logico-

Philosophicus'), p.12.

13 Cf. Wittgenstein, 'Tractatus', op.cit.   'A picture cannot,
    however, depict its pictorial form; it displays it', p.17,
    section 2.172; 'Propositions can represent the whole of reality,
    but they cannot represent what they must have in common with
    reality in order to be able to represent it - logical form ....
    What expresses itself in language, we cannot express by means of
    language.   Propositions show the logical form of reality.
    They display it', p.51, sections 4.12/4.121.

14 Cf. A.J. Ayer, 'Language, Truth and Logic': 'a sentence had
    literal meaning if and only if the proposition it expressed was
    either analytic or empirically verifiable', p.7.

15 Cf. Wittgenstein, 'Philosophical Investigations', op.cit.,
    p. viii, and his critique of the theory of language that words name
    objects and that sentences are combinations of names, pp.2-30;
    for comments on the diversity and multi-dimensionality of
    'describing', cf. p.12, section 24, and p.99, section 291.

16 On these different formulations see Masterman, op.cit., who
    argues on the basis of a detailed analysis of Kuhn's uses of the
    notion: that philosophically a paradigm is not a metaphysical
    worldview, but is an artefact which can be used as puzzle-
    solving device (p.68), and that it has got to be a 'way of see-
    ing' (p.76).

17 Cf. for instance, 'Philosophical Investigations', op.cit.,
    'Think how we learn to use the expressions "Now I know how to go
    on", "Now I can go on" and others; in what family of language
    games we learn their use', p.72-3, section 179; 'if a person
    has not yet got the concepts, I shall teach him to use the words
    by means of examples and by practice.   And when I do this I do
    not communicate less to him than I know myself. ... 'But then
    doesn't our understanding reach beyond all the examples?' - A
    very queer expression, and quite a natural one!', p.83.

18 Cf. ibid., passim; see also H. Garfinkel, 'Studies in Ethno-
    methodology', and H. Garfinkel and H. Sacks, On Formal Struct-
    ures of Practical Actions, ch.13 in J.C. McKinney and E.A.
    Tiryakian (eds.), 'Theoretical Sociology', on the notions of
    'indexicality' and 'reflexivity'.

19 Cf. E. Husserl, 'Logical Investigations', vol. 1, 1970, p.263.

20 This point has been made with most emphasis and insight by
    L. Althusser in 'Reading Capital', part I.

21 See for instance Kant's 'Prolegomena to Any Future Metaphysics',
    and Heidegger's understanding of Kant's notion in 'What is a
    Thing?', pp. 119-21).

22 Marx's early work understood itself as critique (i.e. Critique
    of Hegel's 'Philosophy of Right', 'The German Ideology', and
    'The Poverty of Philosophy), just as much as the later work did
    (i.e. 'Capital; a critique of Political Economy').

23 For a much more developed and insightful, but not wholly un-
    problematic treatment of these kinds of issues in relation to
    Marx, see Alan Blum, Reading Marx, 'Sociological Inquiry',
    vol. 43, 1973.   Several of Blum's themes and formulations, from
    his 'Theorizing', have helped me say what I want to say in this
    paper.

24 See Marx's The Eighteenth Brumaire of Louis Bonaparte, in Marx

and Engels, 'Selected Works'.

25   Cf. K. Davis and W.E. Moore, in their 'Some principles of Stratification' in M. Tumin (ed.), 'Readings on Social Stratification'
pp. 368-77, where classes are equated with strata as the unequal
distribution of prestige.   Max Weber formulates class in relation to status and the market, in H. Gerth and C. Wright Mills
(eds.) 'From Max Weber', Routledge & Kegan Paul, ch.7; and in his
'The Theory of Social and Economic Organization', ch.4.

26   Cf. Enzo Paci, 'The Function of Sciences and the Meaning of Man',
for an analysis of the subject-object, concrete and abstract and
appearance-essence dichotomies in Marxism, which draws upon the
final stage of development of Husserl's phenomenology as a form
of dialectical thought.

27   Cf. the position of Marxism-Leninism, which founds itself on
this dichotomy, in the work of L. Althusser, 'For Marx' and
'Lenin and Philosophy and Other Essays', and the work of the
journal 'Theoretical Practice'.   The Marxist-Leninist use of
the terms 'reading' and 'absences' or 'silences' in texts, particularly in Marx's texts, is not the same as my use of the terms
'reading', 'absence', 'no-thing' etc., in this paper.

28   Cf. V.I. Lenin, 'Speeches at Party Congresses (1918-1922)', 1971,
Progress Publishers, Moscow, in particular the speeches to the
Tenth Congress of the R.C.P.(B.) March 8-16, 1921, pp. 225, 232,
237, 250, 251, 271, 272, etc., where these matters and others
such as the bureaucratization and distancing of the Party from
its class and from the peasant masses are discussed.   See also
A.G. Frank, 'Capitalism and Underdevelopment in Latin America',
for an example of a form of Marxist-Leninist theorizing in which
classes as entities are not the explicit focus, but where the
relationship of dichotomy, and the decision to theoretically re-
view the world this way (that is, class in the sense in which I
am looking at it here) - remain fundamental.   What is important
for Frank is the relationship (of exploitation, contradiction,
dichotomy, zero-sum, or suchlike), between any two things
(countries, towns, regions, etc.) seen as what he calls 'metropolis' in relation to 'satellite'.   Frank dichotomizes the
world in master-slave terms, virtually any object in his theoretical gaze can be a master in relation to one object and a
slave in relation to another (cf. p.34, ibid.).

29   The same kind of remarks could be made about other features of
Marxist discourse and its corpus;   consider the two discontinuities (a) the revolution and (b) the alleged 'epistemological
break' within Marx's thought (between the 'early' humanist ideology and the 'later' science of historical materialism) (cf.
Althusser, op.cit., and A. Cutler in 'Theoretical Practice', 3
& 4).   It is noteworthy that in Marxism-Leninism (b) has at
least an iconic relation to (a), and in some senses could be
said to constitute (a).   However, whatever the relationship, it
is clear that such discontinuities correspond to no point in
time, to no concrete event;   he who thinks them cannot place
himself in a concrete before or after, rather he must continually review his present in these terms, he must continually
reproduce the discontinuity as a threatened presence, something
calling for and involving him in struggle for-against the Party,

the Revolution, the proletariat, materialism in philosophy, the
science of historical materialism, etc.

30   The notion of 'telos' is discussed in the work of Marx and
Husserl by Paci, op.cit. and see also most editions of the
journal, 'Telos'.

31   Cf. Althusser, op.cit., 'Theoretical Practice', op.cit., passim,
and L. Althusser and E. Balibar, 'Reading Capital' (pt.II ch.6
and passim).

32   The clearest statement of class as the difference that is dichotomy, and particularly as master-slave dichotomy (which is part of
what I am interested in - see the third section below), can be
found in the Communist Manifesto (cf. K. Marx and F. Engels,
'Selected Works', pp.31-63, Manifesto of the Communist Party).
'The history of all hitherto existing society is the history of
class struggles.   Freeman and slave, patrician and plebeian,
lord and serf, guildmaster and journeyman, in a word, oppressor
and oppressed, stood in constant opposition to one another ....
the epoch of the bourgeoisie .... has simplified the class anta-
gonisms.   Society as a whole is more and more splitting into
two great hostile camps, into two great classes directly facing
each other; Bourgeoisie and Proletariat' (pp. 35-6).

33   Cf. C.B. MacPherson, 'The Theory of Possessive Individualism'.

34   Cf. A. Gouldner, 'The Coming Crisis of Western Sociology', p.62.

35   Cf. G. Lukacs, 'History and Class Consciousness', 'The Proletariat only perfects itself by annihilating and transcending itself,
by creating the classless society through the successful conclusion of its own class struggle', p.80.   Marx formulates the
proletariat as the self-negation of the bourgeoisie in 'Capital',
vol. 1, 'But capitalist production begets, with the inexorability
of a law of Nature, its own negation.   It is the negation of the
negation', p.763.   'What the bourgeoisie, therefore, produces,
above all, are its own grave-diggers'.

36   Cf. Karl Marx, 'Pre-Capitalist Economic Formations', but as
E.I. Hobsbawm remarks in his Introduction, 'It seems that Marx,
who had earlier welcomed the impact of Western capitalism as an
inhuman but historically progressive force on the stagnant pre-
capitalist economies, found himself increasingly appalled by
this inhumanity', p.50, so much so that he was not averse from
occasionally reconsidering the viability of the primitive
Russian peasant commune and its capacity for development into
a modern form of social organization.   However, Lenin, who
saddled the peasantry to make the revolution and who was then
himself saddled by the peasantry as a problem, was well aware
that 'Socialism cannot be built unless advantage is taken of
the heritage of capitalist culture' (quoted by C. Hill, 'Lenin
and the Russian Revolution', p.144);   see also Lenin, op.cit.,
p.319.

37   Consider Marx's, The Eighteenth Brumaire of Louis Bonaparte,
(cf. Marx and Engels, op.cit., pp.94-167).   Here any articulated theory of class is noticeably absent;   and our desire to
see classes as two opposed things in the world meets with the
resistance of a text which exhibits the political fragmenting
and coalescing of about five or six classes and class fractions
in an historically complex analysis.   But as, with Lenin's

numerous situational commentaries and interventions, Marx's
analysis is to be read as a class analysis in that it shows its
rule as - see contradictions, see dichotomy.

38   That is to say, Marxists have long been embarrassed by the charge
that Marxism is a dogmatism.   They have thus countered by claiming that, on the contrary, it is a method, whether scientific,
dialectical or both.   To this I am countering that if method is
understood as recipe, or explicitly and fully formulable rules of
procedure, replicable and checkable etc., then method is a dogmatism.   Rather, method, in the sense of grounds, or what
provides for the very intelligibility of a text, always remain
implicit, or beyond what can be made explicit by a text;   another
way of putting this would be to say that method as grounds does
not only speak of replicable procedures of writing, but of the
possibilities, and of the responsibilities of reading.   Method
(as grounds) is 'shown' (see below) by examples;   it cannot show
itself;   and any text, whether or not of Marx, comes to be taken
as an exemplary enactment of its internally unformulable method
(as grounds) under the auspices of a reflexive analysis, which is
what I am interested in here.

39   The cultural, social and historical role of difference as dichotomy is vast and daunting to consider.   The epistemological
dichotomies (mind-body, subject-object, self-other) and the
moral-religious-political dichtomies (good-evil, heaven-earth,
angel-beast, freedom-determinism, reason-passions, reason-will)
in their various transformations have done sterling service on
behalf of moral idealizing and political dichotomizing throughout
history.   Irish 'navvies', the British working class, American
blacks, colonized 'natives', have all been formulated as body/
animal/passionate by their masters who formulate themselves as
mind/humanity/reason.   Similarly, such dichotomies ground other
pervasive cultural dialectics such as those announced in the
names high culture-common culture, priest-people, Party-masses,
intellectuals-Party, scientist/expert-layman, doctor-patient.
Perhaps what is needed in this area is a mythological analysis
(as by Levi-Strauss) of dichotomies and their transformations,
which would reflexively engage the mythic character of its own
mythologizing.   On mind-body see Descartes, 'Philosophical
Writings';   Ryle, 'The Concept of Mind';   and for a version in
terms of black-white see Eldridge Cleaver, 'Soul on Ice',
pp. 114-15.   On self-other and subject-object dichotomies analysed in terms of master slave cf. Hegel, 'The Phenomenology of
Mind', pp. 228-40;   Kojeve, 'Introduction to the Reading of
Hegel', chs. 1 & 2;   Sartre, 'Being and Nothingness', part 3,
passim and pp. 285-309, 504-26;   and Nietzsche, 'Beyond Good and
Evil', section 257-61, pp. 201-9.   On sex as a fundamental dimension of or metaphor for dichotomy see for instance Plato's
'Symposium' and M. Kosok, The Phenomenology of Fucking, 'Telos',
no. 8 1971).

40   For Marx on alienation see 'The Economic and Philosophical Manuscripts 1844', pp. 106-20;   for alienation as dichotomy and
dialectic see references to Hegel, Kojeve and Sartre in no. 11
above.

41   In this light, that of the maintenance of the notion of class

and class-rule even under conditions of their acknowledged non-
existence, as mentioned previously, see Lenin, 'Speeches at
Party Congresses (1918-1922)', where it is possible to see this,
together with, and in, the bureaucratization and distancing of the
Party from its class, the proletariat, and from the peasantry.

42 The major discussion of authority produced within the sociological tradition remains Weber's in 'The Theory of Social and Economic Organization', op.cit., ch.3; for a somewhat anaemic discussion of authority within the philosophical tradition of
ordinary language conceptual analysis, see R.S. Peters and P.
Winch, Authority, ch. 5 in A. Quinton (ed.), 'Political Philosophy'.

43 Cf. I. Kant, The Groundwork to the Metaphysic of Morals, in H.J.
Panton, 'The Moral Law'.

44 Cf. Plato, 'The Republic', passim and parts II, IV and VII in
particular: see also Rosen, op.cit. The 'magnificent myth' of
the men of gold, silver and bronze is both meant to be taken
seriously by all classes, not least the Guardians ('Republic',
p. 159-61), but we treat this as a Socratic irony.   In my view
it is just as ironic for Socrates to talk hypothetically to philosopher rulers in the following way; 'you have been bred to rule
to your own advantage and that of the whole community; like
king-bees in a hive; you are better educated than the rest and
better qualified to combine the practice of philosophy and
politics.   You must therefore each descend in turn and live
with your fellows in the cave and get used to seeing in the
dark; once you get used to it you will see a thousand times
better than they do', p.285.   The political abolition of discourse is unavoidable between the blind and the sighted; and it
is matched in modern times by that required by the technical
complexity and strangeness of the language of the natural sciences on the one hand and ordinary language on the other.   The
relationships of the sighted and blind, and of the scientific
expert and layman, are only apparently ones of discourse, moral
and educative ones; they are at least, and perhaps only, abo-
litions of discourse and assertions of unquestionable authority
and rule, in relation to ignorance as the ruled sub-ject.

45 Cf. J. Burnet, 'Early Greek Philosophy', ch. 4, Parmenides of
Elea, pp. 169-96.   The site to which the Goddess calls the
speaker in Parmenides' poem is far 'from the beaten track of
men!'   See also G.J. Seidel, 'Martin Heidegger and the Pre-
Socratics'.

46 Cf. Nietzsche, 'Thus Spoke Zarathustra', pp. 39-53; also 'God
has died.   And let us not be equal before the mob.   You
Higher Men, depart from the market-place', p.297; and pp.335-6
where Zarathustra departs even from them.

47 Cf. Weber, 'The Theory of Social and Economic Organization',
op.cit., p.361 on charisma: although Weber does not use the
sentence, 'It is written ..., therefore ...', I think it gives
the sense of both traditional and rational-legal authority in
his terms; that is, respectively, it covers the personal
ruler's recourse to history, the past, what has 'always existed'
(ibid., p.341) on the one hand, and the 'official's' recourse to
'a consistent system of abstract rules' (p.330), on the other.

For me, even Weber's notion of rational authority is no more
rational or authoritative in the sense of reflexively speaking
to and on behalf of its grounds, than are his notions of tradition and charisma.   There is no news in speaking about the
fateful character of Weber's notion of rationality, but it stands
to be spoken of once again.   Here is Marcuse's version: 'It is
difficult to see any reason, even mere 'technical' reason, in the
'house of bondage' as it closes in around us.   Or was there
irony in Weber's concept of reason, the irony of understanding
and disavowal?   Is he perhaps saying: 'is that what you call
reason?', p.151, Industrialization and Capitalism, in O. Stammer
(ed.), 'Max Weber and Sociology Today'.

48 See Heidegger, 'Identity and Difference'.

49 Some such notion is present for instance in Lenin's 'materialist'
reading of Hegel, see The Philosophical Notebooks, 'Lenin's
Collected Works', vol. 39.

50 On dialectic as method see for instance Marx, 'A contribution to
the critique of Political Economy', pp. 205-14, and Lucien Goldmann, 'The Hidden God', chs. 1 and 5.

51 See also Heidegger in 'Being and Time', p. 262, 'the ultimate
business in philosophy is to preserve the force of the most elemental words in which Dasein expresses itself, and to keep the
common understanding from levelling them off to that unintelligibility which functions in turn as a source of preudo-problems'.

52 Heidegger puts it that 'Only when we turn thoughtfully towards
what has already been thought, will we be turned to use for what
must still be thought'.   But, as against Hegel's turning to, or
conversation with, what has been thought, 'For us the character
of the conversation with the history of thinking is no longer
"Aufhebung" (elevation), but the step-back', 'Identity and
Difference', pp. 41 and 49.

53 For a deep analysis of the ever present threat of nihilism in
thought and its speech, see Stanley Rosen, 'Nihilism'.

54 See in particular Garfinkel and Sacks, On the formal structures
of practical actions, in 'Theoretical Sociology', ed. by J.
McKinney and E. Tiryakian.

55 Wittgenstein's early and later work (see bibliography), could
be taken as examples of the two poles of this debate.   However
both involve, although in different ways, a notion of language
as that which shows its sense as beyond it and beyond what it
can say; and it is for this notion that a deeper reading of them
than they normally get and normally appear to require would
search.

56 See for instance Lenin, 'Materialism and Empirio-Criticism',
and Althusser, 'Lenin and Philosophy and Other Essays'.   What
Marxism-Leninism designates as the struggle of two problematics,
I am here formulating as one unitary problematic which subjects
the thoughtful search for unity in and through the life of theory,
to the search for unity through practice and the political
practice of differentiation and contradiction in particular.

57 On this see Heidegger, 'What is a thing?' and The Origin of the
work of art, in his 'Poetry, Language, Thought'.

BIBLIOGRAPHY

ALTHUSSER, L., 'For Marx', 1969, Allen Lane, London.
ALTHUSSER, L., 'Lenin and Philosophy and Other Essays', 1971, NLB, London.
ALTHUSSER, L. and BALIBAR, E., 'Reading Capital', 1970, NLB, London.
ARMSTRONG, G.A., Notes on Hegel's 'Lordship and Bondage', ch.7 in A. MacIntyre (ed.), 'Hegel', 1972, Anchor Books, New York.
AYER, A.J., 'Language, Truth and Logic', 1971, Penguin Books, London.
BLUM, A., 'Theorizing', 1974, Heinemann, London.
BLUM, A., Reading Marx, in 'Sociological Inquiry', vol. 43 no. 1, Spring 1973.
BLUM, A., MCHUGH, P. et al., 'On the Beginning of Social Inquiry', 1974, Routledge & Kegan Paul, London.
BURNET, J., 'Early Greek Philosophy',1971, Adam & Charles Black, London.
CLEAVER, E., 'Soul on Ice', 1969, Jonathan Cape, London.
DAVIS, K. and MOORE, W., Some Principles of Social Stratification, pp.368-77 in M. Tumin (ed.), 'Readings on Social Stratification', 1970, Prentice-Hall, New Jersey.
DERRIDA, J., 'Speech and Phenomena', 1973, North Western University Press, Evanston.
DESCARTES, R., 'Philosophical Writings', 1970, Nelson's University Paperbacks, London.
FRANK, A.G., 'Capitalism and Underdevelopment in Latin America', 1971, Penguin Books, London.
GARFINKEL, H., 'Studies in Ethnomethodology', 1967, Prentice-Hall, New Jersey.
GARFINKEL, H. and SACKS, H., On Formal Structures of Practical Actions, ch.13 in J.C. McKinney and E.A. Tiryakian (eds.), 'Theoretical Sociology', 1970, Appleton-Century-Crofts, New York.
GERTH, H. and MILLS, C.W. (eds.), 'From Max Weber', 1948, Routledge & Kegan Paul, London.
GOLDMANN, L., 'The Hidden God', 1970, Routledge & Kegan Paul, London.
GOULDNER, A., 'The Coming Crisis of Western Sociology', 1971, Heinemann, London.
HEGEL, G.W.F., 'The Phenomenology of Mind', 1966, George Allen & Unwin, London.
HEIDEGGER, M., 'Being and Time', 1967, Basil Blackwell, Oxford.
HEIDEGGER, M., 'Identity and Difference', 1969, Harper & Row, New York.
HEIDEGGER, M., 'Language, Poetry, Thought', 1971, Harper & Row, New York.
HEIDEGGER, M., 'What is a thing?', 1967, Henry Regnery Company, Chicago.
HILL, C., 'Lenin and the Russian Revolution', 1971, Penguin Books, London.
HUSSERL, E., 'Logical Investigations', vol. 1, 1970, Routledge & Kegan Paul, London.
KANT, I., Groundwork to the Metaphysic of Morals, in H.J. Paton 'The Moral Law', 1965, Hutchinson, London.
KANT, I., 'Prolegomena to Any Future Metaphysics', 1950, Bobbs-Merril, New York.
KIRK, G.S. and RAVEN, J.E. 'The Presocratic Philosophers', 1957, The Cambridge University Press.

KOJEVE, A., 'Introduction to the Reading of Hegel', 1969, Basic
Books, New York.
KOSOK, M., The phenomenology of fucking, in 'Telos', no. 8, 1971.
KUHN, T., 'The Structure of Scientific Revolutions', 1970,
University of Chicago Press.
LAKATOS, I. and MUSGRAVE, A., 'Criticism and the Growth of Know-
ledge', 1970, Cambridge University Press.
LENIN, V.I., 'Materialism and Empirio-Criticism', 1970, Progress
Publishers, Moscow.
LENIN, V.I., 'Philosophical Notebooks', 1963, Lawrence & Wishart,
London.
LENIN, V.I., 'Speeches at Party Congresses (1918-1922)', 1971,
Progress Publishers, Moscow.
LUKACS, G., 'History and Class Consciousness', 1971, Merlin Press,
London.
MACPHERSON, C.B., 'The Theory of Possessive Individualism', 1964,
Oxford University Press.
MARCUSE, H., Industrialization and Capitalism, pp. 133-51, in
O. Stammer (ed.), 'Max Weber and Sociology Today', 1971, Basil
Blackwell, Oxford.
MARCUSE, H., 'One Dimensional Man', 1968, Sphere Books, London.
MARX, K., 'Capital', vol. 1, 1970, Lawrence & Wishart, London.
MARX, K., 'Pre-Capitalist Economic Formations', 1964, Lawrence &
Wishart, London.
MARX, K., 'A Contribution to the Critique of Political Economy',
1971, Lawrence & Wishart, London.
MARX, K., 'Economic and Philosophical Manuscripts of 1844', 1970,
Lawrence & Wishart, London.
MARX, K. and ENGELS, F., 'Selected Works', 1970, Lawrence & Wishart,
London.
MASTERMAN, M., The Nature of a Paradigm, in Lakatos and Musgrave
(eds.), 'Criticism and the Growth of Knowledge'.
MERLEAU-PONTY, M., 'The Visible and the Invisible', 1968, North
Western University Press, Evanston.
NIETZSCHE, F., 'Beyond Good and Evil', 1966, Vintage Books, New York.
NIETZSCHE, F., 'Thus Spoke Zarathustra', 1964, Penguin Books, London.
O'MALLEY, J., 'Sociology of Meaning', 1972, Human Context Books,
London.
PACI, E., 'The Function of the Sciences and the Meaning of Man',
1972, North Western University Press, Evanston.
PETERS, R.S. and WINCH, P., Authority, ch. 5 in A. Quinton (ed.),
'Political Philosophy', 1967, Oxford University Press.
PLATO, 'The Republic', 1955, Penguin Books, London.
PLATO, The Symposium in 'Great Dialogues of Plato', E.H. Warmington
and P.G. Rouse (eds.), 1956, Mentor Books, New York.
ROSEN, S., 'Nihilism', 1969, Yale University Press, New York.
RYLE, G., 'The Concept of Mind', 1963, Penguin Books, London.
SARTRE, J.P., 'Being and Nothingness', 1966, Washington Square Press,
New York.
SEIDEL, G.J., 'Martin Heidegger and the Pre-Socratics', 1964, Uni-
versity of Nebraska Press, Lincoln.
WEBER, M., 'The Theory of Social and Economic Organization', 1964,
Free Press, New York.
WITTGENSTEIN, L., Notebooks 1914-16, 1969, Blackwell, Oxford.

WITTGENSTEIN, L., 'Philosophical Investigations', 1963, Blackwell, Oxford.
WITTGENSTEIN, L., 'Tractatus Logico-Philosophicus', 1961, Routledge & Kegan Paul, London.

Chapter 5

SOCIOLOGY AND SOCIAL STRATIFICATION: ISSUES OF REFLEXIVITY AND TRADITION *
Paul Filmer

> Only when we turn thoughtfully toward what has already
> been thought, will we be turned to use for what must
> still be thought.
>
> Martin Heidegger (1)

INTRODUCTION

This paper introduces itself in demonstrably proposing sociologies
of social stratification for negotiation as essentially reflexive,
and unavoidably uninteresting as such to sociologists who formulate
them.   It proposes the (im)possibility of reflexive sociology as a
paradoxical issue, in the absence of a tradition, as yet formulated
and sharable, for such an enterprise.   It concludes itself in proposing for negotiation demonstrable accomplishments of reflexive
discourse about social stratification.
　　Throughout its sequential course, the writing that is this paper
is organized in anticipation of presenting itself as, in parts, an
analytic address of social stratification as a sociological topic.
It is so organized in parts, rather than as a whole, because attempting to address such a sociological topic analytically has been,
for me unavoidably, to alternate between practices of collaboratively
(re-)creating, with anticipated readers, on the one hand lived and
felt experiences of concrete stratifying practices of collectivity
members, and on the other, analytic (sociological) grounds for
understanding them.   Analytic sociologies, of whatever sociological
topics, are thus proposed as uneasy authorial hoverings between such
practices;   as tenuous, momentary and, in retrospect, perhaps sur-
prising prisings of ourselves out of concrete worlds and back into
spheres of analytic intending.   Analysis, otherwise intended and
practiced, threatens to kill the life of being social, the more
effectively - and disastrously for thought - to dissect it as a way
of finally 'understanding' it.
　　This introduction proposes the paper as an organized whole upon
which I have come after, and not as, writing it.   The introduction,
therefore, may be more interesting to readers if they treat it as
necessarily not being able to be about what when read, the paper

will have been about.   This is not to propose that the paper was
written other than as addressing social stratification as a topic of
sociology: indeed, it relies, for grounds of its senses, upon its
recognizable character as such.   It is to propose, however, that
within that recognizable character it is available for reading coll-
aboratively/creatively - that is to say, for readers' own imaginative
and disciplined re-writings of it that such a way of reading might
be.   Reading collaboratively/creatively is proposed as a way of
being socially for writers and readers in sociology's professional
worlds; and that is a fundamental occasion for this paper, amongst
many others which may be more apparent in its text.

1.   SOCIOLOGIES OF SOCIAL STRATIFICATION AS SOCIOLOGISTS' WAYS OF SEEING SOCIAL STRATIFICATION

Sociologies of social stratification are here proposed as professional sociologists' ways of seeing some practices of members of human
collectivities as sociologically analysable practices.   As such,
they are, simultaneously, ways of doing the stratification that
organizes the particular collectivity that is professional sociology.
And each particular account, such as the one I am proposing may be
read as being constituted in passages of this paper, is an attempt at
the stratification which is (in this case, professional sociological)
membership.
Sociologies of social stratification rest on such contentions as:
there exist, in social worlds, practices carried on by members which
can be rendered as stratifying practices (2).   Sensible sociologists' practices are thus to note, and then objectify these practices as constitutive features of accounts of structures/systematic
organizations (of social relationships) of and as observable socie-
ties/societal forms.   By and in accounting for some practices of
members of collectivities as social stratification, professional
sociologists often constitute such collectivities as societies.
They are also, and often, themselves members of the collectivities
wherein they account for some of the practices of (other) members as
social stratification - but they are members in a special sense only,
a sense which may be captured by describing them as observing-
members.
Both members and observing-members (sociologists) are here seen
as carrying out practices which are constitutive of membership; that
is, they are seen as 'membershipping themselves' by and in their
practices.   Their titular differences are designed to propose, however, that they are membershipping themselves into different collectivities: those of members and observing-members respectively.
Their concrete practices, that is to say, are seen as concretely
different.   Members (in contrast to observing-members) are seen to
membership themselves into those collectivities which sociologists
constitute as societies in and by studying social stratification,
through undertaking those practices which are characterized as
social stratification by sociologists.   Whereas observing-members
are different members in the sense that, instead of undertaking those
practices which they have characterized as social stratification when
undertaken by (other) members, they observe them.   Observing those

practices of (other) members constitutes their practices.   This is
not to propose that sociologists cannot do the practices they are
observing: perhaps they can.   Indeed it may be argued that they
must be able to do them; that the hidden (that is, unexplicated)
resources of their understandings of them may be found in their
experiences of having done them, and in their practical and personal
knowledges of their abilities to do them.   But that is not an interesting topic for consideration here.   What is interesting is the
analytic identity of what sociologists are doing, in observing
(and accounting for) some members' practices as social stratification, with what they propose as the analytic sense of those practices
themselves.   Which is to say that, when sociologists constitute
(other) members' practices as social stratification by and in their
study of them, they are themselves undertaking (concretely analogous
– though different – and analytically identical) practices.   In short,
they, too, are practising stratification.   Indeed, the sense and,
more important, the authority of their studies depend upon them
carrying out such practices as constitutive of those studies.

Sociologists' practices of social stratification are carried out
in two distinct ways: first, in their differentiation of themselves
(as observing-members) from their fellow (other) collectivity members, for the practical purposes of doing sociology at all – without
such differentiation, sociology would appear to be doing no more
than common sense, in that sociologists' accounts of social stratification would be members' accounts, only concretely and not analytically differentiable from any other members' accounts.   That is,
they would be the particular accounts of practices of members which
would not necessarily be recognizable as accounts of social stratification at all; but simply as the accounts, of whatever practices
they accounted for, of the particular members who formulated them.
But in so differentiating themselves, sociologists constitute themselves as a collectivity which is distinct and separate, for all the
practical purposes of producing recognizably sociological accounts,
from the collectivity to which those members belong, some of whose
practices they constitute as social stratification.   Second, within
this distinct and separate collectivity, which is the particular
society that is professional sociology, sociologists differentiate
themselves from one another in offering their individual accounts of
whatever they are accounting for (in this case, social stratification), as contributions to sociology's corpus of knowledge.

2. SOCIOLOGIES OF SOCIAL STRATIFICATION AS SOCIOLOGISTS'
    WAYS OF DOING SOCIAL STRATIFICATION

Parsons, in an essay proposing an analytical approach to the theory
of social stratification (3), demonstrates both distinct ways in
which sociologists constitute their sociology in the stratifying
practices of their society.   First, social stratification is
characterized as:
    the differential ranking of the human individuals who
    compose a given social system and their treatment as
    superior and inferior relative to one another in
    certain socially important respects ... Ranking is one

of many possible bases on which individuals may be
differentiated.   It is only in so far as diffe ences
are treated as involving or related to particular kinds
of social superiority and inferiority that they are
relevant to the theory of stratification. (4)
In so characterizing some practices of members, Parsons implicitly
characterizes himself, as a sociologist, as superior to fellow
(other, non-observing) members, in terms of a socially important
respect; that of science.   And that socially important respect
says that, in effect, detached observation is a more adequate basis
for knowing than is subjective involvement (5).   So that Parsons's
practices, as a sociologist, accord with it in being constituted by
his observing and accounting for (but not doing) members' practices
of (in this instance) social stratification.   Moreover, it is only
in the implicit invocation of the social importance of science that
the sense of the sociologist's claim to superiority may be found.
For if it is socially important, then Parsons's practice of socio-
olgists' science, which is here proposed as observing and accounting
for, and not doing, will be something to which members will consider
it worthwhile giving their attention.   Under what other circumstances would members be likely to consider plausible an account
based on non-participating members' accounts of observations of
their practices, rather than on (and subsequent to) participating
members' accounts of undertakings of them?   Under any other circumstances, presumably, Parsons's (and other sociologists') accounts
could be seen as no more than different accounts, accounts by other
members, of their fellow members' practices.   Thus, then, Parsons
differentiates himself as a member of a collectivity (of sociolo-
gists/observing-members) other than any members' collectivity,
though containable within that latter, wider collectivity.

In proposing his analytical approach to the theory of social
stratification, Parsons is quick to differentiate himself from other
members of the collectivity of sociologists, as an individual talent,
whose analytical approach is proposed as a contribution to the tradition which is sociology.   He does this differentiation at the
outset, as a footnote to his characterization of social stratification as vertical ranking, which begins thus:
Some writers (cf. P.A. Sorokin, 'Social Mobility', New
York, 1927) have distinguished what is here referred
to as stratification as the 'vertical' axis of differentiation of individuals from the 'horizontal' axis.
Correspondingly, when individuals change their status
in the differentiated system, reference is made to
vertical and horizontal mobility.   This usage is
dangerous.   It states the analytical problem in
terms of a two-dimensional spatial analogy. (6)
The differentiation is clearly, if implicitly, between himself and
'some writers'.   Those two words, 'some writers', read interestingly.
This analytical approach is published in a collection of Parsons's
essays on sociological theory.   I read it in the expectation that
the majority, if not all writers referred to in this essay, or in
any of the others that comprise the collection, will be sociologists.
So the term writers may refer to writers who are sociologists - in
this instance, probably, writers who are sociological theorists -

writing on social stratification.   However, I read, also, a mere-
ness about Parsons's use here of the term writers, a sense of a lack
of a need to be more specific, or to award to whom it refers the
significance that might be read as accompanying implied (or explicit) recognition of their writings as contributions to the tradition of the (sociological) theory of social stratification.   Yet
the words 'some writers' are exemplified by Parsons specifically as
Sorokin, a sociologist, and one of his works which, Parsons makes
clear, he sees as a contribution to that tradition.   But his contribution is constituted in usages which Parsons dubs 'dangerous',
because they allow insufficiently for the variety of differentiations involved in social stratification.   The burden of proof in
cases of the use of such concepts, Parsons states, 'should always be
placed on their relevance to social facts and analytical schemes
verified in the social field, not on the logic of deductions from
analogies to physical space and distance'. (7)
    In so limiting social stratification to being constituted, for
his purposes ('regarded here'), only in vertical differentiation,
Parsons implies a claim that his work is more sociological (that is,
more relevant 'to social facts and analytical schemes verified in
the social field') than Sorokin's, which must be read, according to
Parsons's implication, as limited by its dependence 'on the logic of
deductions from analogies to physical space and distance'.   In
drawing such a comparison as a feature of his writing on stratification, Parsons may be read as doing unavoidably, within the collectivity of sociologists, precisely that to which he proposes to
address the attention of those members of that collectivity who are
his readers: that is, he is practising social stratification.   For
his characterization of social stratification (at least for the
practical purposes of his essay upon it, that is, for the practical
purposes of providing for an analytical approach to its theory) is
as practices of and for members ranking one another as superior/
inferior 'in certain socially important respects'.   His approach
proceeds by offering six classes of socially important respects ('a
classification of bases of differential valuation') in relation to
concrete worlds which may be signified by his analytic concept of
the social system. (8) These are his tools for undertaking concrete practices of observation, and their revelation is followed by
a demonstration of their use. (9) The burden, then, of Parsons's
analytical approach to the theory of social stratification is a
concrete demonstration of its applicability and thus the possibility
of its verifiability 'in the social field'.   But the entire enterprise that is this approach rests upon the socially important respect that his careful footnote offers, in terms of which may be
accomplished superior/inferior rankings of members of the collectivity that is professional sociology.   Parsons's writing, that is,
does precisely what it speaks of, and in the terms that it speaks of
it: it does social stratification for readers who care thus to read
it.   And not to read it thus is not to read it as Parsons's essay,
but as any sociologist's essay.

To recapitulate the negotiable proposals that constitute the writing
of this paper so far: sociologies of social stratification are proposed as sociologists' ways of seeing some practices whereby the

collectivity members that they are observing differentiate themselves from one another.   But those ways of seeing such practices
are a feature of the relationships of sociologists who see them to
the members who are doing them.   That is, in seeing some practices
of (other) collectivity members in their own ways (which are, for
practical purposes of this paper, seen as sociology's ways), sociologists differentiate themselves, as members, from those (other,
fellow) members who are doing those practices.   It seems, thus, that
those (other, fellow) members exist for sociologists, in a sense (10)
as their practices.   It is important to note, though, that whilst
they see some of the practices of (other, fellow) collectively
members as social stratification, they do not see (that is, they do
not attend to, address or account for) any of their own practices as
such.   Yet sociologists' practices (which are concrete activities)
in accounting for some (concrete) practices of (other, fellow) members as social stratification share with them a common analytic form
of life.   For sociologists account for (other, fellow) members'
practices in an analytic way, that is as social stratification.
Concretely, as members' practices, they are not necessarily that;
they undergo an analytic transmogrification into that in being constituted as the attentive focus of sociologists' accounts of social
stratification.   Upon accomplishment of construction of these
accounts, the practices are presented by sociologists as what they
have been constituted (accounted for) as: social stratification.
Thus, when sociologists account for members' practices as social
stratification, they render what they account for as accountable for
in their terms: that is a constitutive feature of the practical
accomplishments that are sociological accounts.   Sociologists, that
is to say, present what they have observed in their accounts of it,
as an accomplishment, in and of itself, of what they claim to be
particularly competent to observe and account for.   They enable
themselves, thus, to proceed, in discussion, analysis and explanation of it, as if it had never been, could not possibly be, never
will be anything other than what it is seen and presented as inevitably, unavoidably and essentially being in their presentation of it.

3.   THE PARADOXICAL (IM)POSSIBILITY OF REFLEXIVE SOCIOLOGY

In the preceding paragraphs resides 'the "uninteresting" essential
reflexivity' (11) of sociologists' accounts of social stratification.   To render thus the issue that this paper has so far attempted
to address enables me to consider reflexivity as a constituent,
problematic phenomenon of the practical accounts that sociologists
propose as sociologies of social stratification.   The enterprise
that may be reflexive sociology has been proposed by Garfinkel as
making 'the "reflexive" character of practical activities observable;   to examine the artful practices of rational inquiry as organ-
izational phenomena without thought for correctives or irony'.   (12)
Such an enterprise is not, nor has it any relation to, (sociological)
theorizing (about social stratification, or whatever) which is
practised according to and in terms draw_ from hypothetico-deductive
models.   (13) Instead, for practical purposes of this paper, sociologies (of social stratification) are treated as sociologists'

formulations of sets of (stratifying) practices which are made recognizable as such in those formulations.   That is, they are seen as
being 'made to happen as events, in the same ordinary affairs that
in organizing they describe'.   (14) The terms in which sociologists
construct these formulations are those which they understand as the
terms in which sociologists do their professional work.   Their use
of them to formulate sociologies of social stratification is seen as
sociologists' attempts to put their (shared) language in order for
their (particular) purposes.   That is, they are seen as formulating
their (particular) sociologies on the basis of their (particular)
understandings of the language (of sociology) which (as sociologists)
they share.   Such formulations, thus, imply, in each case, a proposal that sociologists' (particular) sociologies become constitutive features of what each of them understands all of them to be
proposing might (or must) become (their joint) sociology.   Any
understanding of sociologists' (particular) sociologies as such
proposals is a reflexive product of considering them as sociologists'
work at all.   To read writing as a sociologist's writing is, unavoidably and already, to be reading for what sense it may have as
possibly that of sociology's to come.

Yet any sociologist, formulating his sociology, is simultaneously
differentiating himself from other sociologists, and their sociologies, in and because of the language he shares with them.   He differentiates himself in language because in its particular form, his
sociology is a particular use (his use) of sociology's language, in
contrast to any (and all) other sociologists' uses of it.   (15) He
differentiates himself because of language since, by using sociology's language, he proposes a differentiation between his sociology of, for example, social stratification (as potentially a constitutive feature of future sociologies of social stratification)
and all other available sociologies of such phenomena.   I propose
this as exemplifying especially that this paper cannot but try to be
about what I understand as the sharability, or commonness of sociology's language, for it is being written as proposing for itself a
reading, by other sociologists, as a sociologist's (my) sociology of
social stratification.

Thus, my sociology of social stratification is my proposal to
negotiate a differentiation of and for me, as a sociologist, from
other sociologists, through formulating my sociology in sociology's
language, and attempting its exemplification by discussing contributions (cf. Parsons) to the corpus of knowledge that is sociology's
tradition.   In that this formulating and discussing is my use of
sociology's language, it is also my way of differentiating myself
(as sociologist) from any and all (other) sociologists.   I am
attempting to formulate my (sociologist's) understanding of social
stratification reflexively, as what my formulations of it are unavoidably: that is, as practicings, in my writing of them, of that
understanding of stratification.

There is, however, a central paradox to reflexive sociology, which
may be found in what Garfinkel proposes as the uninteresting
character of the essential reflexivity of accounts.   To be interested in the essential reflexivity of sociologists' accounts would be
to be doing reflexive sociology, and thus not doing the practical

sociological inquiries constitutive of sociology (-which-is-not-reflexive).   That is to say, it would not be doing sociology as it is traditionally understood, precisely because to be doing reflexive sociology is to be rendering problematical, and thus the central topic of inquiry, that very tradition in whose (unexplicated) terms sociology is understood as what it is.   The sense, then, in which the essential reflexivity of sociologists' accounts is uninteresting to their formulators lies in this: that sociologists trying to be reflexive are sociologists doing work which is not understandable as sociology; whose sense is not grounded in sociology's tradition of (scientific) discourse.   Thus, in attempting to make the essentially reflexive character of their practical inquiries (into theories or practices of social stratification, for example) available, sociologists, as Garfinkel points out, 'are like members wherever they engage in practical sociological inquiries: though they would, they can have none of it'. (16)   And they can have none of it because sociology's tradition of discourse is not a reflexive one; it is, rather, a tradition developed about that notion of science which exhibits itself as consensual agreement around a set of concrete/substantive concerns. (17) Thus, wherever any sociologist invokes such a tradition as grounds in which may be found the (sociological) sense of his formulations, he surrenders his own authorship of them (what it is about them that makes them his, and no other sociologist's formulations) to the generalized, and generalizable authority of science.   For formulations whose senses reside in a tradition of scientific discourse are meaningful, 'ipso facto', in the degree to which they defy recovery and interpretation as the formulations of subjects. (18) Science's sense is the disimpassioned and impersonal sense of objectivity, whereas to be reflexive is unavoidably to speak as and of oneself.   And to do so requires quite another tradition, one which provides for the reflexive sense of discourse; one which, in the important respects signified above, would be unlike that of (scientific) sociology.

4.   REFLEXIVE DISCOURSE(S) ABOUT SOCIAL STRATIFICATION

This problematic paradox in the enterprise proposed as constituting reflexive sociology, renders reflexive inquiring about such topics as social stratification impossible to conduct as recognizably sociological, according to the provisions for sense of sociology's (scientific) tradition.   It does not, however, prevent reflexive discourse about constitutive features of sociology's topics.   For if sociologies of social stratification are sociologists' ways of seeing some practices of members of human collectivities as sociologically analysable practices, then those practices, whilst being constituted amongst sociology's topics, may be constituted differently in the ways of members of other collectivities of observing-members than professional sociology, according to senses provided for in their traditions.   Two instances may be found in writings of Raymond Williams and E.P. Thompson on those practices of members which are constitutive of class, itself a feature constitutive of social stratification as a topic of sociology. (19) This is not, of course, to propose that either Williams or Thompson formulate any

sociologists's notion of class in their own notions; nor that the
senses of either of their notions are, or might become, sociology's.
Thus they are not invoked here to provide correctives or remedies
for sociologies of social stratification.   Their notions of class
arise from their inquiries after grounds for its sense as a word
signifying some practices of members of human collectivities.
Their inquiries are interesting here in as much as the word class'is
seen as belonging to a vocabulary of words, employed in constituting
collectivity members' practices of social stratification, which is
common to sociology and to Williams's and Thompson's collectivities
of observing members: socio-literary criticism and social history
respectively.   My interest in displaying here my reading of their
inquiries after grounds for their senses of class, lies in examining
them for demonstrations of the possibilities of reflexive discourse
about social stratification.

Williams writes of class as historical practices of class's language, in such modes of speech as literature, criticism and politics.
He points to

a general pattern of change (in) a number of words, which
are now of capital importance (and which) came for the
first time into common English use (in the last decades
of the 18th century), or, where they had already been
generally used in the language, acquired new and important
meanings.   (The changes in their use) bear witness to a
general change in our characteristic ways of thinking
about our common life: about our social, political, and
economic institutions; about the purposes which these
institutions are designed to embody; and about the relations to these institutions and purposes of our activities,
in learning, education, and the arts. (20)

Williams's way of dealing with the examination of meanings (and
changes of meanings) of words is 'not only to distinguish meanings,
but to relate them to their sources and effects'.   He states the
reasoning behind this as a commitment 'to the study of actual language: that is to say, to the words and sequences of words which particular men and women have used in trying to give meaning to their
experience'.   His method is to study 'actual individual statements
and contributions'; its purpose is to 'understand and value' these
statements. (21)

Understanding, presumably, is possible through the commonness of
language; that is, it is a shared understanding of 'the words and
sequences of words', and it is in the uses to which individual
writers have put the language which they share with Williams and
others that provide the grounds for understandability, for sense.
And valuing these words and sequences of words points up the grounds
still further.   For in valuing them, Williams can be seen as negotiating resort to a tradition which is somehow signified by and
in the language he shares with the writers whose works he studies,
and which provides, and provides for, the ways in which he will
value the words and sequences of words that constitute their writings.   Thus, in reading Williams's writing according to its re-
commendations, that is, as inquiring into particular writers' words
and sequences of words, the commonness of those writers', and
Williams's, and our own language(s) of writing/reading makes us

look again at those of our experiences with which they resonate
(which they re-constitute resonantly).   And in looking at them
again, we look at them anew, not only as our experiences, but as
potentially having been their experiences, too.   Valuing their
statements complements understanding them for Williams and, through
our reading of Williams, perhaps for us.   It shows us how we understand the experiences of the writers for whose statements Williams's
writing proposes understanding and valuing, through and as our own
experiences.

In this way, Williams provides for the notion of tradition, in
proposing changes in and of the meanings of such key words as class
as the location of a general pattern of change.   The valuations of
these changes that produce this general pattern equip us, in doing
so, with 'a special kind of map by which it is possible to look
again at the wider changes in life and thought to which the changes
in language evidently refer'.   (22)   More than that, Williams has
a strong notion of one word that encapsulates and organizes class
and all other key words (amongst which words it is itself included):
the word 'Culture'.   It concentrates questions in its meaning, he
proposes, which

are questions directly raised by the great historical
changes which the changes in industry, democracy, and
class, in their own way, represent, and to which the
changes in art are a closely related response.   The
development of the word culture is a record of a number
of important and continuing reactions to these changes
in our social, economic, and political life, and may be
seen, in itself, as a special kind of map by means of
which the nature of the changes can be explored.   (23)

Williams proposes a reading of his writing as the particular task of
describing relations which are found within the general pattern of
change that he sees in these words.   He formulates the relations as
'our characteristic ways of thinking about our common life', etc.
The word culture 'more than any other comprises these relations ...
with all its complexity of idea and reference'.   What he sees in
its history as a word, 'in its structure of meanings, is a wide and
general movement in thought and feeling' exemplified in the 'complex
and radical response' that he sees it as being 'to the new problems
of social class'.   He formulates the relations between culture and
class as constitutive of his notion of class culture - especially
working-class culture.   Thus: 'the body of intellectual and imaginative work which each generation receives as its traditional culture
is always, and necessarily, something more than the product of a
single class'.   (24)   And this is so, not only on historical grounds,
but also because

even within a society in which a particular class is
dominant, it is evidently possible both for members
of other classes to contribute to the common stock,
and for such contributions to be unaffected by or in
opposition to the ideas and values of the dominant
class.   The area of a culture, it would seem, is
usually proportionate to the area of a language rather
than to the area of a class.   (25)

The point is emphasized in Williams's statement that 'men who share

a common language share the inheritance of an intellectual and
literary tradition which is necessarily and constantly revalued
with every shift in experience'. (26) Culture, in Williams's usage, signifies tradition.

Thus, in writing of class as historical practices of class's language in a number of modes of discourse, Williams invites reading of
himself as attempting recovery of shifts in experiences as (re-)
valuings of this inherited intellectual and literary tradition that
are signified by the changes in meanings of the word class that writings such as his propose to reveal. And changes in meaning here
signify changes in the way members use class to constitute features
of their experiences.   Thus the importance of class's language, like
that of each of Williams's other key words, lies in its existence as
a constitutive feature of culture's (the tradition's) language.
Without that, in its commonness, we cannot recover the residua of
shared (re-)valuations of shared experiences that is the tradition
in which we may seek grounds for sense of our living.   For 'it is
clearly of vital importance to a culture that its common language
should not decline in strength, richness, and flexibility; that it
should, further, be adequate to express new experience, and to clar-
ify change'. (27) The flexibility of language is crucial: through
its flexibility I may express the novelty (as difference, rather than
newness) of my experience as a feature of our knowledge.   In its
richness I may express my understanding of the depth of my experience.   And its strength may carry my expressions to you, for what
I hope will be your (and so, our) understanding.   In short, in so
far as my experience is, or can be, knowledge at all, it can be so
only in such expressions, in my use of our language.

Thus, Williams formulates his notion of class as 'a collective
mode (of being, feeling, acting) of that part of a group of people,
similarly circumstanced, which has become conscious of its own
position and of its own attitude to this position'. (28)   And each
class is provided for by its culture, whose constitutive, binary
elements are mediated synthetically by Williams as 'the basic collective idea, and the institutions, manners, habits of thought, and
intentions which proceed from this'. (29)

Thompson writes of class as historical practices of class's acts;
and for him, similarly, a class amounts to
  a very loosely defined body of people who share the same
  congeries of interests, social experiences, traditions
  and value-system, who have a disposition to behave as a
  class, to define themselves in their actions and in
  their consciousness in relation to other groups of people
  in class ways.   But class itself is not a thing, it is a
  happening. (30)
He formulates it, also, as
  a social and cultural formation (often finding institutional expression) which cannot be defined abstractly, or
  in isolation, but only in terms of relationship with
  other classes; and, ultimately, the definition can only
  be made in the medium of time - that is, action and re-
  action, change and conflict. (31)
Class is thus understood as 'a historical phenomenon, unifying a
number of disparate and seemingly unconnected events, both in the

new material of experience and in consciousness'. (32) As such,
it defies characterization as a structure or a category, it is,
rather, 'something which in fact happens (and can be shown to have
happened) in human relationships'. Further, it
    entails the notion of historical relationship. Like
    any other relationship it is a fluency which evades
    analysis if we stop it dead at any given moment and
    anatomize its structure. The finest-meshed socio-
    logical net cannot give us a pure specimen of class
    .... And class happens when some men, as a result of
    common experiences (inherited or shared) feel and
    articulate the identity of their interests as between
    themselves, and as against other men, whose interests
    are different from (and usually opposed to) theirs. (33)
Thompson's formulation of class is as a process to which there is
a deterministic element, in that 'the productive relations into
which men are born - or enter involuntarily - determine their class
experience'. Yet he proposes that this determinism is transcended
where class-consciousness occurs. For class-consciousness is the
ways in which class experiences are constituted in cultural terms.
Thus, though there may be seen 'a logic in the responses of similar
occupational groups undergoing similar experiences', this cannot be
predicated in any law. Thus 'consciousness of class arises in the
same way in different times and places, but never in just the same
way'. (34)
    Above all, however, for Thompson
    class is a relationship, and not a thing ... if we stop
    history at a given point, then there are no classes but
    simply a multitude of individuals with a multitude of
    experiences. But if we watch these men over an
    adequate period of social change, we observe patterns
    in their relationships, their ideas and their instit-
    ions. Class is defined by men as they live their own
    history, and, in the end, this is its only definition. (35)

Both Williams and Thompson need to point up, characterize and utilize notions of tradition, which they both term a culture (Williams
specifies it deeply as an imaginative and intellectual inheritance;
Thompson characterizes its depth by insisting upon the historically
particular and unique character of its constitutive phenomena).
Their notions are signified by our common languages of social stratification - those languages by and in which we are their readers,
they our writers. And their notions are reflexive upon those
languages (in this particular case, on their respective formulations
of class) in order to make them meaningful; that is, to make them
sharable as constituting dimensions of recognizably shared and sharable experience. Their formulations, that is, limit the open
horizon of meaning that the word class, like any and all other
words, carries along with it. (36) They render the word class as
constitutive of their experiential notions and practices, and thus
render those very notions and practices as class.
    To read Williams and Thompson thus, is to read them as writing
reflexively of and in the tradition which affords their language
sense. For their inquiries after the grounds for sense of their

notions of class are not readable as solely concerned with differentiating their formulations of these notions from those of other practitioners in the same, or different traditions of observing. They are, more importantly, readable as attempts to constitute class as members' practical experiences, in different sequences of words from our common language(s).   Such formulations of class involve their formulators' experiences of the dimensions of class, as human experiences.   And to the degree that sequences of words of our common language(s) constitute such formulations, I read them as proposing a guarantee that Williams and Thompson have anything to say at all.   Their inquiries into class as a topic are proposed here as reflexive in allowing me a reading of their accounts of them as sharing an analytic form of life with the concrete practices of which class is constituted.   For to be reflexive on class's language, or its acts, requires that (observing and practicing) members of human collectivities address their own experiences of class as constitutive of the analyses they perform upon class as a topic.

In section 2 of this paper to read Parsons's writing as Parsons's writing, it was necessary to restore his authorship to what cannot but have been his formulations of social stratification because, as a theorizer in sociology's (scientific) tradition, he could not claim any authority for his formulations but that of science. Williams and Thompson, by contrast, propose their authorship as constitutive in significant ways, of whatever authority their formulations of class may be read as having by fellow-members of their human collectivities of (observing and practising) members.   Reading them does not require of this reader that he (I) restore their writing to them as its human source and sense.

Consider, as a way, perhaps, of making this proposal more clearly, that the tradition(s) that afford grounds for the senses of Williams's and Thompson's formulations are not graspable in the unity of their (analytic) commonness at all, but only in their (concrete) diversity.   Read their common language(s), then, as signifying two particular notions of tradition.   First, there are what may be called traditions affording grounds for senses of observing, employed by each in specific forms: by Williams, socio-literary criticism; by Thompson, social history.   Second, there are traditions affording grounds for senses of practices.   The first traditions enable and provide for the juxtapositioning of their ideas with writers on analogous topics, whose senses are constituted in different traditions of observing.   The second traditions enable and provide for their ideas as grounded in the experiences being undertaken by them as members of human collectivities, and thus for the availability of the sense of those experiences to those other members who are their readers.

Another way of formulating such a notion of tradition, as divisible for purposes of conceptualization, is proposed by Oakeshott, (37) who considers tradition as constituted of four modes of experience: Practice (i.e. common-sense acting), Science (i.e. systematic scholarship), History (i.e. past experience) and Poetry (i.e. imagining as a gloss on art).   The unity of these modes as tradition resides in tradition's principle – the principle of continuity.   And it is only this principle that enables characterization of tradition at all: it is nothing in itself, yet it

informs everything that we know, in our saying or doing.   Because
whatever we know is understandable by and in its saying or doing,
and it is tradition's principle of continuity that allows for its
understandability.   Oakeshott writes of it, in relation to political
behaviour:

> Authority is diffused between past, present and future,
> between the old, the new and what is to come.   It is
> steady because, though it moves, it is never wholly
> 'in motion' and though it is tranquil it is never wholly
> 'at rest'.   Nothing that ever belonged to it is com-
> pletely lost; we are always swerving back to recover
> and make something topical out of even its remotest
> moments: and nothing for long remains unmodified.
> Everything is temporary, but nothing is arbitrary.
> Everything figures by comparison, not with what stands
> next to it, but with the whole.   And since a tradition
> of behaviour is not susceptible of the distinction
> between essence and accident, knowledge of it is un-
> avoidably knowledge of its detail: to know only the
> gist is to know nothing: what has to be learned is
> not an abstract idea, or a set of tricks, not even a
> ritual, but a concrete, coherent manner of living in
> all its intricateness. (38)

Read this as gelling strongly with the ways in which Williams and
Thompson inquire into the grounds for sense of class as a word in
our common language (of social stratification).   It proposes, in
effect, that our ways of seeing are our ways of explicating as
knowledge what we understand as our ways of doing, for example,
social stratification.   It is such a generative notion that this
paper proposes for negotiation as the tradition in which reflexive
discourse (about social stratification) grounds itself.   Social
stratification is proposed here as trading upon languages common to
us in our membership of human collectivities of observing and of
practising members.   Membershipping ourselves in the former is exploring the analytic possibility of negotiating agreement that we
are talking together about similarities: in the latter, it is undertaking concrete formulations of the practical experiences which are
the means of doing so.

CONCLUSION

This paper belongs in a collection which I read, understand and
value as seeking to propose for negotiation the tradition that will
provide for senses of (reflexive) sociology.   That tradition's (and
its sociology's) commitment is its insistence upon the human authorship of all human speech, for therein is the humanness of men.
Its practice lies in seeking (and speaking) sociology's 'logos', and,
in so doing, restoring men to social life, and social life to men.
Yet, to give such reasonings, in the way that is much of this
paper, is so far to do no more than to attempt that (social) stratification which is membershipping concretely in existing sociologies'
traditions; it is to leave those things at hand where they lie.
This may be its final irony; for members' and sociologists'
(stratifying) practices remain untouched as yet.

NOTES

* David Walsh made many valuable comments upon this paper during
the many and regular talks that we had whilst I was writing it.   I
am, as so often, extremely grateful for his patience and generosity.
I was also helped considerably by the responses to earlier versions
of this paper of Stewart Clegg, David Harrison and Chris Jenks.
Belonging, as it does, in this collection, what merits it may have
testified to the value of collaborative work with the writers of
other papers in this volume.   Responsibility for its limitations is
my own.

1   'Identity and Difference', p.41.
2   See, for example, Kingsley Davis and Wilbert E. Moore, 'Some
    Principles of Stratification', who introduce their paper thus:
    'Starting from the proposition that no society is 'classless',
    or unstratified, an effort is made to explain, in functional
    terms, the universal necessity which calls forth stratification
    in any social system' in Reinhard Bendix and Seymour Martin
    Lipset (eds.), 'Class, Status and Power', p.47.
3   An Analytical Approach to the Theory of Social Stratification
    (1940), in Talcott Parsons, 'Essays in Sociological Theory:
    Revised Ediction', pp.69-88.
4   Ibid., p.69.
5   'The sociologist ought, therefore, whether at the moment of the
    determination of his research objectives or in the course of his
    demonstrations, to repudiate resolutely the use of concepts
    originating outside of science for totally unscientific needs.
    He must emancipate himself from the fallacious ideas that domin-
    ate the mind of the layman; he must throw off, once and for all,
    the yoke of these empirical categories, which from long continued
    habit have become tyrannical.   At the very least, if at times he
    is obliged to resort to them, he ought to do so fully conscious
    of their trifling value, so that he will not assign to them a
    role out of proportion to their real importance'.   Emile Durk-
    heim, 'The Rules of Sociological Method', p.32.
6   'An Analytical Approach to the Theory of Social Stratification',
    op. cit., p.69 fn.
7   Ibid., p.69 fn.
8   Ibid., pp.75-6.
9   Ibid., pp.78-88.
10 That sense which is constituted in sociologists' practical,
    professional purposes of providing for sociologies of social
    stratification.
11 The phrase is Garfinkel's.   The discussion of reflexivity that
    follows depends upon my reading of his 'Studies in Ethnomethod-
    ology', pp.4-9, and owes much to Maurice Roche's (unpublished)
    Notes on Reflexivity.
12 'Studies in Ethnomethodology', p.9.
13 It is worth noting here that it therefore has little to do with
    Gouldner's notion of reflexive sociology (see 'The Coming Crisis

of Western Sociology', passim, and O'Neill's critique in his 'Sociology as a Skin Trade', pp.209-20); nor does it have much to do with much ethnomethodology (see Alan Blum's paper on Theorizing in Jack D. Douglas, 'Understanding Everyday Life', pp.301-19).

14 Harold Garfinkel, 'Studies in Ethnomethodology', p.1.
15 This notion rests on the assumption that sociologists choose thoughtfully the language that they use, and are, in that sense at least, consciously the authors of what they write.
16 'Studies in Ethnomethodology', p.9.
17 See, for example, Robert A. Nisbet's assembly of the tradition around the concerns signified by sociology's 'unit ideas' in his 'The Sociological Tradition'. The notion of science invoked in this passage is discussed at length by David Walsh in his paper: Science, Sociology and Everyday Life, in Chris Jenks (ed.): 'Knowledge, Rationality and Thought: Papers for a Reflexive Sociology of Education'.
18 'It is a rule in the natural sciences to discard those data of sensation that are too subjective, in order to retain exclusively those presenting a sufficient degree of objectivity .... The sociologist must take the same precautions. The external characteristics in terms of which he defines the objects of his researches should be as objective as possible'. Emile Durkheim, op.cit., p.44.
19 Raymond Williams, 'Culture and Society: 1780-1950', pp.14-17, 307, 318. E.P. Thompson, 'The Making of the English Working Class, pp.9-14, 937-9.
20 Raymond Williams, op.cit., p.13.
21 Raymond Williams, op.cit., p.18.
22 Ibid., p.13.
23 Ibid., p.16.
24 Ibid., p.16-17. Williams's notion of culture, as is often the case in professional sociological, anthropological and literary critical work, is binary (cf. A.L. Kroeber and Clyde Kluckhohn, 'Culture: A critical Review of Concepts and Definitions'). He sees culture as both a tradition of intellectual and imaginative work (received culture) and a whole, ongoing way of life, in the 'patterned', 'structured', etc. 'form' in which it is presented, and of which the 'received tradition' is a constitutive feature.
25 Ibid., p.308.
26 Ibid.
27 Ibid., p.313.
28 Ibid.
29 Ibid.
30 E.P. Thompson, op.cit., p.939.
31 Ibid., p.9.
32 Ibid., p.939.
33 Ibid., pp.9-10.
34 Ibid., p.10.
35 Ibid., p.11.
36 See Alfred Schutz, 'Collected Papers', vol. I, p.44.
37 Michael Oakeshott, 'Rationalism in Politics and Other Essays'. See also W.H. Greenleaf, 'Oakeshott's Philosophical Politics', especially ch. 3.
38 Oakeshott, op.cit., pp.128-9.

BIBLIOGRAPHY

BENDIX, Reinhard and Seymour Martin Lipset, 'Class, Status and Power', Revised Edition 1966, London, Routledge & Kegan Paul.
DOUGLAS, Jack D., 'Understanding Everyday Life', 1970, Chicago, Aldine.
DURKHEIM, Emile, 'The Rules of Sociological Method', 1938 (1964), New York, Free Press.
GARFINKEL, Harold, 'Studies in Ethnomethodology', 1967, Englewood Cliffs, New Jersey, Prentice-Hall.
GREENLEAF, W.H., 'Oakeshott's Philosophical Politics', 1966, London, Longmans.
GOULDNER, Alvin W., 'The Coming Crisis of Western Sociology', 1970, New York and London, Basic Books.
HEIDEGGER, Martin, 'What is a Thing', 1967 (1970), Chicago, Henry Regnery.
HEIDEGGER, Martin, 'Identity and Difference, 1969, New York, Evanston and London, Harper & Row.
JENKS, Chris. (ed.), 'Knowledge, Rationality and Thought: Papers for a Reflexive Sociology of Education (forthcoming) 1975, London, Collier-Macmillan.
KROEBER, A.L. and Clyde Kluckhohn, 'Culture: A Critical Review of Concepts and Definitions', 1952 (n.d.), New York, Vintage Books - Alfred A. Knopf and Random House.
NISBET, Robert A., 'The Sociological Tradition, 1966, New York, Basic Books.
OAKESHOTT, Michael, 'Rationalism in Politics and Other Essays', 1962, London, Methuen.
O'NEILL, John, 'Sociology as a Skin Trade', 1972, London, Heinemann Educational Books.
PARSONS, Talcott, 'Essays in Sociological Theory', Revised Edition 1954, Chicago, Free Press.
ROCHE, Maurice, Notes on Reflexivity, 1972, Department of Sociology, London School of Economics and Political Science, unpublished mimeograph.
SCHUTZ, Alfred, 'Collected Papers' I, 1962 (1971), The Hague, Martinus Nijhoff.
THOMPSON, E.P., 'The Making of the English Working Class', 1968, London, Penguin Books.
WILLIAMS, Raymond, 'Culture and Society: 1780-1950', 1968, London, Penguin Books.

Chapter 6

STRATIFYING SPEECH *
Michael Phillipson

> The spectacle is the heir of the entire weakness of the
> western philosophical project, which was to understand
> activity, dominated by the categories of seeing; further-
> more, it is based on the incessant spread of the precise
> technical rationality which grew out of this thought.
> It does not realise philosophy, it philosophises reality.
> The concrete life of everybody has been degraded into a
> speculative universe.
> > Guy Debord, Thesis 19, The Society of the Spectacle.

Stratifying practices are ubiquitous and this ubiquity provides for
the infinite task of concrete sociological description of such
practices.   But this concrete description stops short of that reflexive and dialectical turn which would re-cognize itself as an
exemplification of its topic; in its stopping short it fails to
listen to and hear its own speech as displaying those very practices
whose being it claims to capture.   Stratifying practices and stratifying talk, as routine social accomplishments, conceal, in the ways
that all practices and talk do through the modes of their Framing,
that which allows for their intelligibility as just such stratifying practices.   To understand the form of life, the way in Language,
that these practices display, the required analytic alternative (to
the infinite concrete description of stratifying practices) is to
make the method which enables their recognition as stratifying practices and the grounds which give them their possibility the topics
for analysis.   The call is for a re-covery or re-trieval which, by
theorizing the methodic character of that movement of being which
generates the sensible character of concrete stratifying practices,
would bring the forms of their organization out of concealment and
point to the grounds on which they stand.

This text treats the practices through which sociological understanding and knowledge are assembled and textually presented as the
topics.   In this way it is sociological work itself which provides
us with an occasion for re-trieving an analytic sense of stratification's grounds.   In circular terms this text can also be read as
a treatment of stratification which provides an occasion for theorizing sociology's grounds.

To talk of grounds is to install ontology as the necessarily
first (but invariably hidden) topic in sociological discourse.
That sociological talk ordinarily rests on what, for it, are essentially uninteresting and therefore implicit and unexplicated ontologies displays its forgetful character; this amnesia is convenient
in the routine accomplishment of sociology for it allows work to
continue without the awkward delays which self-questioning about
sociology's ways within Being and Language would entail. But, for
us, this self-forgetting leaves a hole in the heart of sociological
speech which has fateful consequences for the claims which that
speech makes for itself. Making grounds, or sociology's self-
establishment within Being, topics for sociology is to point to the
invisible presence of ontologies in all speaking and writing and
hence ontology's ineluctable character for any self-questioning discourse. To continue, as does sociology, as if the problematic of
ontology's presence in sociological speaking has been permanently
settled by making it into an absence is to fail to see that the
question of ontology has never been properly raised. In any showing
of a sense of stratification's or sociology's grounds we are, then,
required to move outside the language of the sociological tradition
precisely because the latter's theoretic practices display the tradition as adequately reflexive for its own purposes. From within
its discourse it appears and gives itself as adequately grounded,
but from without the constitution of this sense of adequacy can be
seen as a concealing of that which allows it to claim adequacy.
However a showing of grounds from outside sociology's terms of discourse presupposes inside knowledge of sociology's ways of self-
constitution and the possibility of recurrent movement into and out
of those ways in the course of the showing. This showing necessarily relies on such a circular movement as does sociological work itself when it relies on and moves into and out of ordinary ways of
speaking.
   My treatment of sociological practices and writing as an occasion
for re-trieving a sense of stratification's grounds is done, hopefully, under the auspices of a principled re-trieval and way to re-
covery. The re-covery is carried through under the power of an
'illuminative idea' which opens up a way for the showing. (1) The
way is opened up by a conception of the relation between a text and
its reader as an 'internal relationship'; the 'togetherness' of text
and reader are necessarily lost in those all too familiar modes of
analysis which show and hence reduce 'togetherness' to the status of
product of external features, whether historical/genetic or situational. Treating the relationship between text and reader from the
inside, as a coherence, a togetherness, demands a staying within the
text and a listening to its speech for a reader - ourselves - while
going outside the text is to listen to something other than the text
to show its togetherness for us. This latter movement ultimately
fails, and hence misses the sense of togetherness as a relationship,
because, although it is always forced back to what keeps the text
together for the reader, it fails to treat its own relationship to
the text as the fundamental problematic. Even the external analysis
ends in the position where it faces its own possibility as a togetherness. It sees its inescapable presence within the circle when
it recognizes that the text cannot be listened to from somewhere

outside it, and that it must eventually listen to the mode of its own togetherness with the text.   There can be no extra-textual 'help' for the reader for all such 'help' (critiques, reviews, eulogies, exegeses and so on) itself takes textual form, be it written or spoken, which demands its own togetherness.   Interpretation is always the situated togetherness of dialogue. (2)

1. SOCIOLOGY'S AUTHORITATIVE CALL TO AND CLAIM ON THE READER

While all writing and reading are dialogue, our proposal is that different approaches to writing intend to provide for very different readerships and show this through the different forms of their calls to readers; every piece of writing has a particular kind of call, there can be no 'writing-in-general' which points to 'no-dialogue-in-particular'.   Each call is a convention, it gives itself through methods and rules; for the text to be received according to the writer's intentions in framing the call, the call has to be heeded and followed by the readership, but the problem faced by writing is the reader's freedom to decide what he can make of and with the writing.   In the light of the failure of positivist and realist writing to re-cognize their own transformative character we elect to treat all texts as both 'deep autobiography' (where 'auto's' problem is to show the community within which and to which his 'biography' speaks) and as 'novel' (factitious).   Our problematic here is to listen to sociology's call, to hear how it demands to be read, and to point to the grounds of our own listening togetherness with that call; the form of the practical accomplishment of sociological texts' self-insertion into tradition is taken as an occasion to re-trieve stratification's grounds, to display the tension within which this apparently authoritative self-insertion lives.

Stratification is done in sociology when sociological writing and speaking collects itself under the auspices of an authority which differentiates and elevates itself from other modes of speaking about the social world.   The authority, sociology's ground or being, en-ables stratification as a routine accomplishment of sociological speaking. (3) But the present formulation shows sociological speaking's explicit attempt to differentiate itself from other modes of speaking through Method as grounded on a deeper warrant which collects its speaking with the descriptive practices of everyman. Those sociological practices which attempt to wrench sociological speech away from the site of mundane speaking cover over their analytic community with the mundane; one way of making the forms of that community visible is re-covered here.   Sociological writing and speaking provide explicitly for a stratified mode of together-ness between text and reader or speaker and hearer.

Sociological writing does make reference to its own grounds in its demand to be read in one way - concretely; it is this self-grounding of sociology which is here made problematic, so that, from alternative grounds, the self-grounding is seen as a covering over of that which makes it possible.   This text is a showing, generated (from other grounds to which this text itself, hopefully, points) of the possibility of sociological description.

In its demand to be read concretely sociological writing conceals that which allows it to command.   In the one way, the way 'intended' by the writer, the text is treated as a 'something' which is assembled according to a body of rules that both provide for an unequivocal reading and stand the text on its own without attachments to author.   Sociological texts point to their grounds in their self-presentation as objects whose speech is to be treated like any other object in the world and whose truths have an object-like status. (4)

The sociologist's authority rests on his convincing display that the text is, and is only, what it speaks concretely; this speaking is concretely about the social world and its authority is grounded in ways of seeing the social world and ways of making it available for readers which eliminate the necessity for the writer to show the speaking as his speaking. He has no need to provide for himself as him-self for his speaking has already provided for him as the medium for the articulation of the social world. So his lack of provision for himself can be treated from other grounds as a special kind of provision. A consequence of this lack of provision is that it enables sociology to make stratifying claims about itself as a way to knowledge which, from alternative grounds,are expressed and made available through inauthentic modes of speaking. Inauthenticity, here, makes reference to the self-forgetfulness of sociological writing and speaking; it forgets to listen to, let alone hear, itself. The forgetfulness leads to a way in writing in which author and reader disappear together into the vortex in which they are enveloped by the anonymous Anyman – he who writes and reads for and on behalf of anyone. Where the writer either loses or negates himself in the name of the impersonal 'one' writing becomes decadent through its falling away from that possibility of authenticity in which writer listens to his speaking and invites reader to do the same.

Placing sociology within the interpretive circle shows it both as one way to abstract knowledge of the social and also as a set of practices situated in a world of others and accomplished through the very knowledge which is its subject in the first place. Sociologists can pose problems for themselves only because they are first of all members and can only do the posing through the practices they wish to study. So that to show sociology as living through the practices it wishes to describe is to raise the question of the character of sociological membership of the social world. It is to ask where and how it takes up its stance towards those practices and where and how others locate its practices as ordinary ways of being. Sociology, as a set of situated practices in the world, is itself included in its own problems and questions so that its questions must necessarily recoil back at the questioner, whether or not the questioner is listening for and has the ears to hear them. This recoil requires a regressive movement which is pointed towards origins and opens up ways to a disclosure of sociology's mode of being-in-the-world. The pointing is directed not out of the language but to the movements within the circle; origins, grounds, are not external immutables but are in the interpretive moments which routinely establish sociology's claims.

As an aspiring science sociology aims to produce empirically valid, objective knowledge of the social world; (5) in so far as it takes what it understands as the rationality of science (6) as a prescription for its own practices it recommends these practices as

the way to 'valid' knowledge of the social and sociologists collect
themselves through it.   The collecting entails a differentiation
which sets the validity of such knowledge as sociology produces
against other forms of knowledge which are 'less valid' or 'invalid'
(e.g. that gained through ordinary experience).   In its being within
the life-world as a self-projection through scientific rationality
sociology distances itself from that 'ideological' knowledge which
arises from and supports practical interests.   This differentiating
claim points to the explicit stratifying character of sociological
writing and talk, for that which is scientifically valid requires the
reader to accept its authority as the truth.   The methodic practices
which rest on scientific rationality are presumed to generate texts
which display themselves as in correspondence with or mirrors of the
world.   (7) A reader of a text produced under such auspices 'must'
subjugate himself to it to the extent that he accepts its truth
claims, and its construction is designed to enforce just such acceptance.   Sociological writing achieves its success as a stratifying
practice, that is, it manages to set itself up as 'above' other
claims or as 'above criticism', where it persuades its readers of its
ability to substitute objective for indexical expressions.   (8)
This substitution is a practical accomplishment which rests on sociology's generation of its own ways of conceding truth so that truth
is an 'institutional grammar'.   (9) The accomplishment of public
consensus as the constituting activity of sociological truth is done
through ways of speaking which enshrine and preserve the sociologist,
both for other sociologists and members as 'expert' on the social.
The claim to superiority is rarely explicitly articulated in sociological texts but their organization and their mode of being-in-
language are designed to display their unequivocally superior
character;   the texts speak to their superiority through the methodic
practices in language by which they are constructed.   Their ways of
speaking are sufficient to carry the reader along in willing acceptance for they are constructed to preserve their status as displays
of the truth.

Sociology's claim to be different to other ways to knowledge, that
is the display of difference in the ways in which its texts are constructed, can be seen as grounded in the kinds of methodic reflections from which the texts emerge;   the investigations which constitute these methodic reflections are characterized as possessing
special features which give them privileged status in production of
the social.   But self-reflection in sociology carried out from within and through the mathematizing modes of 'technological - calculative' thought, is limited almost entirely to refinement of its
constructive practices and the definition of concepts, and only
rarely does the turn back address the grounds on which those practices and concepts stand, for sociology's way is to treat itself and
its methods as a set of unsituated practices.   This failure to
treat (even concretely) its own situated character is in itself a
denial of sociology's programmatic intention, for sociology lives
through and stands on its claims to address the situated character
of practices and there is no way such a programme can exclude the
practices of sociology itself without fateful consequences.   Where
reflection's concern is the refinement of existing practices the
being of sociology remains untouched.   In contrast a radically

reflexive and dialectical sociology looks inward and addresses the
possibility of its own production.   The present formulation recovers
a sense of what is hidden by sociological speaking and writing in the
stratifying movements of its own methodic practices (collecting, differentiating, elevating and so on);   the tradition preserves for us
the very moments in which, in the act of writing, sociological speaking congeals itself as stratifying speech, and it is we ourselves who
preserve the tradition when we enter and re-activate its texts on
their own terms.   But this kind of preservation freezes the tradition's texts into building blocks which provide a base for constructive work.   The way of reflexivity and dialectic also preserves the tradition, but preserves it as an ever-open invitation to
a retrieval which overcomes, through its creative negativity, the
very terms through which the texts give themselves.   Along this way
the tradition becomes neither correct orderings, nor a putting to
rights, nor a stockpiling of information, but an occasion for a
dialogue whose topic is always that which grants the constrained and
situated character of its own understanding.   Dialogue addresses
both its own and the tradition's historicity in its continual and
unavoidable transformations of the tradition.   (10)

   Ironically the de-authorization of sociological speech gives it
its authority.   The sociologist, as author, claims authority which
differentiates him from those for whom he writes, whether they be co-
professionals or laity;   the authority claimed in his writing places
him 'over' others for it is a claim to 'know', a claim to 'possess'
knowledge of which others are ignorant.   As a producer of 'new'
'valid' knowledge he claims to increase the stock of things known
about the social world.   But his claim is also that anyone can know
these things for the things are made possible and available through
methods whose truthful character rests on their public availability.
The bases of this authoritative differentiation are found in the
linguistic modes of expression through which sociologists Frame their
speaking.   (11)   Their speech is an authoritative saying - it makes
reference to that which is the grant of their authority.   This grant
is the opening up of a region or site to which others are authoritatively called;   the claim is that the site is on a higher plane, is
further along the way to knowledge, and is thus a calling to those
behind to move up the way to the site of knowledge.

   As theoretic knowledge the only experience sociology could provide
for the reader is an experience with and in language, so that the
reader can only learn something 'new' through his interpretation of
the modes of re-presenting the knowledge.   The theorist re-orders
(transforms) that which is already re-presented by members themselves
so that his task is to ensure the reader's agreement with the re-
ordering;   his methods must do more than the rhetorical persuasion of
'commonsense' for they must secure agreement that 'things' are just
as they are shown to be in the re-ordering.   Any writer's claim to
know, based on the authority which authorizes his authorship (speech)
must have its ultimate ground (its limit) in the horizon of the
writer's present, (12) so that to accept the writer's re-presentation
of the world as true knowledge requires the reader to stand with him
in his present, as disclosed in his writing, and to re-cover the
constitution of his horizon.   But this calls for an impossible unity

which would be the substitution of reader for writer; such a call
and its acceptance by a reader as a feature of writing and reading
sociology hides the togetherness or dialogue that is reading.

Sociological writing, as a display of one kind of theoretic knowledge, beckons to the reader to move up the way to the site on which
it stands, persuading him that he will know both 'more' and 'better'
theoretically from that site. The way (13) consists of sites which
provide for progressively authoritative understandings so that a
site provides a ground from which to methodically look at and talk
authoritatively about the social world. The sites themselves are
framed within and constructed by the sociologist's methods of organizing knowledge so that the knowledge which is sited is a methodic
construction and any attention it commands arises from the impressive
visibility of its methods. The knowledge must point back to the
principles of its construction, it must show or make reference to its
methodic character for it is this which in its terms gives it its
authority. As, for it, its authority resides in this methodic
character there is no need for the author to make substantive claims
for the status of his product for its authority is grounded in its
showing of its own methodic production. (14) By pointing to or
displaying itself as a methodically organized production sociological
writing is adequately reflexive in its own terms; it provides for
itself as a display of that kind of knowledge which differentiates
itself from mundane knowledge through the ways it makes reference to
itself as a methodic achievement. But whether the display points
to a qualitative differentiation between sociological and other ways
to knowledge or is, rather, a more organized form, a bureaucratization,
of that which is already known, is another matter.

If its authority, its ability to subjugate and to demand agreement, resides in its methods and in the ways these are reflexively
displayed in its authoritative ways of speaking, then it is these
methods and the reflexivity of sociological speaking which must be
made the topic if the grounds of the authority claimed by sociologists are to be made visible. Sociological texts must be treated as
texts which make reference to their own organization and in so doing
provide for their claims to knowledge, for it is this self-grounding
character of sociological speech which is our topic.

Self-grounding gives itself as speech which stratifies itself on
different levels. We can see stratification being done concretely
in the way Method is called upon to provide the warrant for the
elevated talk of sociology; but the possibility of this warrant can
be disclosed in the way that ordinary pre-scientific description itself already lives within stratification. A re-covery of Method's
way to elevation points back to the ground of Method in the pre-
scientific life of Language in the everyday world, for while we can
hear the Methodic talk of sociology doing difference and elevation,
we invariably fail to hear that Methodic talk doing community too.
But the community that is done, the way scientific talk collects itself with and shares the ways of pre-scientific description, is a
community constituted through stratifying speech; it is a community
whose way of talking, in failing to listen to itself and turn towards
its own possibility, gives itself as stratifying. Sociology's
self-grounding way in speech, then, both differentiates itself from
and, more primordially, collects itself with everyman's way in speech.

It collects itself with in the ways that it calls for everyman's
agreement; that way of showing and saying what is the case, what
is 'correct', is already encompassed in everyman's way of doing
truth.   Ordinary descriptive speech, for much of its life in the
society ruled by 'technological-calculative' thought, is a display
of the activity of doing truth as correspondence, and the sociologist
collects himself with this way in his bureaucratization of ordinary
speech.   Ordinary description as correspondence, and as the con-
sequent production of phenomena as 'things' 'over there', gives the
possibility of scientific theorizing which both uses and extends the
ways of description.   But does descriptive speech, whether mundane
or formal scientific description, examine its own possibility?   The
authorial demand for acceptance which lies in the activity of truth
as correspondence is present in mundane description and is taken over
by science so that the continuity and community of mundane and scientific speech is done through collecting all description as correspondence.   From within a community constituted through stratifying
speech, self-grounding then proceeds to differentiate itself from
the speech of everyman through the Frame of Method.   Method as an
explicit stratifying points back to its warrant in description as
stratifying.   Sociology's Methodic description only stratifies itself in relation to ordinary description through its self-conscious
display of its concrete commitment to Method.   But, for us, Method
is a metaphor for the exploitative and dominant 'technological-
calculative' thought.

Method does difference but is possible only through the difference
which is already done in the act of descriptive speech itself.   The
authority claimed by the author in the act of speaking-writing is
done through the differentiating claim that the act of speaking itself makes in breaking the silence.   Every self-insertion into the
world in and through descriptive speaking and writing is concretely
a differentiation which says 'Listen! This is the world', where the
description covers over its own methodic accomplishment; but this
speaking shows a tension which, if addressed, may lead us towards
that site where stratification is generated.

Speaking and writing seem to show author as authority, that is,
we hear him as active subject speaking authoritatively; yet we can
also hear the authorial act of beginning as accomplished under the
auspices of an authority.   Author is, as authorial subject, already
subject to an authority which authorizes him.   The concrete idea of
stratification can be heard as making reference to the difference
which is shown in the act of beginning to speak and this difference
gives itself as a tension between the speaker as both authority and
authorized.

Method's self-elevation, which is what we concretely hear as
stratification, is already provided for in that tension which difference is and points to in beginning to speak; difference is
founded not on the distancing that Method achieves through its
mathematizing urge, but in that space which gives the paradoxical
duality of author's subjectitude.   Beginning to speak inserts
author into the tension of that social space within tradition that
provides for him as the subject who subjects and in his subjecting
shows his subjectitude.   Author can only show himself as authority
because he is already under that authority which gives him as the

'Good' subject - 'Good' because he is subject to its authority.
Can we hear stratification as the paradox of author subjecting those
who hear him concretely to his authority only through a subjectitute
which provides for that authority's possibility?

If so, then perhaps author can be formulated as speaking with
authority because his speaking is also a listening that hears that
which authorizes it.   Stratification would then lie in that moment
between speaking and hearing where the speaking, as a listening,
hears its own deep warrant as 'Good' (authorized) speech.   Stratification in this way is the differentiating movement, the in-between,
from one to two, from less to more.   In beginning (to speak or
write) author makes reference to the character of his speaking as a
hearing, as hearing the addition made by his speech, and through this
shows the difference that his speaking makes.   If we can learn to
listen to how the beginning is an accomplishment, a wrenching of
something from nothing, we may come to hear the Reason that authorizes such beginning.   For objectivizing sociology, which begins to
listen at the peril of its own project, the Reason that authorizes
its beginning may show a commitment to the mathematical form of
'technological-calculative' speech.   This generates a mode of being
and speaking where the difference made by its speech is the mathematical difference of addition: it adds some-thing to the already
securely held 'things' that comprise the stock of knowledge of the
common culture.   Difference here is an increase, is that form of
stratification where 'more' (of the same) means 'better', where the
difference made by the amount 'more' that is produced indexes the
'Good' of the speech.   The elevation, the raising, is accomplished
through a raising of the quantity of those 'things' that are already
secure, in a culture where having 'things' secure as 'things' and
ready-to-hand for use, as neutral instruments, is fundamental to the
sustaining forms of social praxis.   The concrete community of
speaker-hearers can then be listened to as a community grounded on a
mathematizing stratifying practice, for it is a community where
beginning to speak makes all the difference in the world.

But we can also hear the tension that the accomplishment of speaking points to as making reference to other possibilities.   The
speaker, as authorial subject, both subjects that which he speaks
about to his authority, but is also subject to the authority of
Language.   Speaker is subject-subjecting-subjected where his
subjection is to the ways that Language uses him.   Here the wrest-
ling of something from nothing, the theorizing, displays speaker's
Languaged relationship to Being, how Being comes to be in Language.
Speaker's way of showing the Reason for speaking, the languaged form
of his life within the ontological difference (the difference between
Being and beings) can point to commitments to other forms of life
than the mathematical, to another 'Good' than the 'Good' of quantity.
By listening to the ways within which the ontological difference is
lived we can find, found, and show a commitment to theorizing which
has a very different sense of that to which it is responsible, and
hence very different resonances, to the mathematical form of life.
For me these resonances have to do with Language as foundationally
metaphoric and mythopoetic, with its granting possibilities of
being-together, and with the dialectic of Self and Other.   Language's possibilities provide an openness that contrasts starkly
with the closures of 'technological-calculative' speech.

2.   PURE OBSERVING AS A PRACTICE AND A WAY OF BEING-IN-THE-WORLD

While analytically sociological speech collects itself with the
speech of everyman (whose community has been formulated as the
'technological-calculative' community of stratified speaker-hearers)
it concretely differentiates itself in ways which explicitly show it
as doing mundane stratification.   Observing, as that practice of
the sociologist which supposedly precedes and gives rise to his
speech, provides a topic through which stratification as the explicit
product of Method, can be addressed.   If the self-transformation,
which becoming a sociological observer entails, is followed and
traced some of the ways in which the transformation is a stratification can be re-covered.

A constitutive feature of sociological writing's self-grounding,
which points to its explicit accomplishment of stratification through
the ways of Method, is that the grounds pointed to and the knowledge
produced are shown as different to those of mundane speakers (those
who do not organize their speaking in sociological ways).   Both
what the sociologist re-presents for agreement and where he represents it from are shown in ways which set them over and against
other ways of speaking.   It is not just that the organized character
of the speaking is displayed but the grounds of this organization are
presented as other than mundane grounds.   (15)   The site of sociological knowledge is moved up a path away from and higher than the site
of the mundane;   this movement to a higher place, further up the path,
is seen as an exemption from membership of the mundane world which
enables the sociologist to look down upon the site of the mundane,
back down the path along which he has travelled.   The self-
transformation which occurs in the climb is one in which the author,
the sociologist, becomes a special kind of observer;   he is special
in that he differentiates himself from the subject on the mundane
site precisely through his ways of observing.

Mundane subjects' practices are constitutive of the mundane world
and one feature of this constitution is their way of observing, but
they are never only observers, they do not locate their being solely
in their observing.   For the sociologist who moves to the higher
site the hoped-for transformation is one which would give him his
being on that new site in his observing;   his observing is his way
to understanding.   That which he observes, the social world below,
enables him to fulfil his being as observer.   His purpose is to
become the 'pure observer'.   (16)   If observing, as that which gives
access or opens a way to things of the world, is the sociologist's
primary way of being-in-the-world his reflecting must be a reflecting
on that observing and its products.   His reflecting, as an activity
secondary to his observing, transforms that which was observed into
modes of speaking and writing in order that his private observation
becomes publicly available in truthful ways.

Observing must eventually become a methodic 'reading' of the
social world because the observer makes his observation available
through language, primarily in ways to be read and occasionally
heard.   The transformation of the visible, seen, and overheard into
coherent texts or speeches points to observing as a reading making
itself readable, but readable in certain ways.

Pure observing as the sociologist's primary mode of being

differentiates itself from other practices in the world and covers
over itself as a practice by re-presenting itself as a passive
observing; the observer becomes a receptacle.   Superiority claims
about this differentiation, displayed in the way the observing is
accounted for, are grounded on beliefs about the enabling character
of pure observing (i.e. that it enables the sociological observer to
do some things, see the truth, better than other practices, such as
those of ordinary experience, or, that learning the truths of the
world comes from pure observing not from experience).

Pure observing is seen as enabling a seeing achieved through a
distancing, a standing back from; this is set against the seeing of
experience in the world which is defined by a closeness to the
'things' of the world that throws out of focus their true forms.
Closeness impedes the seeing of the truth.   Science, as pure
observing, brings the world into focus, whereas the seeing of experience is a myopia which can only see the limited truth of the
near-at-hand.   While the pragmatic system of relevance of experience is a concealing, science is a revealing accomplished through
suspension of pragmatic relevances.   But in so far as the thrust to
pure observing calls for a suspension of all relevances science can
only bring the 'things' fully into focus when it has no system of
relevances.   The thrust then points to an absurd epistemology.
However, if pure observing's distancing were only a horizontal distancing (as being on the same level as that from which the observer
is distanced) the 'things' observed from that distanced horizontal
siting would present themselves, although perhaps in focus, as two-
dimensional, as a flat front facing the observer; they would be in
the same plane as when they are seen by mundane observers in the
course of their everyday experience, and would thus have the same
forms that they have for mundane observers.   To achieve a view which
transcends this frontal self-presentation of the 'things' requires a
movement up from the horizontal which enables the pure observer to
look down upon the 'things', to see behind the front from above on to
their arrangement, an arrangement not given to the distanced horizontal observer.

What enables this levitation of the observer?   He constructs
methods which take him along a path to his higher site and raise him
out of the horizontal to a place from which he can map the 'reality'
behind the frontal presentation of phenomena.   But there is a
question of whether the methods, as a construction, rest on the same
ground as the horizontal observer and the mundane members whose
practices constitute the 'objects' of the observing.   In the light
of the earlier discussion of author's collecting and differentiating
the suggestion here is that, despite the urge of sociological
speaking-writing to show its observings as resting on different
grounds, its methods, while not identical to those of horizontal
observers, do share their grounds and live in their language.

Science's call to the listener or reader to come over and up to
its constructed site in order to see 'things' 'objectively' or
truthfully is a concealing or forgetting of its own mundane grounds,
of its presence within the interpretive circle.   The attempted
transformation into the pure observer conceals the observer's common
grounds with mundane members; this is accomplished in the ways in
which pure observing is represented as a qualitatively different

activity done from another place than the observing practices of
ordinary experience.   The observer bases his truth claims in the
special character of his methodic constructions for it is these which
he and others see as differentiating and raising him and, according
to his claims, giving him access to a realm of truth not available
without those methods.

If methods share the same ground as both distanced horizontal
observing and mundane members' observing within ordinary experience
and are constructed on that ground, what is it that is shared?

1 A view of the 'things' as 'over there', given, independent of
   the observing, at a distance.
2 A grammar, syntax, and partially common semantic for describing
   the 'things' as independent of the describing but in correspondence with them;   descriptions present themselves as de-authored
   and hence the media through which Nature (social world) speaks.
   This includes the primacy given to measurement of the 'things'.
   (17)   Sociological description displays itself as on the way to
   a universal mathematics of the social.
3 A commitment to scientific rationality as an ethic for everyday
   life and the way to knowledge, where the ethic is absolutely
   hidden behind a banner proclaiming commitment to neutrality.
4 A fateful forgetting and concealing of ontology in most description and explanation.
5 A sense of what is 'significant' as a starting-point for constructive analysis (Weber's 'value-relevance', 'point-of-view'
   (18)), which varies according to the content of culture and the
   speaker's situated relation to his tradition, and which provides
   for concept construction.   'Significance' arises not from the
   desire of the theorist to display his commitment to a form of
   speaking, a way in language, but from the peculiar conjunction of
   the 'social world' and the sociological tradition;   'problems'
   (in the world) demand to be treated sociologically according to
   this conjunction so that the scientistic sociologist stands as
   the mouthpiece through which the problem makes itself heard
   (sociologically).

These provide for methodic ways of speaking and writing about sociological practices which incorporate among other features the following:

1 A world-hypothesis.
2 A view of Method as a neutral way of making this world available.
   (19)
3 A view of the world structured according to underlying patterns
   only amenable to truthful treatment by these neutral methods.
   Irony is thus a feature of the display of these patterns for the
   sociologist tells us that although things are not what they seem
   anyone could see them who would (use such methods).
4 A formalizing or bureaucratizing of the 'things' of the world.
   This takes the forms of, re-arranging, re-naming, remedying the
   'things' through ways of collecting and sorting which constitute
   the practices of constructive analysis.
5 A reliance on language (and to a lesser extent on number) as an
   instrument or tool, something to be 'used', for the systematic
   re-presentation of the unifying, objectifying, and defining
   practices of sociology.

Where there is implicit or explicit acceptance by sociologists and others that these grounds and practices open up the way to valid knowledge then the modes of construction which produce such knowledge will be questioned only as to their technical efficacy and not as to the nature of their being as human practices. This confirms the observer in his self-view as the pure observer whose observations are above those of others: technique rules, and the more convincing the display of technical mastery the more secure is the stratifying claim.

What is it in the observing that enables the production of an account that stratifies itself in relation to other accounts emerging from other 'kinds' of theorizing? The claim for sociological observing is that it can see what cannot be seen by the participants because their being is exhausted in the doing (production) of that which is observed; doing, being-in, covers over that which defines the very character of the situation. The observer from his elevated observation site sees that which gives the situation its character (for him) but which is missed by and hidden from those whose activities are constitutive of the situation described by the observer. Its character, for him, is the reality behind the appearance, the invisible made visible. (20)

The authority of the observer's account then stems in part from the opposition of seeing and doing as mutually exclusive; anyone who would observe and see the world as the observer does must stop doing and this removes him from membership. He sees, and then makes available, what cannot be seen by those doing; the exclusivity of doing allows for the superiority of the observer's seeing. But this conceals that seeing is a doing and doing entails a seeing. (21)

The observer's seeing is always active in that he selects that which he sees from his perspective; his field is a field seen from a 'point of view'. Perceiving is a situated activity which constitutes a field for observation within a horizon. For the sociological observer the topography of that field is already partly pre-constituted by him before he even glances towards it by the linguistic tradition, ordinary membership, within which he has his being; we can anticipate that the field will be 'seen' (described) in very particular ways by the observer. His active seeing is a doing through its constitutive character, the constitution itself resting on and employing a received tradition of descriptors, a mixture of ordinary language used in ordinary ways and sociological concepts.

Conversely the activities which constitute the observer's field are doings which entail seeings. An essential constituent of members' doing is perceiving a field within which the doing takes place; doing is done within a perceived context which contributes to the character of the doing (figure/ground; figure/horizon). The intelligibility of doing is partially made available through its perceptual character. In doing the member is also seeing, perceiving, observing; activities observed by sociologists are themselves also observings, observings which are integral to the intelligibility of the activities for the members who constitute them. In much empirical sociology one of the figures in the perceptual fields of those members observed by the sociologist is necessarily the sociologist himself. In order to do his observing the sociologist is necessarily observed by those he wishes to observe; but this observation by members of the observing sociologist is for them an ordinary mode of being, whereas the observing of members by a sociological observer is the mode of being which is, hopefully, constitutive of him, for he hopes to live only as observer.   For members the observing sociologist is merely one among many phenomena within their horizons, nothing special (this is something more than the observing sociologist's hope for he would like to be unnoticed, invisible), whereas for the observing sociologist his ideal is that members' activities constitute the total field of his observing. The observer's ideal is to become fully an observer, to fill, exhaust, his being with his observing, while the observing of the observed members is only one constitutive mode of their being in the world.

As an ideal, pure observing is unattainable and each concrete observing necessarily falls short of its goal;   the observer cannot transform himself into pure observer for he is always situated in the world, a presence for himself and others which demands that he do and be other things in order to accomplish any kind of observing. He exists in other modes of being concurrently with his observing. Existentially sociologists know and recognize that they are anything but pure observers, but in their written descriptions these other modes of being remain behind the text and unmentioned;   they write as if they were pure observers who had accomplished their ideal mode of being and exhausted themselves as men in their observing.   This failure to recoil back on their theoretic life and their situation in relation to their tradition generates an alienated mode of writing. Sociological writing forgets the modes of being which enable and provide for the possibility of observing as one mode alongside others. Sociological language, as the language of pure observation, speaks as though the sociologist were all eyes.

How does the world, seen as below from the higher site, enable the man transforming himself into sociological observer to produce observations?   The sociologist's observations are made available to others, both those on the mundane and those on the higher site, through language;   Language is the House of Being within which both sites have their place and when the observer founds his higher site he does so within and through language.   As language gives him his originary being as a man on the mundane site it is only within this being in language that he can construct a path and find his elevated observation site.   His self-transformation is accomplished within language for it is language which provides the possibility of the alternative site in the first place.   Language throws that light on both sites which discloses and brings to visibility for us their constitutive phenomena;   any differentiation which enables us to distinguish the topography of the two sites is accomplished from within language.   (22)

The differentiation which the observer sets out to accomplish in language through the move to the other site is one which will enable him to claim a privileged status for his asserting and reasoning that are the results of his observing.   His claim is that observer's talk is superior to mundane talk;   the claim is to know better.   The grounds of this self-elevation and claim to authority (that he speaks with the power and authority of the truth about the social) are

constitutive of the site from within which he speaks.   As the site
was made possible by the observer's originary being within language
it too is thus available for a topology and a topography of its
being.

If any of the claims which the observer makes for his speaking
provide for a hierarchic differentiation between his and other speaking then the author may be seen as stratifying himself or, from his
point of view, as being stratified by his practices; (23) he is an
author pointing to the explicit authority given to him by the organization of his speaking, although, as was drawn out in the previous
section, this authoritative differentiation of Method can be listened to as referring back to and grounded in a deeper community which
gives the possibility of the explicit difference.   The presence of
this deeper community can show us a further paradox of the observer's
explicit claim to authority for the topic of his authoritative talk
is the site from which he has ideally elevated and distanced himself.
The attempt to open up a path and found an alternative site on which
his being would be granted as a pure observer is made in order that
he may produce authorized observations of that original site where
he no longer stands.   The observer can claim to be an authority on
the mundane social world on the basis of the ways he elevates himself, through his authoritative talk, above that world.   Indeed the
further away he moves from the mundane site along his path of sociological method and knowledge, the more he develops, polishes and
perfects his organizing principles for constructing and securing
that path, the greater the authority he can claim because the path is
directed, if Method's warrant is to be believed, towards Nature; and
yet the path of Method distances him from the mundane site.   The
path heading towards Nature takes him away from the mundane site
even though the latter can be the only site where Nature presences.

But who accedes to the authority of the observer's speech and
under what terms?   First, there are those who share his site - the
community of observers; and second, there are those on the mundane
site; for both groups his grounds are largely unquestioned and his
concrete claims are acceptable if he makes their methodic construction observable.   But the systems of relevances which provide for
their acceptance differ between the two groups.   The observing
community, with professional relevances, patrol the boundaries of the
enterprise of truth production, while mundane members accept the
claims in ways which allow them to incorporate the claims in their
pragmatic systems of relevances.   The observer produces authoritative speaking whose authority is confirmed when it is read as the
demand for acceptance.   He only has these ways of making others
listen because of the deeper community which provides for his differentiation and because that deeper community is constituted by
speakers who do not listen to the deep grant of their own speaking
and writing; acceptance is a passivity, a letting lie, which cannot
thus re-cover itself.

The paradoxes characterizing the production of superior talk on
the elevated site can be extended.   Although understanding gained
about the mundane site while on it as a mundane member is necessary
for observing and authorship on the elevated site, the transformed
understanding which is produced on this higher site is claimed to be
better than that without which it would be impossible.   Although the

observer's talk is authoritative we have no access to it except
through our originary being in language on the mundane site;   it is
only our prior being in language that allows us to understand both
the possibility of the observer's talk and its concrete substance.
As all talk, in breaking the silence, demands attention, to make himself heard above the talk of the world, the sociologist has to rise
above it and speak in ways which demand agreement.   The bureaucrat-
ized speaking of sociology commands respect which is institutionally
catered for.   Through the claimed authoritative differentiation the
observer places himself above the world's talk about itself, claiming
his talk as the authorized version of the world.   Although it claims
to be authorized and that the authority is dispensed by Nature, this
very claim is self-authorizing in the way it makes reference to its
methodic character and the self-authorizing is deaf to its own
warrant.

How do members of the mundane world come to see this talk about
them as authoritative?   While they may accept the concrete truth
claims of the talk, taking it at face-value, they are only able to do
this because they are already in language and thus already know
something of what the observer tells them about themselves;   they are
within the circle which enables them to 'see' what the observer tells
them and to concur with it.   The showing of the truth of the knowledge relies on its being shown as and in the terms of mundane knowledge and the community of mundane knowledge (constituted by descriptive speech) already lives in and through the ways of stratifying
speech.   (24) So, the all-encompassing character of the circle opens
the possibility that the authoritative claims of the observer,
asserted through the organized display of Method, are not grounded on
a site as elevated or as distanced from the mundane as Method seems
to claim;   mundane knowledge already gives us the possibility of
Method (as a mathematizing) in pre-sociological description.

If there is a recognition that the stratifying differentiation
takes place within language this provides us with an alternative way
of seeing the differentiating activity for we can see that the attempt to move away from the mundane world and to open a new space for
observing can never move outside the circle;   the observer's site is
only locatable within the circle and this provides not for an ultimate or radical break with mundane understanding and description
but for inevitable continuity, overlap, and movement along the same
ways.   It is this continuity and extension of some of the same ways
of speaking (the ever-increasing dominance of 'technological-
calculative' speech), which are constitutive of the mundane social
world, that allows for the understanding and acceptance of the
authoritative claims of the observer;   in spite of the observer's
attempts to cover over these common grounds and raise himself in
principled ways to a superior site, the seeds of acceptance lie in
what the members' and the observers' talk have in common in their
being within language.   The observer's originary being within a
community which lives through the quantitative difference that
speaking calculatively is gives him the possibility of living within
Method's stratifying ways.   Through and within this communal being
the observer selectively builds on what is already provided for by
language (but which is never all that language, as the House of
Being, is) by doing constructive work on a small site within the

infinite region that language opens for us; his selectivity concentrates on the mathematical impulse in descriptive speech and
isolates and extends it.

This recovery of the observer establishing his authority on a
site which gives him an overview of Nature calls for an inquiry
into the mode of his organized speaking as it methodically hides its
own origins.   The observer organizes his speaking so that it displays him as the owner of the social, an ownership which rests on his
individual appropriation of the methods of production of organized
knowledge.   These methods of productive thinking cluster around a
'technological-calculative' (25) view of thought and language as a
means to the formalized production of what is understood as 'news',
'findings', or 'information'.

3.   SOCIOLOGICAL SPEAKING AND WRITING AS THE EXPROPRIATION OF WAYS TO THE METHODIC PRODUCTION OF 'INFORMATION'

The dominance of 'technological-calculative' thought provides for a
reading of 'information' as sociology's way of being; sociology
lives in and through 'informative' ways of speaking. (26) Calculative thought constitutes everything as calculable so that everything stands as equal and indifferent in the face of it.   It faces
a uniformly calculable world, information (as knowledge) about which
is conceived of and produced through organized methods. (27)
Method, through its coercive power, drafts, calls up, and sets up the
theme which always remains subordinate to it.   Method's calculative
ways of speaking are a Framing which sets up themes with uniform indifference, for the world is treated as a possible technical invent-
ory; Method faces a world constituted by mere commodities to be
weighed and divided through its cool coinage of concepts.   All is
available for informative technical reportage through Framing within
which all ordering is channelled into calculative modes.   Framing
orders things through a formalized language which 'informs man uniformly, that is, gives him the form in which he is fitted into the
technological-calculative universe'. (28) Framing's will to formalization passes over the originary nature of natural language and
treats it as a lack of formalization, a 'troublesome residue', which
interferes with the smooth transition to informative speaking in
which all is equally commandeered: 'Formalization, the calculated
availability of saying, is the goal and the norm'. (29) Socio-
ology's way in language, as a Framing, formalizes man's social being
in ordered ways which give that being a uniform availability as information.   In its treatment of world as a uniformly available
world of information it transforms the saying of men's speaking into
indifferent information.   Where truth is correspondence, as in
sociology, saying gets transformed into 'statement' in which the
instrumental-rational element of saying dominates.   Truth, as a
principled statement about a thing that corresponds to its essence,
becomes static and informational, but in this becoming covers over
the prior interpretation both of the way the   thing is turned
towards (and hence how the thing as a being stands within Being) and
of the selection of relevant analytical tools. (30) Sociology
moves within speaking as Statement and in this re-presents itself in

ways which conceal the prior grant of its saying.

The speech of the aspiring pure observer, which is talk that 'has the measure' of the world as commodity, organizes, rationalizes, and bureaucratizes natural language, and to the extent that these activities are given greater rewards than ordinary talk because of the exchange value of what they produce ('news'), the speaking's authority and superiority are assured:

> The use of undifferentiated collective concepts of everyday
> speech is always a cloak for confusion of thought and
> action.   It is, indeed, very often an instrument of
> specious and fraudulent procedures.   It is, in brief,
> always a means of obstructing the proper formulation of the
> problem. (31)

As this provides their way of being-in-language as observers, sociologists have developed the technological-calculative way of speaking, for their way to knowledge is along the path which is opened up through their constructive speaking; the constructions of sociological speech are seen by their producers as additions to our knowledge of the world. As a claimed telling which 'informs' us of things in the world that we did not know about in the ways told, observers' speaking and writing can be heard and read as interpreted information. But, for us, the Framed information is always a transformation of the events which form its topics.

Information is constructed through collecting, differentiating, sorting, and counting procedures which re-arrange and re-constitute the phenomena of the world, and these processes point back to the grounds through which the information claims authority. The interpreted information tells not concretely what we already know (although through our being within the circle of language we do have to understand already in order to understand what the information tells us) but re-collects what is already available and through the ordering of this re-gathering covers over the forms of its originary availability for us and our pre-knowledge of it. This re-ordering is re-presented as something 'new' about the world, as findings not makings, so that the sociologist as owner of the methods of production which excavate 'new findings' about Nature can claim superiority over other ways to knowledge. But the re-presentation of the collecting work in the sociologist's speaking covers over the grounds of his election to talk in those ways by showing itself to be the speech of 'anyman' from within the community of pure observers, or indeed of 'anyman' who would care to see things from that site. To show one's speaking as 'anyman's', however, is also to show it as 'no-man's' so that the region of the sociologist's site is no-man's land. No-man but the sociologist sees the world in the ways it presents itself to those on the sociologist's site; everyman has to methodically transform himself to share the sociolgist's vision. Sociological description's way is to give itself as the re-collecting and re-ordering of no-man-in-particular so that its peculiar context-free vision can be that of no one else but the sociologist; the possible worlds of sociological texts are sociologists' worlds. Within sociological description there is a variety of methodic ways of information-constructing, each of which stands within positivist rhetoric (e.g. explanation, v. description, quantitative, v. qualitative 'techniques') but all ultimately locate themselves on the

same site; the internal differentiation occurs on the move away
from the beginning site of the mundane. They choose different
paths to the same elevated alternative site from which they make
similar claims for the information constructed by way of these different paths.

The grounds of information's claims to be informative can be found
in its provision of an organized context for its interpretation as
something that was not previously known. It is presented in a form
in which it can be treated as a quantitative addition to our stock
of knowledge of the world. Counting comes to be central in sociology because sociology, as an informing, is an adding. In one very
important sense the claim to be news is self-validating for the very
methods which provide the organized context of interpretation are
constitutive of the concrete content as information; findings are
such as the result of constructive work by the observer. In this
way the observer is providing in his speech something new; he constructs something where previously there was nothing and methodically
generates things not before seen as now these things. Through his
interpretation he claims to tell us of the things he has discovered
as being there in the world in the ways he has described them; but
these very claims conceal the problem that for a reader, the things
first of all have their being here (in the text) and only when the
reader has learned to interpret the observer's organized telling can
he then see the things as after all there in those ways in the
world 'already'. The methods of construction then guarantee the
character of sociological telling as a telling of new information
both in their creation of something out of nothing and in their por-
trayal of this something as there all along. Paradoxically the information is both new and old. Science discovers and shows us for
the first time that which was 'there' all the time. For the observer his ability to convince the reader of both the newness and
oldness of the information he provides is one of the strengths of his
telling and an integral feature of his claim to elevate difference;
to tell us something new about that which we ourselves have produced
and which is already there before our eyes is an achievement. The
achievement however, from the standpoint of one trying to display the
circular character of interpretation lies not in the provision of
news but in the ways the methods cover over their own constitutive
and remedial work; the achievement lies in the observer's convincing
display in his telling that he is telling the truth about the world,
about what is there independent of but in correspondence with the
telling.

If a truth claim is being made, and this ability to find the truth
provides the rationale for scientistic sociology, the observer's text
must provide for an unequivocal reading; if the truth lies in the
text there is only one right reading of it, the reading that sees the
truth of the claim. So the observer's biggest problem in writing is
to dispel doubt, queries, ambiguities, and ambivalence in order that
his organized information speaks for and provides for itself in an
authoritative way. The text must leave the reader with neither
doubt nor queries; it is created to give answers which first of all
demand acceptance and only secondarily point to further questions
which might be asked. For the observer who wishes to present his
truth claims the problem is to minimize the interpretive problems for

the reader by showing the 'given' character of the telling; he must
show that what he had to say as the truth claim could only have been
said in that way.   The tradition's ways of speaking are invoked
only as means of access to and display of the truth.   The reader
must be placed in a position in which he subordinates himself to the
text by surrendering to its authority - the authority of truth.
The text must own the reader, take him over as a passive recipient
of the message; while he is reading the reader must be filled by
and so 'become' the text, for there must be no room left for nagging
doubts.   A founding feature of the sociological resolution of this
problem is the de-authorization through which the writer shows the
reader that it is no-man but Nature who authors the text.

The sociological writer writes for a reader who, hopefully, will
concur with his text and his ways of writing provide the pathways
which maximize the possibility of this concurrence.   A main feature
of this writing is the creation of texts which provide for their
being read and taken at their face-value; concrete reading is the
required way of entering the texts.   Sociological texts are organized as calls which through their calculated availability hopefully
pre-empt violent readings (to re-cover the questions to which the
text is an answer) for all that the text has to 'say' (32) is there
on the surface; to listen to the text to hear what it says rather
than what it speaks, or to ask what lies under the text or in the
space between the words (33) is to fail to be the kind of reader the
text needs for they make of the text an interpretive problem and
that is to reject the role of passive surface reader.   The power of
sociological writing can be seen in its ability to induce reader to
read concretely where this induction produces a reader who is forced
not to listen to speech; his reading is not one which listens to its
own way within the text.   In contrast all texts for us are treated
as occasions for that practice of reflexive and dialectical reading
which works with texts in the same way that reflexive and dialectical
writing works with its topics; the practice would then listen to
what the text fails to say to bring to disclosure the unsaid, the
silent space which the text veils.   As any text takes on a life
only in its reading the character of the reading gives the text its
form of life.   The practice of reading, which we see as a listening
and hearing of the text, is the re-trieving activity that brings the
text into being again and re-forms itself as a perennial beginning-
again through its re-activating practices every time a text is entered.   The thinking-reading that listens to itself in its search
for the text's founding grounds is itself the practical founding of
these grounds.   The reflexive and dialectical reader then becomes
he who listens to his reading as that practice of a relationship to
a text which gives life to the text by giving it its foundations and
who, in so doing, points to the origins of his own thoughtful hearing.

The recommendation to readers to do violence to texts follows
from the showing that a writer's constructive action is already a
violence.   Josipovici shows this violence in his description of the
writer's action as 'unnatural' in its cutting up of a seamless whole
for the purposes of explanation. (34) In sociology's case this
cutting up takes the form of a calculative Framing which constitutes
the world as indifferent commodity whose being it can render through

the speech of correspondence.   To outlaw violence is to create a
self-preserving equilibr i um through the texts which denies the possibility of revolution and that alternative beginning whose possibility is contained in any violent dialogue with tradition.   (35)

The sociological tradition through its being within the tradition
of Western thought (which grants sociology its region within Framing
thought) lives in and through various positivisms and has to provide
for its continuity through creating readers who will embody and extend
this tradition; the all-pervasiveness of Framing's calculative modes
facilitates its task.   Its academic way of being is largely geared
to this end for it constitutes itself through the systematic production of passive readers who will lose themselves to the concrete
truth claims of sociological texts.   In its production of texts
which aim at owning their readers sociology simultaneously loses the
possibility of an authentic theoretic life.   Submission to the concrete authority of the texts is a prerequisite for membership of the
sociological freemasonry.   Through its impetus to monopolize the
methods of production and expression of sociological truth and to
control entry to its ranks sociology constitutes itself as a class
even if not as a profession.

While the subordinated reader, as a slave to the text, seems to
be both required and presumed by sociological texts, reading can
never meet these requirements for the reader is always something
more than an empty vessel into which a text is poured.   Even the
beginning reader of sociology comes to the texts with an immense
stock of personal knowledge and a practical mastery of language which
enable him to get some initial purchase on sociological writing; his
transformation into the kind of reader required by the texts (one who
accepts) occurs through an active process of learning how to interpret them, as opposed to other kinds of texts.   What he already
understands and how he understands provide for his entry into the
interpretive circle and his movement within it.   He learns how to
accept the texts by not listening to the saying of their speech;
he learns how to constitute actively the texts as doing what and only
what they claim, reporting on Nature, that is he learns how to read
concretely.

The production of sociologists is first and foremost the production of those who can organize their speaking and writing in professionally acceptable ways, that is who can stand on the site of elevated difference.   The work done from this site, as a dis-covering
of Nature, provides for sociologists' claims to expertise.   But if,
alternatively, sociologists are seen as constructors rather than dis-
coverers then we are less likely to regard them as experts on that
which they are concretely writing about (the world) and more likely
to see them as expert in the modes of production of sociological
texts.   All writing is a claim to know, but can we justifiably extend the attribution of authority and expertise to authors beyond
their responsibility for that which they have constructed as the
medium for their authoritative saying?   And even this does not yet
point to the tension of writing and its responsibility to a form of
Reason.   If this were treated seriously by sociologists then the
movement of sociological work and writing would be re-directed
towards its own theoretic life and would address its own possibility.
Where writing's intentions are neither deeply autobiographic nor

openly factitious I fail to fall in with them for my concern is not only what the text speaks but also the silent saying which gives that which is spoken.   Read as deep autobiography writing becomes a reflexive and dialectical projecting which opens ways that show 'auto's' site within and subjugated-subjugating relationship to Language.

4.   AN ALTERNATIVE WAY IN SPEAKING

The preceding discussion has treated the central problem of sociological authorship as the way in which the author addresses the reflexive and dialectical character of his speaking and writing.   For sociologists, as for others, their activities can be read as the methods for making them accountable/intelligible (36) so that sociological accounts are the methods for their intelligibility;   but where sociology stops short is in its failure to address its own possibility - the grounds of its intelligibility.   As long as it fails to address the grounds of its own theoretic life it will be unable to show its distinctive character, (37) for, in missing the turn back it retains the forgetful character of and so becomes undifferentiable from that mundane speaking which is deaf to its own saying.   To the extent that the texts provide for their intelligibility through concrete reading they do speak to their construction in a way adequate for their practical purposes.   But because they do not address their own possibility we need to go behind the texts to listen to what they say but do not speak in order to disclose their unstated grounds for ourselves.

An alternative approach to speaking and writing is to make the method the topic and through this reflexive and dialectical turn to open up a possibility for reader to enter into a dialogue with the text where the text is read as an insertion into and a pointing towards our tradition which calls the reader to listen to his own reading.   Dialogue would here de-stratify the relation between writer and reader and provide for an open dialectic of Self and Other for its concern is always to hear how the practices of writing and reading speak analytically to the tradition which is their grant. In its reading writing is no longer an informing of reader by a knowledge-producer through the handing down of a given stock of knowledge, but a dialectic which is always moving and pointing back towards that which constrains its own possibility.

Sociology's objectivizing language and concepts are based on a technological view of the relationship between language and the world (as if the two were independent) which sees language as an instrument for mastering a world 'over there'.   This covers over the pre-reflexive understanding and experience in which all reflexive understanding is grounded and which come to expression in language. We receive language from tradition;   we emerge through it, and are constrained by it.   Although we may re-juvenate and re-create it we do not create it.   It gives us our being.   Language, as our way of being which provides for the possibility of world rather than mirroring the world, enables sociologists who live within the restricted world of Framing, to construct possible worlds in their formalizing.   But their ways of doing this and the claims made for

the products cover over and hide the constructive character of the
work and portray it, their language, as in correspondence with
world; the word is transformed into a sign.   To achieve 'community' for this way of seeing they rely on both their concealing
techniques and our everyday understandings of world and language, so
that ultimately the persuasive character of sociological rhetoric
lies, not in some distinctive and separate set of defining characteristics, but in its isomorphism with everyday talk.   By failing to
treat its being within language, and hence its relationship to other
ways of speaking, as problematic it loses the possibility of giving
itself a distinctive character.   It confirms, formalizes, and re-
orders everyday understandings in which world is seen and talked of
as independent of the way of talking about it.   As all ways of
speaking about the world are ordered and organized the grounds of
phenomena are always concealed.   It is this ever-present concealing
which shows a way to an alternative, for sociology, as a 'bureaucratization of the imaginative' (38) in its selection and ordering of
one possibility from all possibilities, can be treated as an invitation to readers and hearers to a dialogue in which the text provides for a listening relationship with tradition.   (39) This alternative, it must be emphasized, is not offered as a remedy or prescription for a 'better' sociology, but as another beginning in
which sociological and all speaking give us occasions for listening
again to and re-trieving a sensible and sensitive reading of our own
origins and way within language.   The leap which is required to
wrench us out of calculative modes of speaking in order to listen
again to that which warrants and constrains our speech is itself a
display of that violent dialogue with tradition which turns the
theoretic life towards possibility and away from information.   Such
a leap would stand as an icon of the Good which breaking out of the
binds of mathematical speech would be.
   One interpretive process to which the sociological process of
understanding the world (and itself as a practice constitutive of
worlds) can be likened is the interpretive reading of a text.   The
sociologist 'reads' social worlds to understand them; this calls not
for the imposition of models on realities but for an openness to
experience and a 'creative negativity' (40) which goes behind that
which is spoken to what was not and could not be said.   While such
reading is always personal and situated and is always a new disclosure (which itself is a concealing that calls for disclosure),
that which is addressed through the 'creative negativity' is the
ground of community, analytic membership, that which gives me my way
in language.
   The unavoidably situated and perspectival character of reading
the social world points to the necessity of addressing the character
of that reading, for the reading is the experience, it is the understanding, reconstitution and transformation of tradition; addressing this understanding is an overcoming which moves from the indexical particulars of situation and perspective to that which grants
their intelligibility.   Reading a portion of the social world becomes an occasion for addressing the understanding itself for the
latter is constitutive of the reading.   If a reading is to understand itself, which would be a move towards de-alienation and self-
realization, then it must address the text both as production (its

methodic character, how it constitutes a world, the question to which
it is an answer) and its own methodic way of understanding that production.   As the reading is always personal (my reading) the reader
can claim no more for it than that it discloses a truth for him;   but
in trying to re-cover and re-present the character of the reading itself, his methodic way for locating the methodic character of the
text, he both displays his recognition of its limited truth and its
ambiguity and opens up a way for dialogue.   Its limited truth is
reader's sense of his own analytic self-insertion into tradition, but
the very setting down of this sense, while an unconcealing for the
reader, is also a concealing and it is this which calls for dialectic.
Language gives itself as a concealing and in this shows itself as an
eternal dialectic.

The life-world, in the same ways as texts provide for multiple
interpretations, makes available for observers possible worlds whose
deep grant gives methods for their situated assembly and production;
the observer's problem is to provide a reading of these methods from
within his position and its horizon which shows their and his
grounds.

The texts read or worlds observed have horizons and the observer's
horizon can overlap with theirs through language;   but there is no
way of re-covering or re-constructing their methods as independent of
the observer's ways of re-covering.   His ways of re-covering display
his participation with them within language and he must therefore
address these ways for his reader for his participation makes reference to the possibility of community.   But he can only point to them
because his text, as a display of his way of reading, can always be
seen by its reader as an answer to an unstated question and as
necessarily not saying things which cannot be said.   These can only
be formulated by the reader for himself and can only be concretely
pointed to by the writer in the course of his writing.   Even formulating a question always rests on an assertion, so that a concrete
question in a text is necessarily silent about the assertion on which
it rests, leaving the reader to formulate the unsayable assertion.

If making problematic the subject/object dichotomy (by an analytic
which shows the grounds of 'subjecting' and 'objecting') which is an
inescapable presupposition of sociological and all accounting, is a
feature of such an approach to reading and writing, then the reader
will be concerned to display his reading not as master of or slave to
the world or the text but as a participation with it.   In this participation the world of the text or the world as text, which in turn
is described and describes itself as a world 'over there' independent
of the ways of 'saying' it, is experienced as a disclosure of Being;
but this unconcealing only arises out of doing violence to the text,
seeing what the text did not and could not say.   Participation is,
then, an overcoming, and disclosure, as a historical experience, is
the truth of the text for me, here, now, where 'me', 'here', and
'now' point back to both historicity and the insertion of the analytic self into tradition in ways which display the communal grounds
of its theoretic life.

My text, as a display of my reading of the world as text, is
constituted by the methods for rendering it intelligible;   these
methods are always ordered ways within the infinite horizons of
language, and are therefore shareable and given for I did not create

language; I display myself (my reading as constitutive of myself)
through these ways.   I do not use them, I am them for I have no recourse to anything other than the ways of language; thus in some
senses they use me because I cannot escape them - they pervade me.
This is not to say that I am constrained by language in some deterministic sense, but that, in so far as I treat language as a topic it
is 'always ahead' of me, for it withholds its nature from me so that
I can never possess it.   Heidegger shows such with-holding as 'in
the very nature of language', (41) and it is the constraints of this
with-holding which give us both our possibility and our problematic.

To the extent that my reading displays the truth for me of the
world which I read and makes reference to the grounds of that truth
and the methodic ways that the world's intelligibility is provided
for, I have offered an authentic account, for the project would then
be displayed as the self-realization of unique but constrained possibilities.   Authenticity entails a recognition of the situated,
historical character of one's own truths and the impossibility, in
stepping out of the impersonal instrumentality of everdayness, of
stepping outside the horizons of the language in which one lives and
by which one makes these truths available. (42) As our mode of
being, the discourse or dialogue can always be terminated by choice
when we have said what we want, but this termination is not authoritarian for that is the way of science and absolute truth.   The
history of discourse is open because it follows the infinite contours and ways of language.   It is circular in that it is not progressive, accumulative, or ascending to a higher site of knowing,
and it always takes its origins,its own accomplishment, as its topic
by turning back on itself while recognising the impossibility of
perfectly completing the re-coil as a concrete achievement:

We must first turn, turn back to where we are in reality
already staying.   The abiding turn, back to where we already
are, is infinitely harder than are hasty excursions to places
where we are not yet and never will be, except perhaps as the
monstrous creatures of technology, assimilated to machines.

The step back into the sphere of human being demands other
things than does the progress into the machine world.

To turn back to where we are (in reality) already staying:
that is how we must walk along the way of thinking which now
becomes necessary. (43)

The authenticity, which is available for a reader, points to the
writer's commitment as it is shown in the text's methodic ways of
speaking about itself.   Writing's problem is to point towards the
invisible commitment which gives the visible its possibility.
Visible commitments (to science, self, a 'movement' and so on) are
always embedded in speech which conceals the deep grant of their
possibility.   The text is a pointing to the writer's commitment,
although this commitment can never be fully said by the writer:
the reader necessarily goes behind what is spoken to what the writer
could not say, and locates for himself the writer's commitment in his
reading, which in turn is a display of his method and commitment.(44)

If I rely on objectivist ways of describing I display myself as
telling what 'anyman' could tell from my position, (i.e. reading/
seeing the world from where I stand).   But not only can no other man
take 'my position' 'anyman' is also 'no-man' and 'no-man' is, by

definition, groundless.   The claim to be reporting on Nature 'over
there', from the outside, covers over my participation in that
Nature and thus conceals the way I live within Nature and the life-
world.   By a writing which assumes a perfect reciprocity of concrete perspectives I conceal both the uniqueness of my perspective
and the forms of my analytic community (the dialogue with and within
tradition) and hence the originary truths which language grants me
in the ways it inserts me into tradition.   In the way it conceals a
writer's commitment with an aura of absolutism, universality and
finality which put him in a community of thinkers outside history,
objectivist talk in sociology is inauthentic.   This leads us to ask:
what is required of writing and what possible community could be
formed in a movement towards authentic ways of speaking, that is,
speaking that in listening to itself recognizes and addresses itself
as a speaking that conceals and hence can only point to its commitments?

An alternative is membership of a reflexive and dialectical
community of authentic speakers whose speaking concretely treats
topics as occasions for the addressing of those topics' grounds;
the speaking, while concretely displaying a speaker's uniqueness,
would open a way for dialogue within the common medium of Being -
language, whose topic would be the very possibility of community
itself.   The problematic would be the re-trieval and disclosure of
the forms of community within the language of Being.   Commitment as
a sociologist, that which gives the ground on which the observer's
speech rests, is pointed to in what is spoken and what is spoken
derives from the writer's way of being-in-the-world as a sociologist,
that is from what he did and experienced in order to produce the sayable.   The sociologist's methods of producing his reading of the
world are his praxis - his text points back to the praxis within
which its sensible character and being arose;   this can be seen as
the unity of his experience - all those features of his being to
which his text makes reference - and his text, as language, provides
a horizon within which others can meet it by learning to listen to
what it says.   Language as the House of Being provides us with
communal facilities but gives to each of us our own space within it,
so that writing makes reference to the social space within which, and
the grounds on which, the writer stands.   To see it as speaking
truths which are independent of the ways of their speaking is to fall
back into the inauthentic objectivist mode.   If the objectivist
sociologist were to speak without his concepts, which are the bringing of Method into expression, he would, like the emperor without
his clothes, lose the grounds of his authority (Method) and his talk
would be immediately assailable as talk, not from ground which dis-
covers the world, but from his position;   his relationship to the
means of his own productions would be apparent to all.   Speaking
(theorizing) which employs distinctive formalizing concepts can be
authentic provided that the speaking treats itself as an occasion
for the address of these concepts' possibility, for this reflexive
and dialectical turn shows and situates the concepts as constitutive
of the writer (and not 'anyman') and his situation within the interpretive circle.

In re-covering a sense of stratification as a methodic practice
through a treatment of sociological ways to knowledge this writing

tries to point to a way of speaking which eschews self-elevation.
Such writing, hopefully, distances itself from the claims made for
the products of pure observing as superior products and from the
commitment of that activity to the formalized speaking that lives in
its informing; but this writing's call would be for a recognition
of the way it displays difference within the community that language
provides for, of itself as a pointing to the grounds of that community in the speaking, of the dialectical accomplishment of this differentiation as the tension of ruling-ruled, and of the possibility of
bringing the rule to visibility (that the writing make reference to
the rule in order to successfully differentiate and provide for
itself).   This way of speaking seeks no final say; pure observing
as a showing of absolute truth seeks to have the last word, but in
the alternative way of speaking there is no last word, no final say,
only a possibility of discourse.   As the final say scientific truth
(statements about 'what is') necessarily elevates itself, transcends
history, claims independence of those who brought it to disclosure,
and shows itself as non-situated.   The truth of the alternative
discourse is to be found both in its situated historicity, and in
the forms of its encounter with the constraints that its ways in
language provide for.   It is both an openness and a withholding
which invite dialogue.

This writing is not a claim to see sociology 'better' than it can
see itself but an attempt to provide for the grounded character of
stratification as it is displayed in sociological writing.   A claim
to 'see better' would stratify itself by transcending and reducing
sociology.   Non-dialectical and unreflexive description which, in
making a claim about something, calls for agreement, is stratifying,
and hearing this as stratifying can lead us to the paradoxical difference that subjecting is.   As a region within Framing speech,
formalizing sociological description distances itself from that which
is described because it is Framed in terms which methodically establish it as the product of observing which is above and counter to
that which is described; description in its describing is constitutive of the phenomenon as its phenomenon and in this establishment of
possession it makes it something other than and thus necessarily less
than what it may be for others.   Because of the being of saying and
the being of the phenomenon description stops short of, for it can
never be, a complete saying.   But when this stopping short is regarded, for all practical purposes, as a complete saying, then the
saying stratifies itself as definitive in relation to that about
which claims are made.   Definitive claims and descriptions are self-
stratifying.   Can description escape this self-stratification where,
in addressing its own possibility, it recognizes the paradox and ambiguity that, as difference, its own subjecting is?   Where it sees
itself as an irony in its describing of things that are ultimately
indescribable in so many words, it is at least beginning to take the
consequences of this seeing seriously.   In re-cognizing its limitations the writing-reading dialectic of the alternative beginning is
aware of the danger referred to by Proust of displaying not the reflexive practice itself but only the desire to be reflexive:
'... if words are chosen not by our thought according to its essential affinities, but by our desire to depict ourselves, this desire
is represented and we are not'.   (45) Any attempt to show theoretic

activity as methodically grounded and secured is itself an exemplification of that which it describes; in trying to disclose or
point to origins of theorizing, the talk is concretely about some
things, it describes them.   But this is not a stratifying description if the impossibility, the paradox, and the irony of the project
are recognized and shown in the description. (46) To accomplish a
complete re-covery of his Method and ground writer would have to
transcend and so reduce himself; the impossible requirement would be
for the writer to capture himself by being outside and above his own
Method and ground.   But author, in re-presenting a re-trieval of
those forms of analytic constraint through which tradition grants
and holds him, through modes such as, a pointing towards, a making
reference to, a showing the way to, places the onus on the other to
listen to the speaking, follow the pointing, and locate the grounds
of that re-trieval by hearing the unsaid; in this way the claim is
fulfilled by the other and not by the author.   The project is to
write and speak in a way that invites other to formulate writing's
and speaking's grounds and to listen thoughtfully to the accomplishment of his own reading and formulation.   This project would stand
as an icon of the fateful necessity of thinking and speaking ourselves out of the fascinating bonds of the mathematical form of life.
Its 'telos' is nothing less than the destruction of the hegemony of
the technological-calculative community with its founding modes of
knowledge-production and their supercession by theoretical practices
which show themselves as grounded in and responsive to the foundationally metaphoric and dialectical life of language.

* This paper formulates my response to extensive collaborative
work with both the other authors of this collection and Chris Jenks
and Dave Walsh.   Thoughtful readings by Alan Blum and Peter McHugh
of an earlier draft of this paper led me to listen again to and re-
formulate certain passages (notably the discussions in Section 1 and
Secion 4).

NOTES

1 J. Deely, 'The Tradition Via Heidegger', Martinus Nijhoff,
   The Hague, 1971.
2 Borges us shows us our problematic: '... a book is more than a
   verbal structure; it is the dialogue it establishes with its
   reader and the intonation it imposes on his voice and the changing and durable images it leaves in his memory.   This dialogue
   is infinite ... A book is not an isolated being: it is a relationship, an axis of innumerable relationships'.   J.L.Borges,
   'Labyrinths', Penguin, London, 1972, pp. 248-9.   Our problematic is the dialogue the sociological text attempts to provide
   for with its readers.
3 For the formulation of an alternative ontology in which stratification is a constituent mode (see Merleau-Ponty's description of
   Being as 'Wild' or 'Vertical'); his notion of Being as 'dimensionality' shows stratification as ontologically inescapable.
   M. Merleau-Ponty, 'The Visible and the Invisible', North-Western
   University Press, Chicago, 1968.

4 Proust alerts us to the danger of that way of reading which does
   not listen to itself:
      ... reading becomes dangerous when instead of waking us
      to the personal life of the spirit, it tends to sub-
      stitute itself for it, when truth no longer appears to
      us as an ideal we can realise only through the intimate
      progress of our thought and the effort of our heart, but
      as a material thing, deposited between the leaves of
      books like honey ready-made by other, and which we have
      only to take the trouble of reaching for on the shelves
      of libraries and then savouring passively in perfect
      repose of body and mind (M. Proust, 'On Reading',
      Souvenir Press, London, 1972, p.43).
5 M. Weber, 'The Methodology of the Social Sciences', Free Press,
   Chicago, 1949.
6 For a formulation of science's form of life as the public and
   consensual character of its display of method, see D. Walsh,
   Science, Sociology, and Everyday Life, unpublished paper,
   Goldsmiths' College.
7 For an analysis of the inadequacies of correspondence theories
   of truth, see P. McHugh, On the Failure of Positivism, in
   J. Douglas, 'Understanding Everyday Life', Routledge & Kegan
   Paul, London, 1971, p.320.
8 The distinction between objective and indexical expressions is
   discussed in H. Garfinkel, 'Studies in Ethnomethodology',
   Prentice-Hall, New Jersey, 1967.
9 McHugh, op.cit., p.334.
10 In what follows my formulation owes something to my reading of
   Heidegger's way of showing, especially his 'On the Way to
   Language', Harper & Row, New York, 1971.
11 Framing is discussed in a later section.
12 Husserl calls this 'horizon-certainty'. E. Husserl, 'The
   Crisis of European Sciences and Transcendental Phenomenology',
   North-Western University Press, 1970, p.374.
13 For Heidegger 'way' is 'that by which we reach - which lets us
   reach what reaches out for us by touching us, by being our
   concern', op.cit., p.91.
14 Heidegger speaks of Method in the sciences as holding 'all the
   coercive power of knowledge' and as pressing the sciences 'into
   its own service', op.cit. p.74, and 'In the sciences, not only
   is the theme drafted, called up by the method, it is also set up
   within the method and remains within the framework of the method,
   subordinated to it', ibid.
15 The ordered character of the speaking is referred to in Schutz's
   description of sociological concepts as 'second-order' constructs.
16 The thrust of this movement into observing, ordinarily discussed
   in relation to problems of suspending personal values in sociological observing, is similar to Husserl's early attempts to
   develop a method (the reduction) which would give access to a
   realm of pure consciousness; for others too the accomplishment
   of a pure activity through bracketing is a goal (e.g. the phon-
   etician's attempt to hear 'pure sound'). Ironically, then,
   the empiricism of sociology in its urge to suspend values points

directly to a pure phenomenology.

17 Science transforms the world into the image of its own desires.
    See G. Josipovici, 'The World and the Book', Macmillan, London,
    1971, p.154.
18 Weber, op.cit., p.22.
19 The counter to this is to see Method as inseparable from its
    object; for, in that Method has already delimited what we shall
    see it is necessarily already interpretation, but only one poss-
    ible interpretation; see R.E. Palmer, 'Hermeneutics', North-
    Western University Press, Chicago, 1969. See also, Heidegger,
    op.cit., p.74.
20 However if Merleau-Ponty's notion of 'chiasm' is followed every
    visible is also an invisible, so that our showing here is a mak-
    ing visible of that which the covering practices of sociology
    conceal. In like way this text can be treated as necessarily
    concealing that upon which it rests, and therefore open to form-
    ulation by the reader. (See M. Merleau-Ponty, op.cit., p.264.)
21 It also conceals that the making available (as text) 'what is
    seen' is a transformation of the seen. To frame the seen as a
    boundaried and capturable scene hides the multi-layered trans-
    formations which the movement and way from sight to text contains;
    the predominance of visual metaphors in sociological speech points
    to the problem. Debord's Thesis shows its fateful character.
22 If topology speaks about the providing of a space for a site then
    topography comprises the description of its features. For an
    elaboration of this distinction in relation to the movement of
    Heidegger's writing see O. Pöggeler, 'Heidegger's Topology of
    Being', in J. Kockelmans (ed.), 'On Heidegger and Language',
    North-Western University Press, 1972, p.107.
23 In one sense the talk is not 'his' speaking for his authorship is
    concretely covered by the claims of Method to be Nature's medium.
24 Palmer, in discussing the understanding as dialectic, shows the
    paradox of the grasping of meaning in reading where it is necess-
    ary to understand in advance what will be said, and yet this
    understanding must come from the reading. Palmer, op.cit., p.16.
25 Heidegger, op.cit., p.105, p.132.
26 The following paragraph draws heavily on Heidegger's discussion
    of Framing, op.cit., pp.131-2. The Frame is shown too in
    M. Heidegger, 'Identity and Difference', Harper & Row, New York,
    1969.
27 'On the Way to Language', p.74, p.91.
28 Heidegger, op.cit., p.132.
29 Ibid., p.132.
30 Palmer, op.cit., pp.22-3.
31 Weber, ibid., p.110.
32 See Heidegger, op.cit., p.122, for the distinction between
    speaking and saying.
33 See M. Merleau-Ponty, Indirect Language and the Voices of
    Silence, in 'Signs', North Western University Press, Chicago,
    1964, p.43, for an elaboration of this.
34 Josipovici, op.cit., p.174.
35 For a thoughtful interpretation of Heidegger's way towards the
    other beginning and his violent readings of the tradition, see
    W. Marx, 'Heidegger and the Tradition', North-Western University

Press, Chicago, 1971.
36 Following Garfinkel, op.cit., p.1.
37 See McHugh, op.cit., pp.334-5.
38 K. Burke, 'Attitudes Towards History', Hermes Publications,
    California, 1959, p.225.
39 See Palmer's discussion of Gadamer's dialectical hermeneutics,
    op.cit., pp.194f.
40 Palmer, op.cit., p.233.
41 Heidegger, op.cit., p.74, p.81.
42 Macomber offers an illuminating treatment of Heidegger's showing
    of the instrumentality of the impersonal 'one' and the event of
    authenticity, see W. Macomber, 'The Anatomy of Disillusion',
    North Western University Press, Chicago, 1967, pp.80ff.
43 Heidegger, op.cit., p.851.
44 And so on. This 'and so on' typifies and names the problem
    pointed to at the beginning of finding, doing and showing a
    principled reading of a text or world. The showing of the
    principle opens up a region for discourse and speaking and allows
    them to continue.
45 Op.cit., p.59.
46 The paradox can be recognized too in the word 'project' which,
    as a 'throwing forward' is carried through to locate something
    which requires a re-covery, a re-gress, a going backward. The
    pro-ject needs to be also a re-ject for the doing of re-covery
    and re-construction.

BIBLIOGRAPHY

BORGES, J.L., 'Labyrinths', Penguin, London, 1972.
BURKE, K., 'Attitudes Towards History', 1959, Hermes Publications,
California.
DEELY, J., 'The Tradition via Heidegger', 1971, Martinus Nijhoff,
The Hague.
GARFINKEL, H., 'Studies in Ethnomethodology', 1967, Prentice-Hall,
New Jersey.
HEIDEGGER, M., 'Identity and Difference', 1969, Harper & Row, New
York.
HEIDEGGER, M., 'On the Way to Language', 1971, Harper & Row, New
York.
HUSSERL, E., 'The Crisis of European Sciences and Transcendental
Phenomenology', 1970, North-Western University Press, Chicago.
JOSIPOVICI, G., 'The World and the Book', 1971, Macmillan, London.
MACOMBER, W., 'The Anatomy of Disillusion', 1967, North-Western
University Press, Chicago.
MARX, W., 'Heidegger and the Tradition', 1971, North-Western
University Press, Chicago.
MCHUGH, P., On the Failure of Positivism, in J. Douglas (ed.),
'Understanding Everyday Life', 1971, Routledge & Kegan Paul, London.
MERLEAU-PONTY, M., 'The Visible and the Invisible', 1968, North-
Western University Press, Chicago.
MERLEAU-PONTY, M., Indirect Language and the Voices of Silence, in
'Signs', 1964, North-Western University Press, Chicago.
PALMER, R., 'Hermeneutics', 1969, North-Western University Press,
Chicago.

PÖGGELER, O., Heidegger's Topology of Being, in J. Kockelmans (ed.), 'On Heidegger and Language', 1972, North-Western University Press, Chicago.

PROUST, M., 'On Reading', 1972, Souvenir Press, London.

WALSH, D., Science, Sociology and Everyday Life, 1972, unpublished paper, University of London, Goldsmiths' College, London.

WEBER, M., 'The Methodology of the Social Sciences', 1949, Free Press, Chicago.